Smart Negotiating

HOW TO MAKE GOOD DEALS IN THE REAL WORLD

James C. Freund

A Fireside Book
Published by Simon & Schuster, Inc.
New York London Toronto Sydney Tokyo Singapore

FIRESIDE
Simon & Schuster Building
Rockefeller Center
1230 Avenue of the Americas
New York, New York 10020

First Fireside Edition 1993

FIRESIDE and colophon are registered trademarks
of Simon & Schuster Inc.

Designed by Irving Perkins Associates
Manufactured in the United States of America

10 9 8 7 6 5 4 3 2 1
10 9 8 7 6 5 4   (PBK)
Library of Congress Cataloging-in-Publication Data

Freund, James C., date
    Smart negotiating : How to make good deals in the real world /
James C. Freund.
        p.   cm.
    Includes index.
    1. Negotiation in business.   I. Title.
    HD58.6.F74   1992
    302.3—dc20   92-19572
                                                            CIP

ISBN: 0-671-73027-4
        0-671-86921-3 (PBK)

ALSO BY JAMES C. FREUND

Advise and Invent
The Acquisition Mating Dance
Legal-Ease
Lawyering
Anatomy of a Merger

To my wife, Barbara Fox, a world class negotiator.

In fact, to this day, I still don't know whether
she was bluffing on the "now or never" position she took
seven years ago over the issue of whether our wedding
would be in January or in June. But if it was a bluff,
I wasn't willing to call it—which is surely one of
the smartest negotiating decisions I've made in my life.

CONTENTS

BY WAY OF INTRODUCTION

All of us negotiate. We make some deals and miss out on others. Sometimes we achieve more than anticipated; on other occasions we leave a lot on the table.

Remember the negotiating scene in the hit movie *Pretty Woman?* The wealthy businessman (Richard Gere) tells the stunning hooker (Julia Roberts) that he has a business proposition for her—he'll be in town until Sunday and would like her to spend the week with him. Roberts looks up from her bubble bath and says, "You're talkin' twenty-four hours a day—it's gonna cost you." Well, Gere urges, give me a ballpark figure. She does a quick mental calculation and replies, four thousand dollars. Out of the question, he responds, and offers two thousand dollars. Make it three thousand dollars, she says. Gere doesn't hesitate: "Done!" Roberts, blurting out an ecstatic expletive, dunks her head underwater. Later, as Gere is going out the door of the hotel suite, Roberts confesses: "I would have stayed for two thousand." He turns around slowly, pauses a beat, and replies: "I would have paid four."

I'm a lawyer who negotiates for a living. My views on the subject aren't theoretical or academic—they're rooted in over twenty-five years of professional experience. But I also write about negotiating, lecture on the subject to lawyers and business executives, and teach a course on it at law school. My approach to negotiating is a blend of these practical and instructional components.

In this book I'm going to introduce you to what I call "smart negotiating," as it takes place daily in the real world. I'll be coaching you through a wide variety of negotiating situations, pointing out the pitfalls, calling attention to the opportunities. My goal is to prepare you to negotiate for yourself or others—or to supervise people who are negotiating on your behalf—with confidence, flair, and a sense of direction.

Much of my experience consists of negotiating major corporate deals—primarily mergers and acquisitions (often referred to as "M&A") involving hundreds of millions of dollars. Some, like those where I represented TWA and Federated Department Stores, were initiated by hostile takeover bids; the bulk of the deals, such as Dun & Bradstreet's numerous acquisitions and divestitures, have been consensual. Over the years I've dealt with many top executives and most of the leading investment bankers and lawyers in the M&A business.

But this book is *not* a replay of those big deals. You can't really sharpen your negotiating skills by hearing about what happened in a major corporate transaction—there are too many crosscurrents and complications that obscure the basic elements. So I'll keep the war stories to a minimum, other than an occasional reference that reinforces the specific point under review.

The challenge for me has been to sift out the central principles from the welter of other details surrounding these negotiations and then apply them to everyday bargaining situations. The examples I use, although taken from real life, have been simplified to make the major issues stand out in bolder relief. Once you've grasped the key negotiating principles that are involved, you should be able to use them in the more complex situations you encounter.

BUILDING UP FROM THE BASICS

My friend Rich, who's a fine tennis player, told me that he recently took a series of lessons from a professional at a resort where he was vacationing. "To my surprise," Rich said, "there wasn't one thing the pro told me that he wouldn't have said to a rank beginner. It was all basic stuff, breaking down the mechanics of my strokes, urging me to move my feet, bend my knees, watch the ball . . ." When I asked Rich whether it had been worthwhile, he replied, "Absolutely. It was just what I needed—the ideal way to pinpoint and correct some problems that had crept into my game. I'm now playing better than ever."

My aim is to improve your negotiating skills in much the same way the pro helped Rich's tennis game. We'll start with the basics and build on them, adding the fine points and nuances when we've established a firm foundation. This is essential for a beginner, but it also makes good sense for experienced negotiators. Let's face it, most of us don't pause at regular intervals to analyze our negotiating techniques or evaluate our skills. As a result, our styles may have developed some kinks over the years, which undermine our attempts to achieve prime results.

I stress the fundamentals, but my approach isn't simplistic. In the real world the essence of smart negotiating is a *process*, which doesn't lend itself to sound bites or instant gratification. You have to probe beneath the superficial bromides. It's not enough to recite the general rule, like "Don't bid against yourself"; the real question is, when should you *disregard* the rule? "Don't lose your cool" may be good everyday advice, but when do you *need* to show some emotion?

THE CASE OF THE TORN TWENTY

To get you thinking like a smart negotiator, let's do a warm-up exercise.

Here's a little drill I use when I address groups of businessmen or lawyers, as well as my law school negotiating class. The situation is fanciful—nothing like the practical, realistic negotiating problems we'll soon encounter—but it does get the juices flowing and will also serve as a sneak preview of some issues that come up later on. So check your incredulity at the door, pretend these are big bucks in dispute, and get ready to negotiate.

Someone once advised me that when traveling, I should tip the concierge upon my *arrival* at a hotel rather than upon departure. The theory is that I would purchase better service by paying in advance, thereby obligating the concierge to look out for my welfare. Let's assume that you've received the same advice from a friend, are intrigued by the notion, and await a chance to test it out—perhaps in another setting. The moment arrives tonight, while you and your spouse are dining at a restaurant.

When the waiter—whose name is Walter—first comes over to your table, you say to him, "I would really like excellent service tonight, Walter. My guess is that the bill will total around eighty dollars. If you're willing to hustle and give us your full attention, your tip will be twenty dollars—roughly twenty-five percent, instead of the normal fifteen percent, or twelve dollars, that you might otherwise expect."

At this point, you take a twenty-dollar bill out of your wallet with a flourish—but then, just as you're about to hand it over to Walter, you have second thoughts. Is this wise? Once Walter actually has the money, what's to stop him from ignoring your table? You are, in a word, torn—anxious to go through with the experiment but fearing the consequences. So what do you do?

You guessed it! You tear the twenty-dollar bill in half, giving Walter one part while keeping the other, and say, "You'll get the other half after dinner if the service is outstanding."

Walter gives you a quizzical look, shrugs, and pockets his half of the bill. You proceed to order and eat your meal. The food is all right, but the service is mediocre—not at all what you were hoping to generate by your offer. (Perhaps the halfhearted quality of your gesture contributed to the waiter's lethargy.) So when Walter brings over the check (which, in fact, is close to $80), you take out a ten and two ones, and say, "I'm sorry, Walter, but the service was simply not what I anticipated. It doesn't deserve anything more than a routine fifteen percent tip. So here's twelve dollars. Please give me back the other half of my twenty-dollar bill."

Walter is outraged. "That's not fair," he cries. "I think I did a terrific job of serving you. I earned the twenty dollars."

"No, Walter," you reply calmly, "the issue was whether your performance would be to *my* satisfaction, and it wasn't. I offered an overly generous tip as a reward for fine service, but that's not what we got. So hand over the other half."

Walter remains firm. "No way. And besides, I need the extra money to pay my bills."

"Is that so?" You rise from your seat, conspicuously pocketing the twelve dollars. "Look, I'm going to walk out of here, and then you'll have nothing."

Undaunted, Walters replies, "Go ahead and leave. You'll be out twenty dollars."

Your voice gets louder. "I may be out twenty dollars, but at least you won't have it."

The dispute is escalating rapidly, until at last your spouse breaks in. "Hey, wait a minute. This is crazy. The torn bill means that *both* of you lose. Can't you try to work this out—to *negotiate* a settlement?"

WHAT'S YOUR STYLE?

All right, here's a situation that is certainly ripe for negotiation. How do you go about it?

If you're like some negotiators, you would take a tough line. "Here's twelve dollars, Walter. Take it or leave it. You're lucky I'm willing to give you *that* much after such crummy service." And if Walter doesn't budge, you would set a deadline coupled with a threat to walk out. Is that your style?

At the other end of the spectrum, some people who dislike conflict and try to avoid confrontation might simply throw in the towel and give Walter the $20, if he hewed to his tough line.

There's another popular style of negotiating in between those two. You're offering $12; Walter's holding out for $20. So without prolonging the agony, you offer to split the difference—right down the middle at $16.

A fourth approach might be taken by those who believe in what they call negotiating "on the merits." Their technique is to lessen the emotional content of the encounter, get behind the parties' posturing and explore their real interests, examine a number of options, and search for objective criteria to validate a fair resolution. If you follow this approach, you would probably want to discuss with Walter the standards typically used to evaluate excellence of service, then measure the perceived quality of Walter's effort against those standards—where it rates on that $12 to $20 scale.

Personally, I don't consider *any* of these approaches well suited to resolving this particular problem. That first macho technique may work, but it runs the distinct risk of having Walter ignore his self-interest and tell you where you can shove your ripped bill. And the second approach, just forking over the other half of the bill, is less a technique than a capitulation.

The third method might not be so bad if you knew that Walter would *accept* your "split the difference" proposal, but you don't. So the problem it causes is that you've now shown your willingness to pay $16, *while Walter is still at $20!* Even if you're able to move him off that figure, the deal is likely to be struck in the vicinity of $18. In effect, you've surrendered something—namely, significant information about the level at which you're willing to compromise—without getting anything in return.

(By the way, if *Walter* had proposed the split, he would face a comparable problem—the prospect of a deal ending up around $14— but with the added penalty of having undermined his moral fervor about being entitled to the promised $20.)

The "on the merits" approach has much to recommend it in theory, but you would be in for one long night! The standards of excellent service are tough to pin down, it's not clear where you're heading, and in the end you may find yourself shelling out more than you need to.

So, if none of these approaches is satisfactory, what other way might you proceed?

AN INVENTORY OF STRENGTHS AND WEAKNESSES

It's always useful to start out a negotiation by taking an inventory of your strengths and weaknesses, as well as those of the other side (insofar as you're aware of them). Let's do that here. Who do you think has the stronger position heading into the negotiations—you or Walter—and why?

Did you pick Walter? If so, you must think that he'll end up with close to the $20 he expected. Perhaps you were influenced by the "equitable" argument Walter will undoubtedly make—that he had been led to believe he was going to get the $20, he had relied on this in rendering the service, and now he's being let down hard. Maybe your intuition tells you that with a standard as subjective as quality of service, you'll fold your cards in the end and hand over the $20— saving your self-righteousness for the friend whose absurd notion got you into this mess. Other than these intangibles, however, I don't see any compelling rationale why it's preferable to be Walter in this situation. On the contrary, I think *your* position is far superior, for at least three reasons.

The first has to do with the underlying legal situation, an important factor in every dispute. Sometimes it's complicated and you need legal advice. But not here—everyone knows this one cold. The fact is that Walter has no legal right to *anything*, not even the $12 you offered. Strictly as a matter of law, you could stiff Walter—tip him zero—and although he might cry bloody murder, he would have no legal recourse. So your threat to walk out without leaving him a dime has real teeth—as it might not, for example, if the restaurant included a standard 15 percent tip in the price of the meal. If and when Walter cools down and evaluates his options, he will have to take account of this hard reality.

The second reason, which is a little more subtle, has to do with expectations and the economics of the situation. The waiter will get $12 if he accepts your offer. If he refuses your offer and ends up with zero, then he has "lost" $12 from what is now his minimum expectation. Compare this with the view from your perspective. You're prepared to pay $12—that's your offer. If you end up "paying" $20 (by not getting back the other half of your bill), then you're only out of pocket an additional $8. The differential in loss potential between your $8 and his $12 should make Walter realize that he has more "invested" in working out a deal than you do—even at your minimum $12 level.

The third reason pertains to what might be termed the "desire" factor. The premise here is that the party with the stronger desire to make a deal is at a disadvantage vis-à-vis the party who is more indifferent to whether or not an agreement is eventually reached. Since Walter depends upon his tips for a living—an assumption bolstered by his statement about needing the extra money to pay his bills—I have a hunch that his desire to emerge from this unpleasant experience with *something* for his trouble is likely to weigh more heavily on him than whatever might be motivating you.

THE LOCATION OF THE LOOT

Given your greater leverage, you should do well in the negotiations—at least if Walter sees his own self-interest clearly. Your technique should be designed to keep the combative Walter on a rational plane. You don't want him to get so befogged by emotion and anger that he turns down a good settlement and ends up with nothing, just for the satisfaction of knowing that you're out $20.

In addition to appealing to his self-interest, what else is important? I think Walter has to emerge from the negotiations with *something* of a tangible nature—and I don't mean just the $12 you've already put on the table. He needs an extra amount, not only for the money itself, but for the psychological satisfaction of *seeing you move.* And you know what? He *deserves* something. Not because of the quality of his service—I'll take your word that it was mediocre. But because of the leverage *he* possesses, by reason of . . . By reason of what?

By reason of his possessing one-half of the twenty-dollar bill.

Why is this? Let's imagine that instead of what actually happened, you had promised Walter $20 but *hadn't* given him half of the bill. He can still claim he was duped or appeal to your sense of fairness—or, better yet, direct his appeal to your less agitated spouse. But Walter has very little in the way of leverage, because now you can walk out the door with total impunity *and* a full wallet.

Under these circumstances Walter would be wise, after testing your flexibility, to accept the $12 being offered—which, after all, you could take off the table at any moment. As for your part, you would be justified in hanging tough, although you might want to sweeten the pot by a dollar to show you're not such a bad sort.

Now, how would the situation differ if instead of half, you gave Walter the *entire* twenty-dollar bill in advance? Clearly the fact that Walter now holds *the money*—not just a worthless piece of paper—bolsters his position. But why is this so? After all, whether Walter has the entire bill or only half, you'll be in the hole for $20 if you walk out. What's the distinction?

It's this. If Walter has the *whole* bill and you walk out, it's all over; Walter wins. But if he only has *half*, then when you walk out there's a good chance he'll come running after you, shouting, "Wait, wait, I'll take the $12!"—at least if he's rational. From his point of view, $12 is clearly better than the severed greenback. (Still, if Walter turns out to be a zealot, he might prize the fact that you're out the full $20 above considerations of his personal fortune—which is precisely why taking a hike is a risky way for you to play this negotiation.)

POSITIONING YOURSELF FOR COMPROMISE

Getting back to the split-bill scenario, and assuming you'll end up paying something more than $12 (say, $14 or $15), does that mean you were unwise to select $12 as your initial offer? Should it have been lower to give you more room? Higher? What do you think?

To my mind, $12 was the right offer for you to make. Anything higher and you would have been voluntarily offering to overpay for mediocre service. Anything lower and you would seem to be penalizing Walter for your own defaulted expectations, which could lead to ill will and irrational behavior on his part—precisely what you *don't* want to see happen. By wrapping yourself in the mantle of the "usual" tip, your position has an equitable underpinning. You've managed to highlight the distinction you're trying to make between ordinary and excellent service and thus make your subsequent reluctance to go much higher more credible.

Now, let's assume you've decided for various reasons to end up by giving Walter $15. How do you plot the journey there to make sure it seals the deal? Do you jump to $15 in a single bound? Should you creep toward it in one-dollar (or fifty-cent) increments? Do you insist that Walter come down off his $20 demand before you move at all? Do you bluff? Threaten? Cajole?

Well, that's what *smart negotiating* is all about. There's no single "right" answer here. But just for kicks, let's check out one possible technique. After a few minutes of discussion, you look down at your wristwatch and say, "Listen, Walter, I'll stay here for no more than two minutes. If you hand me back the other half of my twenty-dollar bill in the first minute, I'll give you a tip of fifteen. If you hand it back in the second minute, I'll give you twelve. If you don't hand it back by the end of the second minute, I'm going to walk out of here and you'll get zero."

The clocks starts to tick. What does Walter do? I'll tell you what I would do if I were Walter. I'd grab the $15! The proposition you've made is both too specific and too simple to implement for Walter to ignore. And now that you've offered a decent compromise, you're unlikely to feel any further moral qualms about your conduct.

EXPANDING THE PIE

Let's look at one final twist. Since it's always useful to try to see things from the other side's perspective, pretend that you're *Walter*. Say that tempers have cooled, but negotiations over the split bill have thus far gotten nowhere. It's time to introduce a more creative element into the problem. Up until now the parties have been dealing with a finite universe. But can a solution be structured that will "expand the pie"—creating additional values that make the customer more amenable to a "richer" settlement? Can you think of anything, Walter? Assuming that you would really like to get the other half of that twenty-dollar bill, what might you suggest?

Actually, I've given you a hint by referring to "the pie." You go back to the kitchen and emerge carrying two servings of apple pie. "Look," you say, "we want our customers to be satisfied. Here's some delicious dessert, on the house."

At any rate, those are a few of the myriad possibilities inherent in the situation. My own guess is that this contretemps will be settled at about $14—$2 over the customer's initial offer—with neither party overjoyed, but each satisfied enough to do the deal rather than face the consequences of failing to reach a resolution.

THE BASIC SKILLS AND THE GAME PLAN APPROACH

The heart of smart negotiating lies in your mastering certain basic skills and adopting a logical approach to the negotiations. The skills involve such crucial factors as leverage, information, credibility, and judgment. No special qualifications are needed. Negotiating success isn't dependent upon accidents of birth or formal educational background. Most of the meaningful attributes—the ability to read people, a willingness to challenge and resist, flexibility, the capacity to persuade, a healthy dose of common sense—are available to anyone.

As for the approach, the problem is that too many people—even those who bargain as a routine part of their business lives—never bother to develop a systematic approach to negotiating. They embark upon, conduct, and even conclude negotiations without going through the steps necessary to obtain good results:

- They fail to assess in advance their realistic expectations for the deal.
- They start either too close to their goal to achieve it or so far away as to put the deal in jeopardy.
- They lack a sense of how to make the journey from opening position to ultimate goal—of how to manage the bargaining and concession process.

- They aren't able to seal the deal—to make sure their counterpart accepts the ultimate compromise instead of using it as the prelude to yet another round of bargaining.

I don't like the idea of winging it. To borrow an analogy from sports, *I'm convinced that you need to approach each negotiation with a well-conceived game plan*—just the way a football team prepares for each week's contest. Of course, you can't follow the game plan blindly. You have to remain alert to unexpected revelations, new developments, emerging risks and opportunities. But if you start out with a sense of where you're heading and a well-conceived path to get there, you'll make out much better over time.

I'll explain and illustrate the basic negotiating skills in the chapters that follow, after which we'll explore the game plan approach to smart negotiating. Then you'll be ready to take on certain additional factors that complicate a negotiator's life, such as the role of agents in advising and bargaining for their principals, the special problems involved in trying to resolve disputes, the need to deal with threats or other attempts at intimidation, and how to convert a handshake into a written contract. Finally, at the end of the book, you'll find for ready reference a checklist of all the major points covered.

THE GOAL OF MUTUAL SATISFACTION

But first let's spend a few minutes talking theory. Just what is negotiating all about?

Some people compare it to chess, with the two sides matching wits, making moves, thinking ahead, and so on. But the comparison ultimately breaks down because in chess there's a winner and a loser—in fact, winning is the object of the game. In a negotiation the ultimate goal is for *both sides* to reach a mutually satisfactory agreement. That's the only way it works; either they both "win" or there's no deal. (This is why the worst confrontations usually occur in a dispute between a man of principle and someone who can't stand to lose, where the merits are with the man of principle!) As a result, much of your energy is spent trying to make the other side feel comfortable with the outcome, which is definitely *not* what motivated Bobby Fischer.

Reaching a mutually satisfactory agreement, however, is no piece of cake—which isn't surprising when you think about it. Here's the problem. Assume there was a neutral third party with excellent judgment and access to all pertinent facts. This neutral, if asked by the parties, could presumably suggest a fair resolution of the matter being negotiated. But the real question is, would both of the parties *agree* on that resolution if it were presented to them? Even if they would, since no such neutral is involved in the typical negotiation, will the two negotiators be able to *arrive* at that resolution on their own? Finally, even if they manage to get there, will they *realize* that they've reached a meaningful juncture? After all, there's no one around to proclaim that this is the right place; and if experience serves, each will probably feel that *the other* has a distance yet to travel!

The goal of *mutual* satisfaction is what makes negotiation unique. You miss out on a crucial dimension if you think of bargaining solely in terms of getting your own way and fail to focus on the need to bring the other party along. It's winning him over that counts—not winning over him. That's why, except in a dispute, words like "adversary" and "opponent" don't accurately describe the person on the other side of the table. I prefer using more neutral terms, like "counterpart" or "the other party."

If, however, you're totally preoccupied by the need to win over your counterpart, then you probably aren't taking such good care of your own interests. For that reason, when I negotiate, I look for the *favorable middle ground*—where my client is pleased with the resolution and the other party is satisfied enough to do the deal.

COMPETITIVE VS. COOPERATIVE BARGAINING

Most of the practical literature on negotiating tilts toward one or the other of two schools of thought on how to go about bargaining—what might be termed the "competitive" and "cooperative" models. Much of the negotiating that goes on today in a business context is competitive (or positional) bargaining. Perhaps that's because the crucial issue—price—is almost invariably handled that way. The seller of property asks for a price above the amount the buyer is willing to pay; the buyer offers an amount below what the seller will accept; and they grapple competitively through successive positions toward a price poised somewhere in between. The ultimate compromise, while perhaps not totally satisfactory to both parties, at least represents a figure at which each is willing to do the deal. And most other issues of importance take their cue from the price negotiations.

Contrasted with this is the cooperative approach to bargaining, best exemplified in the book *Getting to Yes*, by Roger Fisher and William Ury. The premise here is that if adversaries could truly sit down together—cool their emotions, put their cards on the table, focus on their real interests instead of positions, engage in a mutual search for common ground, apply objective criteria, and be creative—then they would swiftly reach wise agreements without harm to the relationship.

But although the goal is laudable and many facets of that method have value, I don't think the cooperative approach correlates with what's going on in today's business world. Nor, I fear, does it address the needs of most Americans who negotiate nowadays. Rather, what makes us feel comfortable with the ultimate result of a negotiation—however bumpy the journey to achieve it—is a *process* that provides for some familiar maneuvers, some give and take, before culminating in an agreement. We need to see the other side move from its opening position—to feel the satisfaction of having engaged in a strenuous undertaking—in order to arrive at the finish line reassured that we got the best deal possible and didn't leave too much on the table.

This is particularly true in the corporate world. When the negotiations have been hard fought but are ultimately resolved, then you can go to your superior in the company—or I can go to my client—and say, "Hey, look at what we accomplished!" But when the other party walks into your conference room that first day and says, "Listen, these are our mutual interests, and here's the deal we can make to resolve them neatly," then even if what he proposes is acceptable, my bet is that you would caution yourself: "Whoa! I better slow this down and look displeased. I can get *more!*"

There's a lot of talk about *fairness* among disciples of cooperative negotiating, but you won't hear that concept mentioned much in these pages. In my experience, it's rare for both sides to have congruent notions of what's fair under the circumstances; and there's seldom a single objective test that compels acquiescence. *Satisfaction* is the gospel I preach. If the parties are ultimately satisfied with the result—in large part because of what they went through to get there—

then they're likely to feel that the result is a fair one, which is all that's really needed.

So, although I applaud many of the precepts of cooperative bargaining—and hope I live long enough to see a world where this approach to reaching agreement becomes widespread—I'm convinced that as an overall technique it misses the mark in today's deal-making atmosphere. And that's because the *positional dance* it seeks to eliminate is, in fact, the key to unlocking the terms of agreement on which the parties can come together.

Now, don't get me wrong. I'm no apologist for the way that competitive bargaining is generally conducted nowadays. Many positional bargainers employ tough coercive tactics I find objectionable. Some simply go in and wing it, without any plan. Others get bogged down by blind adherence to familiar axioms that may not be applicable to the situation. And most competitive negotiators—absorbed by themselves and *their* positions—spend too little time thinking about the other side. By contrast, a cooperative bargainer often worries *too much* about the other side's wants, needs, and problems instead of focusing more on how to *influence* that party's thinking and conduct.

THE COMPOSITE APPROACH TO NEGOTIATING

Rather than adopting an either/or approach to competitive vs. cooperative bargaining, I want you to treat negotiating theory as you would the menu in a Chinese restaurant, selecting some items from column A and some from column B—plus a few specialties of the house. For example, you should

- recognize the durability of the *competitive* bargaining mode in the business world, realizing it can't be ignored—
  but refuse to be limited by the rigidity of thinking and approach so often associated with the positional style.
- acknowledge the many valid points and techniques associated with *cooperative* negotiating—
  but be aware of its shortcomings in coping with everyday business problems and in satisfying the needs of both parties for a positional process that validates their efforts.

What's needed in *smart negotiating* is to take and apply the best of both worlds. From the *competitive* side, the emphasis on

- leverage;
- information;
- gaining advantage.

From the *cooperative* side, the importance of

- problem-solving (including the other party's problems);
- a convincing rationale;
- creative thinking.

And then add my emphasis on such matters as

- having a negotiating game plan;
- achieving credibility;
- using good judgment to maintain a proper balance.

This composite approach to negotiating doesn't provide you with a quick fix, nor does it guarantee that you won't feel impatient and frustrated. But if both sides share a mutual interest in reaching an agreement, then it should help you attain your goal within a reasonable time span—and, if done right, with egos salved and personal relationships preserved.

It takes a lot of energy, however. The keynote is *awareness*—paying attention to everything that's happening (and that should be happening). In order to negotiate effectively, you need *both* eyes wide open—one to check your counterpart and the other to keep watch on yourself:

- You're focused on vital real-world considerations—such as each side's relative strengths and weaknesses—and *not* on trivia like the place of the meeting.
- You're alert to the games people play—*yourself* included.
- You're aware that few things are truly neutral, so you're sensitive to the advantages and disadvantages that often lurk below the surface of a complex or technical issue.

- You're mindful of credibility factors, not only with regard to your counterpart, but also to *yourself*—do you, in fact, deserve to be believed?
- You're trying to influence your counterpart's thinking in ways that work to your advantage, while avoiding the transmission of inadvertent messages that could harm your cause.
- Finally, you're not losing sight of the big picture—the need to devise the right strategy and tactics to achieve the favorable result you seek, no matter what obstacles are strewn in your path.

A PERSONAL VIEWPOINT

The negotiating I engage in generally involves money, securities, property, services, or contractual relations. I distinguish this from negotiations over political hostages and international treaties, or the kind of dickering that goes on in a House-Senate budget conference—where larger issues often dictate the agenda—as well as from pitched battles over child custody between ex-spouses and other highly charged emotional contests. I'm not experienced in those arenas, and I don't tout my advice as applicable to them (although some of the same principles may apply). This book is about the kinds of negotiations that take place in our everyday business and personal lives. Of course, broader issues may intrude, and emotions can get out of hand, but there's a good chance that reason will prevail—provided you play your cards right.

The negotiations in this book are being conducted by Americans in the United States. Bargaining conventions and styles differ markedly from country to country, but I'm going to stick to what I know best. So forget about cultural differences, quaint customs, and language problems—the real world here is located somewhere between Main Street and Wall Street.

I've also made a special effort to keep my own profession from becoming too intrusive. You don't need to be (or, in most instances, even hire) a lawyer for the negotiations I'll be discussing. And in the few instances where the law directly affects the subject matter under discussion—primarily in the area of disputes—I'll provide you with the basic legal framework.

With a few exceptions, I've tried to focus each chapter on a single facet of the subject—while recognizing, of course, how interwoven the various strands of negotiating are. It may help to think of the chapters that follow as an array of Nautilus machines in a fitness facility, each singling out specific muscles for individual attention, but with the goal of ultimately putting them all together into a fully sculpted physique.

Just so you know where I'm coming from, I consider myself an ethical and fair-minded bargainer. I'm opposed to misrepresentation, to the kind of dissembling that seeks to achieve an unfair advantage. I don't believe in chiseling; I scorn dirty tricks. I'm not looking to win at any cost or to make those on the other side feel as though they've lost. I like to base my arguments on reason, to have a solid rationale for my positions, and to try to be persuasive. In turn, I'm willing to listen, in case the other side's rationale might persuade me. And where possible, I prefer to conduct the negotiations in an atmosphere free of rancor or personal animosity and to conclude on good terms with my counterpart.

Nevertheless, I don't like to end up with substantially less than I consider myself or my client entitled to, based on all the factors affecting the negotiations. It's gratifying to end up with *more* than we expected, and I generally try to land in that territory if possible. But I don't look upon achieving something extra in each deal as an article of faith, as long as we get our just desserts. On the other hand, I definitely do *not* like to feel that I've been taken advantage of or jerked around; and when my antennae sense this happening, I stand up on my hind legs and let the world know about it.

It goes against my grain to see deals muffed that should be made—whether because of intransigence, overtrading, miscalculation, misinformation, erroneous assumptions, or whatever. I recognize that some deals simply don't make sense. But when one is itching to occur, I feel a sense of failure if I can't concoct and carry out a strategy to bring the two sides together.

Finally, I'm well aware that negotiating isn't something you can master just from reading about it. You need to get out there and *do* it. But even for experienced negotiators—as many of you undoubtedly are—I believe this book provides practical techniques, strategies, and insights that will pay off handsomely for you at the bargaining table.

PART I

The Basic Negotiating Skills

1 A PREVIEW OF THE BASIC SKILLS

This chapter is like the overture to a Broadway show—a sampling of the major themes you'll be hearing more about later on. These themes embrace what I consider to be the four basic skills of smart negotiating. Stated succinctly, they are

Leverage—An appreciation of the leverage factors at work in each situation, plus the ability to apply leverage (when it's with you) and cope with it (when it's against you);

Information—The knack of ferreting out and evaluating useful information regarding the other side, while protecting information about your side you would rather not reveal;

Credibility—The ability to make those on the other side believe you mean what you say, as well as to assess whether or not they're bluffing;

Judgment—The ability to strike the right balance between gaining advantages and reaching compromises, in the substance as well as in the style of your negotiating technique.

All these skills are interrelated in a negotiation, and the interplay among them is significant in itself. To observe this, let me recount the facts of a typical negotiation without commentary. Then we'll go back to review the elements of this negotiation that bear on the four basic skills. Keep your eyes and ears open to what's going on here, and before reading my critique try to form your own opinion about the negotiating involved.

THE CASE OF THE OVERREACHING SUBTENANT

Ted is a tenant in a residential apartment building in Bigtown with a lease that has fourteen months to go, terminating December 31 of next year. Although his lease explicitly prohibits carrying on a trade or business from the premises, Ted has been using his apartment as an office to operate a consulting business under the name "Ted Talks." In early November of this year Ted's landlord, Leland, discovered what Ted has been doing and presented him with an ultimatum: either stop conducting business from the apartment or be evicted and held responsible for the balance of the lease term.

Ted has no choice. Caught in the act, unable to convince the landlord to overlook this breach, dependent on his consulting business, and lacking funds to afford a separate office, he must move out. Leland gives him until the end of this year. Fortunately Ted's lease permits him to sublet, and with two months to find a subtenant, he advertises the apartment for rent. The first week he has no takers. Then, in mid-November, Susan materializes. She's moving from another city into Bigtown to begin a new job on December 1. He shows her the space; she's definitely interested.

Ted's rent (New York City rates!) is $1,500 a month. The real estate market in Bigtown has been relatively static since he signed the lease, so he asks Susan to pay the same $1,500 per month under the sublease—"no profit, no loss," as he puts it. When Susan asks him why he's moving, Ted doesn't mention his problem with Leland but alludes to having found "larger quarters" he likes better, trying to give the impression that he's under no time pressure to leave.

Susan, who would be willing to pay that much if she had to, decides to negotiate. She offers $1,200. Ted, who doesn't want to subsidize $300 of Susan's rent, holds out for the full $1,500. The issue is unresolved.

Susan then brings up three other items:

- She wants occupancy from December 1, when her job begins. Ted, not yet having found another place to live—despite his remark about "larger quarters"—would prefer to wait until the end of December, when he must move out.
- The paint in the vestibule of the apartment is peeling badly. Susan wants Ted to have it repainted at his expense (which he estimates to be about $300). Ted thinks she should pay for it.
- Susan asks him to leave behind the television set, which is worth about $200. Ted wants to take it with him.

After some discussion Susan says that if Ted is willing to satisfy her on those three items, she'll raise her offer on the rent to $1,300. Ted rejects this proposal but remains interested in continuing the negotiations. They decide to think it over and resume discussions the next day, Susan pointedly remarking that she has another apartment to see later that afternoon.

As Susan is about to leave Ted's apartment, she notices an envelope on the desk addressed to "Ted Talks" at this address. Already suspicious about his vague reasons for leaving, she decides to take a long shot. "Do you run a business here?" she asks.

A lengthy pause. "Why do you ask?" Ted replies warily.

"Because I saw this envelope," Susan says, holding it up, "and I assume that the lease prohibits conducting business from the apartment."

Another pause. "Well," Ted says, recovering a bit, "*You* aren't going to operate a business here, are you?"

"No," she replies.

"Then you've got nothing to worry about."

Susan decides not to press the issue but now suspects the real reason for Ted's premature departure, which may mean he's under pressure to move out quickly. She also has a hunch, based on other exchanges between them, that no one else is currently bidding on Ted's space. So when she returns the next day to resume the negotiations, she decides to get tough. She goes up only $25 (to $1,325) on the rent and sticks on all three of the other issues—even the TV, which she doesn't really need since she has one of her own.

"As far as I'm concerned," Susan says, "either you acquiesce on all of these issues or there's no deal. As a matter of fact, that other apartment I looked at yesterday is cheaper than this one." (This last statement is literally true but misleading. She didn't like the other apartment at all and hasn't yet found a decent alternative to Ted's place.)

Ted, provoked by Susan's sudden toughness, would like to say "Then there's no deal. Good-bye," and usher her out of the apartment. But he realizes that she may prove to be his only hope. So he bites his tongue and—because he thinks her "final offer" is a bluff— decides to make an accommodating counteroffer. His proposal is to split everything except the television, which he considers to be his.

He offers $1,412.50 on the rental (halfway between their positions), a fifty-fifty division of the painting costs, and a December 15 occupancy date. He sits back, convinced that he has been eminently reasonable.

Susan, believing that Ted will go farther on each point—even the TV, which isn't that expensive an item—replies that this isn't good enough for her (although, in fact, it would be). "You know my position," she says.

Ted, annoyed that his compromise proposal has produced no progress, hardens his own stance. "That's the best I can do," he says—even though it's not.

With neither Ted nor Susan willing to budge an inch, they're at a standstill. Do you think this deal will get done? At the very least, it won't be easy.

Now let's step back and examine what was going on here and, in particular, how it relates to the four basic negotiating skills involving leverage, information, credibility, and judgment.

ANALYZING THE LEVERAGE

Let's begin with leverage. Where does it appear in this scenario, and how do the parties handle it?

Obviously a principal negative leverage factor is *necessity*. When you're forced to do a deal, you can't afford to hold out for optimum terms. Here, necessity is working against Ted. The fact that he has to vacate the apartment puts more pressure on him to reach an agreement—even on imperfect terms—than if the subletting were voluntary. (And, by the way, Ted is right to try to dispel signs of this pressure by adopting a calculated air of nonchalance.)

A negotiator who's up against necessity should try to neutralize it by using other leverage factors to his advantage. The prime offset for a forced seller of property (or here, a lessor of space) is to generate *competition* for the deal. Unfortunately for Ted, however, he has no other takers for the apartment; and in my book, inventing one who doesn't exist would be improper. (This does *not* mean, however, he has to *concede* that the cupboard is bare.) And just to make things worse for Ted, Susan is actually trying to use competition against him, by alluding to that other apartment she has under consideration.

Desire is another possible offset to necessity. If the person acquiring the property (or, here, renting the space) wants it badly enough, that provides a strong motivation to make the deal. Susan likes Ted's apartment; but based on her hard-nosed (and thus risky) position, she appears able to live without it.

Then there's the leverage factor of *time*, which is definitely working against Ted here. If he had more time, he might be able to develop some competition for Susan. In this case, however, it's partially offset by the pressure on Susan to find a place in Bigtown as soon as possible.

THE ROLE INFORMATION PLAYS

Let's turn now to the subject of information, which can play many roles in a negotiation—as a means of helping a party understand the other party's interests and motivations, evaluate credibility, predict the direction things may go, and so on. But perhaps the most central role for information is to assist in the appreciation of leverage.

Witness the shift in mood that takes place after Susan spies the "Ted Talks" envelope—information that reveals possible negative leverage affecting the other side. Susan is alert in spotting the envelope and insightful in making the connection to pressure on Ted from the landlord. Then, once she has this clue, she attempts to establish the fact by questioning Ted directly. What other channels might she have pursued to pin this down? One possibility would be to shield her suspicions from Ted, obtain the landlord's name from him on some other pretext, and then contact Leland to see what she can find out.

After a slow start, Ted bobs and weaves fairly well, shifting the inquiry to whether the ban on business will interfere with *her* occupancy. But his first pregnant pause lets him down; he just isn't prepared for this line of questioning. As for Susan, after getting underway like Perry Mason, she doesn't follow up so well. She fails to keep Ted focused and responsive and never poses the key question of whether he's being forced to leave.

The information we glean in negotiations is often fragmentary and incomplete. As a result we're frequently forced to reason by inference and assumption and then to act on that basis. Susan draws a strong inference from incomplete information and decides to go with it, hardening her bargaining stance on the assumption that Ted has to move out and thus must make a deal. As it happens, her *inference* is correct; let's reserve judgment, however, on whether the *action* she takes is appropriate. If the inference had been incorrect, Susan would have overestimated her leverage—the kind of illusion that can often prove a real impediment to reaching agreement.

STRIVING FOR CREDIBILITY

When you take a strong bargaining stance or convey information that appears to increase your leverage, your effectiveness depends on whether the other side believes you. Your strongest weapon in providing information is the truth. With it, you may still have trouble convincing your counterpart, but at least you've got a firm platform for support. When the facts you're brandishing aren't authentic, then—in addition to the ethical question raised—the task is much tougher. This is just what happens here. Susan isn't believable with her "other apartment" pitch; Ted never considers it to be real competition. Likewise, his "moving to a larger space" story lacks credence, even before Susan discovers the envelope.

The crucial credibility question, however, is the one raised by Susan's "final offer" posture. Ted doesn't believe her; he thinks she's bluffing and will eventually increase the amount of rent and reduce her other demands. So he takes the risky step of ignoring her stance and proposing his own compromise. It's risky because if Susan *isn't* bluffing, she might react by walking out—never to be seen again, even if Ted were to change his mind.

Ted's assessment of Susan's *willingness* to accept less favorable terms is correct. What he fails to take into account, however, is her appraisal of the relative leverage. On *this* basis, she *isn't* prepared to move—at least not yet—because she's convinced that Ted will ultimately yield. But for reasons we'll come to in a moment, Ted doesn't find the firmness of her position credible.

Ted's "the best I can do" compromise proposal is calculated to send a message of fair dealing. But it carries little credibility in terms of being his final position, beyond the fact that he has made the effort and might be loath to make another. The awkwardness of his $1,412.50 figure on the rent, his readiness to split on other issues, even the speed with which he introduces his "solution"—these factors suggest to Susan that there's a further point to which Ted is willing to retreat, if pushed.

These observations illustrate what a tricky business credibility is and how easy it is for the other side to misconstrue your words and deeds.

JUDGMENT AND THE PRINCIPLE OF BALANCE

But even if Susan believes she holds all the cards—which she can't be sure of—she takes too strong a position too early in the negotiations. She doesn't observe what I call the principle of balance. You can't win 'em all; the other side needs to score a few, too. You have to strike the proper balance between getting a leg up and working out a compromise. And to achieve a suitable equilibrium, you need judgment and perspective.

From Susan's point of view, the key issues are the amount of rent (the biggest dollar item by far) and the date she can move in (so as not to spend December in a hotel room with her possessions in storage). Painting the vestibule is nothing more than a small dollar issue, which she can arrange for as easily as Ted. As for the television, it's not only unnecessary but overreaching on her part. To make it a basic component of a nonnegotiable demand destroys Susan's credibility as to how final her "final offer" really is. Ted simply doesn't believe that she won't budge—at least on the TV.

What's the result of all this? Well, after Ted's "the best I can do" compromise proposal, Susan is faced with either having to back off her "final offer"—always a difficult proposition, considering the loss of face—or possibly blowing the deal. How much better for her to have negotiated further to arrive at, say, a $1,375 rent, early occupancy, splitting the cost of the paint job (if completed before she moves in), and letting Ted keep his TV—a compromise that I have no doubt he would have accepted. Now, they may never make it.

THE LT SAGA

If the Ted and Susan saga sounds contrived, just pick up the newspaper. This kind of negotiating is going on in real life, too. For example, on September 6, 1990, all the New York papers carried banner stories about Lawrence Taylor, the New York Giants' standout linebacker, who had finally signed his contract after a forty-four day holdout.

Taylor (or "LT," as he's known to the football cognoscenti), was slated to receive $1.2 million in 1990 (the last year of his expiring contract) and asked for a new four-year contract for $9 million. The Giants offered him $4.25 million over three years. After a good deal of haggling, Taylor came down to $5.5 million for the three years, and the Giants inched upward to $4.5 million. The deal was struck at $4.6 million over three years.

Those were the basic facts. But now look at some of the factors that, according to the participants and the press, resulted in the settlement occurring at that time—and at a price much closer to management's position than to LT's.

The key factor everyone pointed to was that the season opener for the Giants was scheduled for the following Sunday against their big rival, the Philadelphia Eagles. This became the real pressure point in the negotiations, because LT just didn't want to miss that contest. It wasn't so much the $90,000 per game paycheck that was at stake, it was simply (as one scribe put it) "impossible for Taylor not to open the season." As LT himself said when he reported later that day to training camp: "Now is the time to play football. That's what I do best. I'm not a negotiator. I'm a football player and I'm here to work."

Taylor knows who he is. But the Giants' general manager, George Young, is a negotiator—and he was counting on LT's "professionalism." In Young's words, "It was hard for me to comprehend his not wanting to play against the Eagles. He's a competitor." Or as a reporter put it, "His need to play is greater than his need to be paid full value."

In our lexicon, this was a case where the leverage factors of powerful desire and time pressure were working strongly against Taylor, and the Giants took full advantage of them. But there's more to the story. In the negotiations, Taylor's agent had apparently taken the position that if LT could be traded, other clubs around the league would be prepared to pay him more than the Giants were offering. So he asked the Giants for the opportunity to check this out. (In our terms, Taylor's agent was trying to drum up some competition as a countervailing leverage factor.) General Manager Young, who suspected that no one would offer more and didn't believe that Taylor would leave New York anyway, agreed to let LT's agent call around the league. When Young proved correct about the other teams, the specter of competition collapsed, reinforcing the Giants' view of Taylor's value and leaving him no alternative but to sit out the season without pay.

By the way, the one team that expressed real interest in Taylor was—you guessed it—the Philadelphia Eagles! Of course, they denied the rampant speculation in the press that this was just a stall to keep LT out of the opener. But their refusal to put an offer in writing, despite Taylor's agent's request, undermined their credibility.

Why was Young so sure that even if someone offered more, Taylor wouldn't leave New York? Young said that he always felt Taylor wanted to finish his career in New York, where he had started out. But according to one reporter, there may have been another important factor. Taylor had recently put a lot of money into a big sports bar and restaurant in the shadow of Giants Stadium. The success of this endeavor was directly dependent on his presence as a Giant. "That's why the bar was named after him," said the reporter, "and not his accountant." So the threat of LT leaving town to play for another club simply wasn't realistic.

This illustrates the central role that information plays. It affected the leverage by providing another, more tangible reason for LT's presumed desire to remain in New York. It also undermined the credibility of his willingness to go elsewhere, thus negating his efforts to kindle competitive fires.

But if Taylor didn't want to go anywhere else, the Giants, for their part, didn't want to face the season without LT. So although Taylor got a lot less than he asked, the Giants ended up paying somewhat more than they wanted to pay. I would like to think that the Giants—even with so much leverage working for them—recognized the principle of balance.

After the contract was signed, Taylor was able to wax philosophical about the whole thing: "I'm happy to be back. I can put aside my pride for a while. Nobody gets exactly what he wants. It's good money." And by the way, LT's pride wasn't put too far aside. This contract made him the highest-paid defensive player in the history of pro football—a point of real principle to Taylor all along and the kind of intangible factor that's often needed to cement a deal.

And yes, LT did get to play that Sunday. After only three days of practice he made seven tackles and three quarterback sacks, forced a fumble, and led the Super Bowl–bound Giants to a 27–20 victory over the Eagles!

2 LEVERAGE—THE ABILITY TO COPE WITH (AND EXPLOIT) AN UNLEVEL PLAYING FIELD

Most bargaining situations contain a variety of factors that either favor or disadvantage a party. A level playing field may be the conventional negotiating model, but it's just as common for one party to arrive at the table less voluntarily or to want the deal more than his counterpart. When the playing field is unlevel for whatever reason, it creates leverage—either for or against you.

A smart negotiator knows how to deal with real and apparent bargaining leverage. Strategies and tactics that are suitable to a level playing field may not be effective when the field tilts. In any negotiation you should be taking account of these dynamics—reaping the advantages available when you've got the clout, husbanding ammunition if your wagons are encircled, and maneuvering for position when the weight teeters.

THE CASE OF HARRY'S DWINDLING NAVY

To help in isolating the principal factors that create positive or negative leverage, let's use an example involving that intrepid trio, Tom, Dixie, and Harry. It's Memorial Day weekend, but Harry's not celebrating. He has a real problem. The poor guy is out of funds and is being pressed by creditors to pay his debts by July 1.

So, with no other course of action open to him—and after a final winsome cruise over the holiday—Harry reluctantly decides to sell his prize asset, a sailboat named *Wildabout*. On June 1 he places an advertisement in the local paper that, after describing the craft, states: "Asking $10,000, but will consider all reasonable offers." In fact,

Harry would like to get $9,000 for *Wildabout*. If necessary, he'll accept $8,000, which will be just enough to satisfy his creditors.

Only two potential buyers materialize—Tom and Dixie. Tom craves *Wildabout* and is willing to pay $9,000. Unfortunately, however, he won't be able to close until August 1, when he'll receive the proceeds from the recent sale of his last boat, *Piper's Son.*

Dixie is interested in *Wildabout* but isn't overwhelmed. She's also quite dollar conscious. There's another boat for sale (*Land O'Cotton*), at a $7,800 price, that she likes almost as much. Dixie offers Harry $7,500 for *Wildabout*, which he turns down. She doesn't make a further offer, although she's prepared to go higher. Dixie has funds in hand and would be prepared to close immediately.

NECESSITY, DESIRE, COMPETITION, AND TIME

A number of factors can create leverage in a deal. Sometimes they operate in tandem, multiplying each other's effects. At other moments they work at cross purposes, vying for predominance and neutralizing the overall impact. One important leverage factor, for example, is which side has more invested in getting a deal done. Costs sunk into a transaction—not just dollars, but also time and effort—create weakness. It's not so easy for the "investor" to walk away from the deal.

In corporate settings, a major motivator may be whether some executive's prestige is on the line, tied to the successful completion of the deal. If so, he or she is likely to stretch more on price, to be more flexible and accommodating in seeking solutions to divisive issues. Sometimes the nature of the bargaining situation itself creates the leverage. If, for instance, one party to an ongoing agreement wants to revise the agreement before it expires, then the other party—who prefers the status quo—starts out in the driver's seat.

Let's go back to Tom, Dixie, and Harry and single out four of the most common leverage factors—*necessity, desire, competition,* and *time.*

NECESSITY

The epitome of necessity, and of the negative leverage it creates, is the seller who is forced to sell. It's the ability to walk away from the table if acceptable terms can't be worked out that puts backbone into your bargaining posture. By contrast, sitting there glued to your seat, afraid to do anything that might cut short the negotiations, forced to endure whatever indignities the other side chooses to inflict, can be a truly excruciating experience.

Harry, unfortunately, is in the position of being forced to sell *Wildabout* in order to pay his debts. If he doesn't receive top dollar, he can't just terminate the discussions and say, "Well, I'll sell *Wildabout* later on, when I can get a better price." This puts him at a real disadvantage and may force him to accept less than what he could otherwise hold out for.

DESIRE

Since necessity may not always be present—and even when it is—a crucial consideration is desire. Who *wants* the deal more, and how strongly does he or she feel about it? Disparity of desire creates a real advantage for the cooler party, the one who's more willing to risk losing the deal.

The potential buyers of *Wildabout* differ in this regard. Tom wants the boat badly, especially since he has already sold *Piper's Son*. A buyer who's too avid tends to overpay. Dixie is less anxious and has a viable alternative in *Land O'Cotton*. Although the desire factor can sometimes change in the course of the deal, Dixie holds a strong hand now, which could cause her to hang tough.

COMPETITION

In a sale, as well as in various negotiating situations, a critical factor is whether or not other potential buyers are vying for the right to make the acquisition. Competition puts pressure on a buyer to pay top dollar, while stiffening the seller's resolve to hold out for it.

Necessity may be working against Harry, but at least he has two bidders to play off against each other. If he were to lose one, he would be in real trouble. Meanwhile Harry will have to decide whether to make each of them aware of the competition. Like most sellers, he'll probably do so, in order the send the usual warning: Hey, don't get too hard-nosed with me, because I've got an alternative.

TIME

But does Harry really have an alternative, once you add in the factor of time? Time pressure cuts across all other negotiating considerations. A party acting under a deadline that has no impact on the other side often makes decisions and takes actions that vary from what his or her conduct might be under more relaxed circumstances. Unfortunately these decisions and actions have a way of playing right into the other party's hands.

Harry is acting under time pressure from his creditors. That July 1 deadline looms ominously, impairing his freedom of action. Tom has his own time restraint; he can't put his money on the line until he collects the proceeds from the sale of *Piper's Son*. Harry's deadline may cost Tom his shot at *Wildabout*. It also has the effect of eliminating, for practical purposes, the competition Harry has been stoking between Dixie and Tom.

Dixie, with no time pressure and plenty of funds available to close the deal, should be able to use time to her advantage. This could change, however, if she were suddenly to come under time pressure herself. That might happen, for instance, if she was forced to make up her mind by a certain date whether or not to buy the other boat, *Land O'Cotton*.

DON'T IGNORE APPARENT LEVERAGE

In many cases the leverage factor is obvious to both parties—for instance, a forced sale under a mortgage foreclosure. At times, however, one of the parties may be unaware of the source of leverage—for ex ample, where a highly motivated buyer conceals his avid desire from the seller. And sometimes one party's belief that his counterpart enjoys positive leverage (for example, that there are other buyers for the seller's property) or is subject to negative leverage (that the seller must sell by a certain date, for instance) turns out to be just plain wrong.

Exerting leverage in negotiations (or having it used against you) depends to a large degree on appearances—and appearances can be deceiving. Overestimating your own strength or underestimating that of the other party has blown many a deal. Overestimating the other side's relative strength or underestimating your own often results in your paying too much or receiving too little.

So, at the outset of any negotiation, always remember to take these initial steps:

- Try to gauge your own strength or weakness:

1. If you're strong, make sure your counterpart knows it.
2. If you're weak, work hard to keep him from realizing it.

- Try to gauge your counterpart's *actual* strength or weakness.
- Surmise whether his *perception* of his strength or weakness accords with reality:

1. If your counterpart believes he's stronger than he actually is, educate him to the real facts.
2. If he thinks he's weaker than he actually is, *don't say a word!*

WHEN THE BALANCE TIPS YOUR WAY

To analyze the implications of leverage and how you should handle it, let's start out with you in the catbird seat and your counterpart behind the eight ball. This can come about because of *negative* leverage affecting your counterpart—a seller who is forced to sell, for example. In that case your job is to discover the existence of any imbalance that would work in your favor. It can also relate to *positive* leverage that *you* possess. For instance, you're a seller who isn't under time pressure or forced to sell, and there are multiple eager buyers. Here your main objective will be to make sure the buyers know what they're up against.

Assume that you're Dixie and you find out that Harry needs $8,000 to pay his creditors by July 1, and—since Tom can't get his act together before August 1—you happen to be the only possible source of funds. You're riding high.

Communicating strength where it really exists might seem simple, but it presents two problems. The first is that you may not be believed (a subject we'll cover in chapter 4); the assumption here, however, is that your strength is credible. The second problem is that you come across as so smug, so arrogant, so overbearing, that your counterpart retaliates by taking actions that aren't in his rational interest.

Don't let this happen. Convey your strength quietly, letting it speak for itself and keeping personalities out of the way. Try not to be confrontational, which could cause Harry to bluff or harden his position. Just let the facts sink in—not calling for a response, but hoping to influence Harry's deliberations in the quiet of his own caucus. Let's face it, your chances of getting Harry to bow, scrape, and congratulate you publicly on the strength of your position equate roughly with the likelihood of a real-life defendant confessing on the stand à la "Perry Mason."

When it's your good fortune to hold all the cards, I feel you should behave reasonably, treating the Harrys of this world with courtesy and respect. Forget about crusades, retribution, and power games. On issues where you're immovable, tell Harry so, quietly but unequivocally. That way he won't be operating under the delusion that there's room to negotiate, which will save frustration down the road. Don't cut off Harry's rebuttals and arguments, even if they're fruitless; he needs to go through this process.

To avoid appearing arbitrary, express a rationale for your position. Don't seek to justify your position with such unsatisfactory refrains as "This is how we always do things" or "That clause is in all our agreements," ignoring Harry's rational arguments in favor of a contrary result. And don't insist on total victory. Couple issues on which you're unbending with others on which you can be more flexible, so that Harry isn't made to feel helpless. (More about this in chapter 5.)

Remember, too, that leverage factors aren't necessarily permanent. They can change swiftly in the course of the negotiations. This could happen here, for instance, if Tom could lay his hands on some funds earlier or Harry's creditors were to give him an extra month to pay up. So when things are running strongly in your favor *today*, try to conclude a deal promptly, before the situation changes. And that holds true even if you might drive a harder bargain by letting Harry perspire some more.

U'RE AT A CLEAR DISADVANTAGE

..... switch to a situation in which you're at a clear negotiating *disadvantage* and both sides know it. For me, this happened in the final sad days of People Express. My upstart airline client, after a bold run for the roses, had just about run out of money. To avoid bankruptcy, it desperately sought out a purchaser. But of all the carriers, only Texas Air was willing to talk turkey. If you want to know what it's like to be behind the eight ball, try negotiating with Frank Lorenzo and his lieutenants under those circumstances. We swallowed hard and made a deal, but believe me, it was painful.

If you were Harry in the *Wildabout* negotiation, complete with unrelenting creditors and a Tom who can't get his funds together, you would be at a clear disadvantage. Does this mean you're without resources? Not at all. But you have to aim for limited objectives, distinguishing between what is achievable and what's not.

This distinction often turns on the nature of the particular issue. With a subject like price that has various rational outcomes, the odds are clearly against you. But with issues that are usually handled a certain way, or where one conclusion is much more reasonable than any other, you've got a fighting chance. Your substitute for leverage is to wrap yourself in the twin mantles of "reasonableness" and "conventional practice," hoping that your counterpart is fair-minded and respects precedent.

Let's see how this plays out on four different issues in the *Wildabout* negotiations, beginning with price. Assume that Dixie is willing to pay the minimum $8,000 that you need for your creditors. My bet is you'll fail to move her to a higher level. If, for instance, you say, "Well, I've got Tom in the wings here, and he's willing to pay nine thousand dollars," Dixie's response is, "Hey, Harry, if you can get nine thousand dollars for *Wildabout*, grab it. That's a terrific price." And when you reply, "But as you know, I've got this little time problem," her simple retort will be, "If you need eight thousand now, Harry, then you'd better deal with me." And that's all you're likely to get.

The second issue concerns the gangway linking the boat to the dock, which belongs to Harry (the marina doesn't supply them). The question is whether or not the gangway is included in the sale at the $8,000 price. The issue wasn't addressed specifically; Dixie thought the gangway went with the boat, while you wanted to retain it for possible future use. In the absence of an understanding between the parties, there's no "right" or logical way for this issue to come out once it's addressed; it could go either way. If Dixie insists that it be thrown into the pot, I think she's going to end up with a "freebie" gangway.

The third issue involves the marina rental fee for *Wildabout*. Since you've prepaid it for a period running through September 30, you ask Dixie to reimburse you for the prorated share of the cost from July 1 (the date she buys the boat) through September 30. Your argument is entirely logical: she'll have the use of the space for that period, so she should bear the cost. Dixie doesn't have any rational counter-argument. She could stick to her guns, in which case you might have to give in eventually. But in my experience the Dixies of the real world don't play the game that way. When the logic is irresistible, they usually end up conceding the point. I think that would happen here.

The fourth issue is one that you feel strongly about. At the July 1 closing, which happens to be the due date of your obligations, you need a certified or bank cashier's check to be able to pay off your creditors immediately. Instead Dixie proposes to give you a regular uncertified check, which doesn't represent immediate funds and can't be used until it clears several days later. (Presumably Dixie is looking to keep the interest on the funds for herself in the interim.) You invoke the conventional practice in sales of major items such as automobiles, art, jewelry—*and boats*—requiring that payment be complete when title and possession pass, which calls for a "cash" type of check. I think Dixie will bow to precedent and back down on this one.

A point of style is worth noting here. When you're the beleaguered party, there's one sure way to guarantee that your powerful counterpart will feel no compunction about nailing you to the wall, and that's for you come on in a shrill, hectoring style. Forget the frustration you undoubtedly feel; this is not the time to throw your piddling weight around. On the other hand, don't wrap your requests in weak, apologetic tones, either. Your appeal to reason is best handled with quiet self-assurance, accompanied by a thoughtful rationale.

When the merits of an issue don't prevail, and assuming it isn't a deal breaker, then it's best to give in—not on the principle, but to the power. Your attitude should be, Okay, I won't prolong the agony on this point; but, Dixie, you owe me one! Perhaps—just *perhaps*—some small tremor of remorse will greet your next meritorious issue.

The toughest moments to handle are naked displays of power by the other side. Dixie might, for example, drop her price, or renege on a concession previously granted, or suffer a convenient loss of memory, or persist in a totally irrational position. The temptation to tell her to "get lost" is overwhelming. But you can't afford this self-indulgence if you need the deal. Try to be constructive. Maybe there's some fat around the edges you can strip out of the final resolution. Perhaps you can revive something you didn't get earlier to swap for your concession here—especially where there's a logical tie-in. Keep your focus on *solutions*. Don't let yourself become part of the problem.

WHEN THE LEVERAGE FACTORS CONFLICT

In the two previous situations, the relative leverage was clear—either for or against you—and both sides knew it. The typical case is more in balance. Either the actual leverage doesn't tip so far in one direction, or, if it does, the parties aren't aware of the imbalance.

We've seen how competition can partially offset necessity, how time can work at cross purposes with desire, and so on. Don't become obsessed with some positive factor that's working in your counterpart's favor, or paralyzed by a disturbing negative that's undermining your interests. Rather, keep your eyes open for overlooked countervailing factors to mitigate the leverage. Better yet, sprinkle some helpful new ingredients into the pot.

Picture yourself as a seller. You know full well that a purchaser who concludes that you must sell and that you lack an alternative buyer will take a very tough line. You have to work hard to keep this from happening. Always try to get another buyer interested, even if it's a long shot. That way you can truthfully make reference to "other current interest." But what if nobody else is available?

Put yourself again in Harry's place. Tom is now completely out of the picture, so Dixie is your only buyer. She has offered $7,500 in response to your $10,000 asking price. Assume that Dixie does *not* know that you've struck out in coming up with another buyer—a fact you're under no obligation to reveal. She is also unaware that you need to close by July 1; but since that time pressure does exist, you have to move things along briskly—a potential tip-off. What might you do to offset Dixie's leverage, without lying or creating a fictitious alternative purchaser?

Here's one possible tack for you take: "Dixie, for reasons I won't go into, I would prefer to complete this deal by July 1. If you're agreeable to closing by that date, I'm willing to let you have *Wildabout* for the bargain price of eighty-five hundred. If you're not, then I'll probably try to get a higher price by advertising more widely."

Now, note what you've done here. While acknowledging that you would like to close by July 1, you make it appear more a preference than a necessity, at the same time discouraging further discussion of the reasons for your haste. You offer Dixie an inducement to meet your schedule by a "temporary" reduction in your asking price to $8,500. (If she decides to negotiate, you still have some room to go before hitting your $8,000 minimum level.) You don't invent another current purchaser; rather, you sidestep the issue by referring to a possible wider circle of buyers. This invokes the specter of *potential* competition. It's not as forceful as actual competition, yet Dixie can't afford to ignore it entirely.

To sum up, there are three ways to balance the leverage in a bargaining situation. If the factors, taken as a whole, are really in equilibrium, then make sure to get all the relevant facts out in the open. If they tilt in the other direction, then either try to generate new leverage to offset the pressure or, alternatively, keep your counterpart from fully grasping the negative leverage you face.

On this last score, make sure to conceal any overt signs of pressure you're feeling. Mask (don't mop) your sweaty brow, avoid that dejected slump in an upright chair, rule out anxiety-ridden glances at your wristwatch. Never behave as if you had no other options. There's no ethical requirement to acknowledge weakness. And as we'll see in the next chapter, there are various ways to block or avoid questions on the subject without resorting to falsehood.

Finally, you should probe your counterpart for signs of vulnerability. Don't underestimate *Dixie's* problems—even if you don't know about them yet. Those problems are your opportunities.

WHEN YOU'RE RUNNING A QUASI-AUCTION

From a seller's perspective, a clear case of positive leverage occurs where two or more willing and able suitors are vying *simultaneously* for the prize, *and* the seller doesn't care which one ends up as the winner. (If the seller cares who wins, there's a wholly different dynamic at work. If the competition is sequential rather than simultaneous, then the seller's task is more difficult; it's that old "bird in the hand vs. two in the bush" quandary.) But if the seller has *two* birds in the hand, he's running an informal quasi-auction.

You're Harry. Assume, for example, that your creditors relent and give you until August 1 to pay up. This makes Tom, who still craves *Wildabout* and will have the necessary funds by then, a viable buyer. Further assume that *Land O'Cotton* is sold to someone else, so that Dixie no longer has that alternative. As a result, her level of desire for *Wildabout* goes way up. Now you can play Tom and Dixie off against each other.

This is the kind of situation sellers crave. In most cases the seller will want each buyer to know the other is there. The idea is to spur them on, in true auction spirit, to bid boldly against each other—the competitive juices flowing right into the seller's pocket. The prime example of this for me came in representing Richardson-Vicks, when it was under siege by Unilever. Once the Richardson-Vicks board decided the company had to be sold, it invited three well-heeled and eager purchasers to the party—Procter & Gamble, Pfizer, and Colgate. We set up the three buyers in separate conference rooms and conducted a veritable shuttle service, letting each of them go at it to see who would prevail with the best price and terms. Proctor & Gamble eventually took the expensive prize.

A buyer can attempt to counter this leverage by refusing to bid unless the seller is willing to deal on an exclusive basis. In my experience, however, this type of pose by a buyer, especially one who has previously shown real interest in the property, is often a bluff that ought to be called. At the very least the seller should condition his willingness to deal exclusively on the buyer offering a whale of a preemptive price.

In a spirited bidding contest, one of the bidders will sometimes take a hard-line position on a nonprice issue that the other bidders haven't taken. Here's the speech I like to deliver (as the seller's lawyer) to such a bidder and his lawyer:

Look, the seller is going to make the ultimate decision among these offers based on the merits. Obviously price is paramount, but other considerations may also be important. My goal is to present the seller with as much comparability as possible in terms of these other issues. Your competitors have *not* insisted on this particular point. I suggest you see your way clear to doing the same, because otherwise you may lose the deal—even if your dollar bid is as good as any on the table—since the principle at stake is such an important one for the seller.

A warning like this has real force with an insecure executive of the bidder, who won't want his boss to think he's blown the deal. It also works particularly well when the issue involves a legal point. The last thing in the world the bidder's lawyer wants is for his client to lose the deal because he demanded protection that may not have been needed; after all, none of the lawyers for the *other* bidders insisted on it.

By the way, a seller in the driver's seat should be sure to negotiate all the crucial terms of the agreement while the auction is still in progress. Once the seller selects one suitor over the others and tells the prospective buyer that he has won the contest, the leverage can shift abruptly. This is particularly true where the winner has prevailed by paying a helluva price. All of a sudden he thinks he actually deserves some contractual protection! And let's face it, the seller is not about to risk letting him off the hook over some lawyer's legalese, especially now that the other bidders have either disappeared or would be tough to deal with if the seller had to go back to them hat in hand.

LEVERAGE WRAP-UP

By way of summary, here and at the close of each of the following chapters, I will provide my three picks for

- a basic point (*Keynote*) from the chapter worth stressing;
- a common error (*Blunder*) negotiators make in the area under discussion;
- a notable omission (*Lapse*) that often occurs in dealing with this aspect of negotiating.

Keynote

The first basic skill of smart negotiating is an awareness of the leverage factors at work, plus the ability to apply leverage when it's in your favor and make do when it's not. Where leverage is concerned, appearances are often crucial—and appearances can be manipulated. As a negotiator, you should always be responsive to leverage; but you must learn to distinguish between the real thing and the ersatz variety—as well as how to cover up your own weaknesses.

Blunder

Negotiators with leverage in their favor often misuse it, adopting arrogant and confrontational postures, which cause their counterparts to toughen up in retaliation. Don't squander your riches. Let your strength speak for itself. Never furnish your counterpart with an excuse to respond irrationally.

Lapse

There's a tendency to be overwhelmed by negative leverage factors that hamper your freedom of action. Your counterpart may be *talking* a good game, but what's really going on underneath? There can be elements you're unaware of that hamper his freedom of action—in which case you may not be in such bad shape after all.

3 INFORMATION—THE ABILITY TO FERRET OUT (AND PROTECT) VITAL FACTS

Good information is an essential commodity for you as a negotiator. It gets behind the other side's positions and provides you with insight into your counterpart's motivation and intentions. The more you know, the better you can judge what price will swing the deal, how an issue is likely to play out, what arguments should be stressed or scrapped. And as we've just seen, the *appearance* of leverage depends largely on who knows what.

There are many ways to gather useful information: by consulting public records, for example, or by hiring investigators, speaking to knowledgeable third parties, and using intermediaries. Here we'll focus on the most significant means: the information you can elicit from your counterpart before and during the negotiations, together with its unavoidable corollary—what your counterpart can pry out of you.

THE CASE OF THE VALUED EMPLOYEE

Keyes is a valuable employee of Printco, a financial printer, who is responsible for the care and servicing of a number of the company's biggest corporate accounts. He has been working under a three-year employment contract, which has six months left to run. And there's a substantial accrued bonus payable to him eleven months from now— but only if he's still employed by Printco. (Keyes wasn't too careful in the prior contract negotiation.)

A few days ago Boss, the Printco chief executive, told Keyes that he would like to negotiate a three-year extension of his employment contract. Keyes replied that he was willing to talk. But just before negotiations got under way, two tidbits of information rose to the surface. Keyes heard rumors that Printco might be sold to a big conglomerate in the near future. And Printco heard rumors that its competitor, Hotlead, has been trying to lure Keyes away from the company.

WHAT INFORMATION ARE YOU SEEKING?

Assume you're Boss, preparing to negotiate. What information would you like to find out? And why will it be useful? Here's a partial listing of items and motives you might be interested in knowing about:

1. Does Keyes enjoy working at Printco?

   • The more he does, the more likely he'll extend the present arrangement. The less content Keyes is, the more you'll have to tempt him with contractual goodies.

2. Has Keyes actually been approached by Hotlead (or other competitors) to jump ship?

   • If so, he's likely to be more feisty in the negotiations, knowing that his services are in demand and that he has something to fall back on if the Printco proposal doesn't satisfy his needs.

3. Does Keyes control his customers personally, or does their real loyalty run to Printco? In other words, if Keyes leaves Printco, how many of his accounts will follow him? (Assume, for these purposes, that his present contract lacks an effective noncompete provision—an oversight on Printco's part.)

   • If the bulk of Keyes's accounts will go with him, that gives him real leverage, and he's likely to hang tougher in the negotiations. If few will depart, then it won't be the end of the world if Keyes leaves, and you don't have to be as generous in order to keep him.

4. What attitude does Keyes have toward his accrued bonus?

- The more he wants or needs it in eleven months, the less motivated he'll be to leave Printco when his present contract is up in six months, and the less free-wheeling he's likely to be in the upcoming negotiations.

Now, shift over and assume you're Keyes. What morsels of information about Printco would you like to know for purposes of the bargaining, and why? Here are a few:

1. Why is Printco initiating the negotiations a full six months before the end of your present contract term?

    - The answer may provide an important clue as to Printco's motivation, its desires, and the strength or weakness of its bargaining posture.

2. Is Printco about to be acquired? If so, has the buyer made it a condition of the deal (or an element of the price) that key employees like you agree in advance to stick around for a number of years?

    - If an acquisition is on the horizon, this might account for the early commencement of negotiations. And if your continued employment is an important element in Printco's deal, you may find yourself possessing some real leverage.

3. Regardless of the actual facts, what is Printco's *assumption* about the loyalty of your customers?

    - The more Printco fears your ability to control your customers, the more leverage you'll have in the negotiations—even if, in truth, you don't exercise that much influence.

PRYING THE INFORMATION LOOSE

All right, if that's what each of you wants to know, how do you go about finding it out? For openers, you should try to adopt a low-key style that doesn't send a warning signal to your counterpart. If Boss has "cross-examination" tattooed on his forehead when he sets out to inquire about the accrued bonus, Keyes's defenses will quickly go up in place. Ferreting out useful information is hard work, but try not to look as if you're working at it. Even a direct question should be posed in neutral, nonconfrontational terms, at a time and place that you've chosen to arouse minimal suspicion.

In terms of timing, try to gather the information as early as possible. Your best shot at eliciting a candid response occurs *before* the negotiation starts, when your counterpart isn't as alert to the possibility of a connection between the probe and the bargaining.

You should, of course, be as fully informed as possible when you sit down to bargain. Still, you might glean more useful information *during* the negotiations. There's much to say for a period of small talk at the outset anyway—introducing yourself and getting to know your counterpart if you've never met before, setting a good mood for the bargaining that follows. Keep in mind that the more *you* talk, the less information comes your way. So resist the temptation to chatter. Encourage your counterpart to speak. And listen attentively—not only to the words, but for any clues transmitted between the lines.

In the postmortem caucus with colleagues that follows after most negotiating sessions, I often find myself speculating on the significance of something our counterparts *didn't* say that I expected them to cover. These kinds of inferences can be helpful. Don't rely too heavily on them, however. There may be perfectly valid reasons for your counterpart's omission that have nothing to do with the spin you've chosen to put on it.

COMPARING DIRECT AND INDIRECT PROBES

There are two basic ways (with numerous variants) to go after information from your counterpart. The first is *direct*. You ask a specific, pointed question, seeking a candid and responsive answer. (You do *not*, however, go on to add, "I need to know this because it will be helpful to me in the negotiations.") So, for instance, Keyes might say to Boss, "I've heard rumors that Printco is being acquired. Are those rumors true?" It may take a little gumption on your part to pose such a straightforward question in search of confidential information, but it's good gumption to have.

Let's assume that Printco is, in fact, engaged in acquisition talks, a tidbit that Boss would rather not reveal to Keyes at this time. The virtue of a direct question is that it puts the other side in a quandary. On the one hand, a truthful reply may give away too much too early. Even an equivocal response invites Keyes to follow up with further probing questions. On the other hand, if Boss flatly denies the rumor, then he has misled Keyes in a manner that's not ethical. Since neither course is satisfactory, Boss is forced to cope in some other way. (Both the ethics and the coping are discussed later in this chapter.)

The disadvantage of the direct approach is that it highlights the subject. Boss now knows exactly what Keyes is interested in and can try to protect the information. If the questioning had put him less on his guard, he might have let slip something valuable, from which Keyes could have inferred the true state of affairs. So the other way to go after information is *indirectly*—coming at the point obliquely, in hopes you might learn something from which you can draw a reasonable inference.

For instance, say that Boss wants to size up what control Keyes exercises over his customers. In the course of a business encounter that takes place before the negotiations have even commenced, Boss might begin with some broad general questions about customers, encouraging Keyes to talk freely about them. This gives Boss the opportunity to explore the origins of particular associations, to probe gently into whether certain relationships have gone beyond business to become social, and so on.

Now if Keyes is suspicious, he may guard this information. Even if he doesn't suspect anything, he's likely to play up his strength with customers in a conversation with his superior. But here, at least, it's not tied in to the negotiations. And if Boss handles his probe in a low-key manner, Keyes might just let something significant slip—for example, that his largest customer recently exhibited some independence by using another printer who quoted lower rates for a small job. It's more likely to happen this way than if Keyes had been alerted by direct questions from Boss: "How loyal are these customers to you? Do any of them use other printers?"

The disadvantage of the indirect technique, however, is that by not putting Keyes on the spot, Boss may never get any useful information about the customers. Keyes, if he wants to, will be able to bob and weave around that particular loyalty lapse without being forced to address it forthrightly. Of course, Boss can always switch to a specific direct inquiry later on, if the open-ended questioning fails to produce anything usable. But, then, unless Boss is careful, it may look as if he were being a little sneaky in the earlier rounds.

So how does a negotiator decide which technique to use? There's no hard and fast answer, but here's my general rule of thumb. If the information you're after is clearly relevant to the subject matter of the negotiations, and there's no other downside risk to your putting it on the table, you might as well do it directly, phrased in such a manner as to compel your counterpart to give you a straight answer. On the other hand, where the information sought is more nebulous—but still wouldn't be *consciously* revealed—then it may be worthwhile to orchestrate an indirect strategy, aimed at eliciting an inadvertent disclosure.

So, for example, assume you're Boss. On the point of whether Keyes has been approached by Hotlead, you might as well ask him the direct question, even if the two of you have already commenced negotiations. After all, his options as to employment form an obvious element in Keyes's decision whether to extend his contract. And a competitor's attempt to poach on Printco's employees is something in which you're clearly interested.

On the point of Keyes's attitude toward his accrued bonus, however, you're better off dealing indirectly. After all, the answer you could anticipate receiving to a direct question on the subject won't give you much to go on. ("All things being equal, Boss, I would rather collect the bonus, but it's not going to keep me here if we're unable to reach satisfactory terms.") But if, under more oblique prodding, Keyes were to let slip a specific need he has for funds next September—for instance, he's sending a kid off to college—or if he shows interest in a *one-year* contract extension, then you might be entitled to infer that the bonus looms large on his personal horizon.

PROTECTING SENSITIVE INFORMATION

Now I want you to change roles from the party probing for information to the *recipient* of the probe. And let's assume you know exactly what the prober is after, which is something you would like to protect. This, too, calls for some advance planning, anticipating the potentially "soft" areas and deciding how to respond to inquiries.

Spontaneity may be refreshing, but under pressure it can prove your undoing.

NEED FUNDS, LACK BIDDERS

Let's leave Printco and use a different example here. Assume that Mr. Cellar is selling his house, and Ms. Byre is quite anxious to buy it. Cellar starts out asking $200,000; he would like to get at least $185,000, although conceivably he might take less. Byre, who wants to make a deal at around $175,000 but is prepared to go as high as $190,000, offers $150,000. Cellar pooh-poohs Byre's offer and doesn't budge. Byre violates the precept of not bidding against oneself (discussed in chapters 8 and 9) and raises her offer to $160,000. Cellar still hangs tough, although hinting he might be prepared to knock $10,000 off his asking price ("I don't even have five-percent leeway built into that price.")

Now, consider the significance to the bargaining if the following information were to be introduced into the picture. Say that Ms. Byre becomes aware that Mr. Cellar has already gone to contract on the purchase of another house, for which the closing date is coming up, and he needs the funds from this house to pay for that one. She also finds out that Cellar has no ready, willing, and able buyer for this house other than Byre.

The leverage resulting from these nuggets of information—involving the factors of necessity and competition—would give Ms. Byre a real advantage in the ensuing negotiations. By playing hardball, she may well be able to pressure Mr. Cellar down to her desired $175,000 level. Conversely, if Cellar had no immediate need for funds and other buyers were actively bidding for the property, then Byre might consider it necessary to strike an immediate deal with Cellar at the $190,000 level, in order to end up with the house of her dreams.

Let's assume Byre suspects that Cellar needs funds quickly and poses a direct question to him: "Do you need the proceeds from the sale of this house to pay for your new home?" What's more, she also asks him, "Is anyone else bidding on the house?" Pretend you're Mr. Cellar, faced with these direct queries and stuck with the worst of all worlds: you need the funds and lack other bidders. How should you reply to Ms. Byre's direct questions on these topics? How do you steer a safe course between the twin shoals of revealing valuable information and telling a lie?

LYING—THE CLEAR "NO-NO"

I don't intend to explore the legal implications of lying. You should know, however, that if you induce your counterpart to make a deal by fraudulently misrepresenting a material fact—and assuming his reliance on your misrepresentation is justified—then he can hold you liable for damages. Even under lesser circumstances, the resulting contract may be voided. In addition, lawyers who negotiate for clients are subject to certain ethical rules, which can lead to disciplinary action for violations. But even if this weren't the case, I would urge you to shun lying like the plague. It violates all precepts of fair dealing between responsible individuals.

I believe most right-minded people share that sentiment—at least in theory. The problem, however, is something that lies at the core of negotiating. The fact is that many of your actions and statements are *designed* to mislead your counterpart, to facilitate an inaccurate assessment on his part. You *want* your counterpart to believe you're more immovable on price than you really are. You *don't want* him to realize the relative unimportance to you of the point you're about to concede, so that your concession will motivate him to make a substantial move on another front. But where should you draw the line?

POSING THE ETHICAL ISSUE

Most of us engage in some forms of puffery. Sellers exaggerate the value of what's being sold. Buyers feel no compunction about overstating the firmness of their latest bid. Lawyers inflate the strength of their client's case. This sort of hype is viewed as part of the game; everyone expects it, and the system accepts such behavior. At the other extreme, misrepresentations of fact that relate directly to what's being bought and sold are clearly off limits. You can't put zircons into a Tiffany box, move the odometer back ten thousand miles, or concoct a nonexistent account receivable.

On the other hand, many phony rationales are used to justify positions taken in negotiations (for instance, the reason stated by one party as to *why* he can't give a certain protection requested by the other). This is what I call "creative motivation." I don't encourage this sort of thing, but the reality is that it's generally condoned on the theory that one side isn't entitled to see the inner workings of the other side's mind. *So, be warned, negotiators: take* nothing *at face value, and examine closely all ostensible rationales.*

The questions that create a dilemma for the negotiator usually relate to matters that are *collateral* to the subject matter of the negotiation. They don't go to the quality of what's being bought and sold; rather, they relate to the leverage factors that affect the bargaining between the parties—such as Mr. Cellar's need to sell quickly and the unavailability of other alternatives.

Say that, as Cellar, you were to lie blatantly in response to Ms. Byre's question about other bidders, inventing another buyer who is ready, willing, and able to pay $180,000 on the spot. On hearing your reply, Byre panics and concludes an immediate deal at $190,000. Put aside any legal question; do you feel you've done something wrong? I do—and I bet you do, too. That's not a proper way to negotiate. Still, a less blatant response, hinting obliquely in the same direction, might enable you to rationalize any feelings of misbehavior.

I wish I could provide you with an all-purpose guideline on what's permissible and what's not, but I can't. In the end, like so many aspects of negotiation that depend on good judgment, this one comes down to your own sense of what's appropriate. I will pass along, however, something that has been suggested as a legal test and that also works pretty well on a practical basis. The key is whether the deception causes some *unfairness* in the bargaining situation. Put another way, does the nature of what's said make it likely that the speaker will *succeed* in deceiving the listener? This may turn on whether the listener was *justified* in relying on the false statement. As a result, the more specific the statement ("I have another buyer at $180,000"), the more likely it crosses the line into "no-no" territory. When the remark is less precise ("My house is a real steal at $200,000"), chances are it will be considered puffing or simply the speaker's own opinion.

BLOCKING TECHNIQUES

So, Mr. Cellar, what *should* you do when that assertive Ms. Byre demands answers to tough questions about your need for funds and the presence of other buyers? The method you use has to block the flow of harmful information but not give your counterpart reason to infer the bad news from your response. Ruling a particular query out of bounds, for instance—"None of your business!"—runs the risk that Byre will infer from your sensitivity that she has struck pure gold. And even though she can never be as sure of her surmise as when you've revealed the truth, she may still proceed on the basis of that inference.

Surely, however, you can do better than that. We've all watched an adroit politician bob and weave around the questions of a skilled reporter. Here, your interrogator is likely to be considerably less adept and might even feel uneasy at pressing the inquiry. You may get away with ignoring the funds question entirely, if not by silence, then by changing the subject ("By the way, let me show you the handy ice maker in the refrigerator.")

But since silence and non sequiturs also risk generating a negative inference, a better tack may be to deflect the inquiry, channeling your reply into a less sensitive area. Typical of this genre is the response that purports to answer the question but in fact addresses a different one. For instance, on the "other buyers" query, you might reply, "Funny you should ask. The broker was just saying the other day that this would be a perfect house for a doctor who has his office at home."

You can also provide a general answer to a specific question. For example, in responding to an inquiry about your "new home," a reply such as "Obviously, I'll have to live somewhere—I'm not about to take to the streets" may get you off the hook. This also illustrates, by the way, the use of sarcasm or hyperbole, which can be an effective technique with a less than persistent questioner. Specific answers to general questions may also derail the line of inquiry.

A frequently effective riposte is to proffer your own question back to the interrogator, particularly one that probes an area your counterpart might not want to discuss. On the funds question, for instance, you might turn the spotlight onto *Ms. Byre's* sources of financing. Showing that two can play at this game may ease the pressure of her direct inquiry.

Generally, my own preference is to take an assertive tack. On the "other buyers" issue, if I were Cellar—and assuming that a person of means recently expressed interest in the house (although hasn't yet made an offer)—I might say, "I don't have a firm offer at this time. But I do have a potential purchaser who, if he decides to buy, is clearly capable of paying two hundred thousand. Are you willing to take the risk that I'll pass up your much lower bid for a possible higher offer?"

Or if I had no nibbles at all and therefore decided to rule the "other buyers" question out of order, I might couple it with a warning along these lines: "I don't want to get into that. Make up your mind on the merits of the property. I'm telling you"—*and here I would slow down and emphasize each word*—"it . . . will . . . take . . . two hundred thousand . . . to . . . buy . . . this . . . house."

On the "paying for another house" question, I might try something that concedes the need for speed (which, after all, I won't ultimately be able to disguise) but attempts to point Byre in a different direction as to *why* the need exists. Perhaps something like this: "I love this house. It was a wrench for me to decide to sell it. But now that I've decided, I want it to happen quickly. You'd be well advised to get me signed, sealed, and delivered before I change my mind and take it off the market."

THE NEED TO DEBRIEF

The flow of information in a negotiation is constant. Many of the clues you receive that bear on intention, motivation, credibility, and leverage are no more than faint traces. They require further validation—in the form of repetition, corroboration, or similar reactions by others—in order to form more indelible impressions.

For this reason, when several people are involved on your side of the deal, it's useful to have a postmortem or debriefing caucus shortly after each negotiating session. That's the best time to discuss any inklings of information. The impressions are fresh in your mind, and the exercise of voicing them may rouse complementary (or contradictory) inferences from your colleagues. If you wait a few days, it's difficult to remember precisely what occurred—the words that were used, the meaningful omissions, the body language, and so forth.

There are, of course, subjects other than information that you'll want to explore in such a caucus, all feeding into an assessment of your strategy for upcoming sessions. You might have to check some things out before reaching any conclusion; a little more perspective on certain matters may be desirable. But those fresh first impressions can be potent indeed and shouldn't be ignored.

INFORMATION WRAP-UP

Keynote

The second basic skill of the smart negotiator is the ability to uncover and evaluate any information about the other side that may increase his leverage and at the same time guard any information about his position that may decrease it. Information is so central to negotiating that you have to develop plans regarding it *in advance*. What do you need to know? What's the best way of finding it out? What is your counterpart likely to be looking for from you? What's the best way to protect information you would prefer not to disclose?

Blunder

If you're unprepared when a tough question comes your way, you may respond in a manner that inadvertently gives away just what you're trying to protect. Be sensitive to the inferences your counterpart may draw. Work out your sidestepping strategy in an unpressured atmosphere to avoid finding yourself forced to reply in the heat of the moment.

Lapse

For some reason—politeness may be the chief culprit here—we too often fail to pose the key question directly. When we do inquire, it's handled in a more roundabout fashion, which is easier for the other side to duck or counter. As a result, we don't obtain significant information or even building blocks from which to derive a valuable inference. Don't be afraid to pose tough questions to your counterpart. The worst that can happen is you'll be told it's "none of your business," a response that itself often transmits some valuable information your way.

4 CREDIBILITY—THE ABILITY TO BE BELIEVABLE YOURSELF AND TO SPOT THE OTHER SIDE'S BLUFF

"Eighty-five thousand dollars, that's my top price—I won't pay another nickel." Sound familiar? You bet. The buyer asserts his position strongly, trying to make the seller stop negotiating and sell at his price. It's a tactic often employed, and not limited to buyers or issues of price.

But the real question is how *credible* is the assertion? Should the speaker be believed and his position acknowledged? Or is his seemingly firm stand merely a bluff? And the related question—when *you* are the speaker and your statement is *true*—is how do you make *yourself* believable?

TRANSMITTING AND RECEIVING POSITIVE INFORMATION

Before examining the credibility of our negotiating positions, I want to touch on another area where authenticity is the keynote: the transmittal and receipt of information. We've discussed how to block your counterpart's access to information you consider *adverse* to your interests. The flip side is how do you convince your counterpart that the *helpful* information you're telling him is genuine? How does a seller, for instance, persuade a buyer that the seller *really* does have a higher competing bid for the property?

The credibility you've been able to achieve over the course of the negotiation thus far plays a major role here. The more truthful your words—the more your counterpart has come to trust your actions—

the greater the likelihood that your favorable information will be believed. But if you've engaged in sharp practice or been caught dissembling, you'll face real skepticism—just when you have something positive to report. It's the familiar boy-who-cried-wolf syndrome, in spades.

In terms of what you say, I offer two bits of advice. First, the more removed the positive information is from the actual negotiations, the less it's suspect as a ruse designed to gain advantage. Second, the more precise and specific your statement is, the more you're likely to be believed. So resist the temptation to overstate your case.

The recipient of such information has to approach it with caution, particularly when the statement (if true) provides real leverage for the speaker. Here's a useful rule of thumb: The more the recipient's actions are likely to be influenced by the statement, the greater the speaker's temptation to exaggerate or even dissemble.

We all have our own ways of assessing the credibility of what we're told. Some people assume that any sentence beginning with certain words—like "To be perfectly candid," or "In all honesty," or "Frankly speaking"—is automatically suspect. Others put great store in nonverbal clues to deception—shifty eyes, perspiration, fidgeting, the hand over the mouth to "suppress" the intended falsehood. Still, the best con men ooze sincerity, looking you right in the eye while lying through their teeth. At any rate, don't hesitate to use in your negotiations whatever system you subscribe to in your daily life.

THE CREDIBILITY OF "FINAL" POSITIONS

Now let's turn to the credibility of negotiating *positions* taken by the parties—particularly when one of them says, "This is it. There ain't no more." The fact is that a "final" position can be genuine or a bluff. If the position is *unacceptable* to the other party, then either the deal is dead (if the statement is true) or the speaker will back down (when his bluff is called). The situation I want to focus on, however, is where the other party would, if necessary, *be willing to accede* to the terms of a final position—but not lightly, and particularly not when he smells a bluff.

If you're the speaker and your position is genuine, you need to transmit that reality so that your counterpart doesn't stand firm out of a misreading of your bona fides. If, on the other hand, you're a speaker who is bluffing, you have to be convincing way beyond your bona fides! And if you're the listener, you need the savvy to distinguish between the real thing and the ersatz variety.

By the way, in negotiating there's only one thing worse than to be caught bluffing. It is *not* to be bluffing, but to have the other side *think* you are. This is in stark contrast with the game of poker, where having your opponent read your actual strength as a bluff can be terrific. He stays in to bet, and you rake in the sweetened pot.

So let's examine a this-is-it position

- When it's genuine,
- When it's a bluff, and
- How to tell the difference from the other side of the table.

THE PIZZA CONSULTATION

Peter owns a small chain of pizza restaurants, Peter's Pizza Parlors. Connie, a business consultant, is pitching for his business, claiming she can increase efficiency and improve margins. He's definitely interested. They turn to negotiating the terms under which Connie's services would be engaged.

WHEN YOU'RE FOR REAL

There are two aspects to convincing your counterpart that the rock-solid position you're taking is the real McCoy when it really is. The first, which we'll discuss here, is to show how meaningful the point is to you, on the premise that people don't usually become immovable over lightweight issues. The second aspect—that you've gone as far as you're willing to go—is covered in chapters 9 and 10 as part of the concession pattern and compromise technique needed to persuade your counterpart that you've traveled the distance.

The crucial insight here is to recognize that *you will not be able to achieve "sticking" credibility by taking a "this is it" position on multiple issues*. Try and you'll simply demean the lot. Rather, what carries the day is your ability to *differentiate among issues,* so as to impress upon your counterpart how important *this* one is.

Let's face it, your counterpart is likely to be somewhat dubious about the finality of the positions you take, expecting that most of them are really negotiable. By limiting your firmness to several key issues, you're conforming to his expectations. Just as in art, where negative space defines form, or in music, where silence outlines sound, so in negotiations, *you gain credence for your inflexibility on a few choice issues by your willingness to give ground on the rest.*

To be analytical about it, let's divide a negotiator's attitude toward his positions into four categories: *immovable, staunch, malleable,* and *pliant.* (Obviously, the other side may not assign a particular issue to the same category.) I'll illustrate each with an issue that develops in the Peter's Pizza Parlors talks.

IMMOVABLE

This is an unbending position. Come hell or high water, the negotiator won't back off or trade. And it can be a real deal breaker. The one issue on which Peter is immovable involves his competition, the two other pizza chains in the area. If he's going to spend money on Connie's recommendations in order to gain an advantage over his competitors, he doesn't want her to turn around and give them similar advice. So Peter insists that Connie agree not to act as a consultant to either of the other chains for a term of years. The only aspect of this he's willing to discuss is the duration of the restriction.

Connie isn't happy about this restraint, since the experience she gains from Peter's assignment would be ideally suited to the other chains. But it's not a deal breaker for her, just one among a variety of issues that have actual or potential financial significance.

STAUNCH

This is a position that's deeply felt and likely to be maintained during the course of the negotiations, but it's not sacrosanct. Perhaps at the end of the day some movement will occur, especially if the other side is equally tenacious, and the movement unlocks something else of importance or clinches the deal on otherwise advantageous terms.

For Connie, a staunch position is her requirement that 50 percent of her fee be advanced at the outset of the assignment, with the balance paid 25 percent upon delivery of her recommendations and 25 percent within thirty days thereafter. She has consistently used this as her basis for payment to discourage clients from holding up the bulk of the fee. She fears that any variance not only will expose her with Peter, but also will be used against her by future clients. Still, she's not so inflexible about it that she won't consider a compromise, if that's what it takes to get the assignment.

As for Peter, who has no intention of welshing, while he would prefer for cash flow reasons to hold back more of the money, the *size* of the fee interests him more. His mind is open about the terms of payment.

MALLEABLE

This is a reasonable position for a negotiator like Connie to take on an issue. It represents an outcome that she would like to achieve, yet one she fully realizes may have to be traded, compromised, or yielded. Chances are, however, that making her give it up will cost Peter something. For Connie, her fee falls into this category. She has quoted Peter $25,000, a figure she considers realistic for the assignment. Still, at times she has been forced to reduce her fee for tight-fisted clients. So she has some room here.

Peter realizes that her fee is negotiable. As a purchaser of services, however, he doesn't want it to be so thin that Connie skimps on the service, the reduced amount of the fee no longer warranting four-star treatment. So he'll want to spend less than $25,000, but not so much less that Connie is uncomfortable with the final number.

PLIANT

This is a position that isn't firmly held. It may not even be particularly reasonable. And it's likely to be disputed by the other side, which will probably end up prevailing—perhaps without the need for any trade-off at all.

Peter has one of these. He has asked Connie to come back six months after completing the assignment and, for no extra charge, to evaluate how things are going. Peter would like her to perform this review but doesn't really expect her to do it for nothing. Even if the charge weren't stated separately, her up-front fee would no doubt be increased to accommodate this added feature. Connie feels the same way. She's happy to do it, but not for free.

It would be nirvana if you were able to make the other side believe that all your positions are either immovable or staunch—even when they aren't—but it puts too great a strain on your credibility. In the typical negotiation, your counterpart will assume implicitly that on some issues you'll be pliant, on many you'll be malleable, on several you'll be staunch, and on the rare bird you'll be immovable. My hunch is that you would have a hard time convincing the other side that you're different from most bargainers in this regard, unless your name happens to be Schweitzer and you operate out of a jungle hospital.

SENDING BLUE-CHIP AND BARGAINING-CHIP MESSAGES

To achieve credibility, you have to start by dividing your positions on the issues into categories similar to those I've outlined, or at least into two camps: what some people call the "blue chips" (including both immovable and staunch postures) and the "bargaining chips" (covering both malleable and pliant positions). Then you can begin to send different messages on each.

In order to be credible on the blue chips, you have to convey a sense of the importance you ascribe to them right from the outset and consistently throughout the negotiation. If you don't start early, your resolute attitude may come across as a manufactured afterthought. As the moment of truth nears, you can't suddenly elevate to deal-breaker status a point you treated casually in the early rounds. Inconsistency undermines the aura of credibility you're trying to create. Conversely, while you never want to suggest the relative unimportance of bargaining chips—or else you'll get no credit for giving them up— there are ways to imply that you don't hold them in the same esteem as the blues.

So, in our example, Peter ought to state his immovable position on "no consulting with the competition" in unmistakable terms at the first meeting: "If I'm going to hire you, Connie, it will only be if you promise not to do any work for those other guys, who are out there every day trying to eat my lunch." If she agrees right off the bat, fine. If not, then Peter is well advised to keep returning to the issue until she realizes he means business. In fact, Peter can buttress his posture by refusing to discuss other issues until this one is resolved.

Likewise, Connie should stress her staunch "standard payment schedule" issue the first time the question of money comes up, emphasizing that it wasn't just devised for this particular job: "My fee would be twenty-five thousand dollars, Peter. In accordance with my standard practice, fifty percent of the fee is payable when I undertake the assignment." If, instead, she broaches the $25,000 without mentioning that she wants 50 percent down, when she finally gets around to mentioning it, the payment schedule may seem less inviolate than the amount of money (even though in her mind it's more so). If Peter balks at the terms, Connie shouldn't let the issue fester, but ought to engage in a spirited and reasoned defense of her position.

A negotiator who takes an immovable or staunch position should articulate a solid rationale to justify it. Peter's "exclusive" point is more than just antipathy for his competitors; it's good business. If Connie recommends efficiencies that result in reduced expenses, thereby allowing Peter to drop his pizza prices—and giving him a vital edge over the competition—he doesn't want Connie helping them figure out how to match the cuts. For her part, Connie should attempt to make decent rebuttal arguments, explaining how her services are custom-tailored for each client, the disparate nature of these seemingly competitive businesses, and so on. Negotiating often comes down to a battle of cogency. The more logical your arguments in support of a point, the greater your chances of resolving it on satisfactory terms.

How about the bargaining chips? Connie's fee isn't cast in stone; it differs for each job she undertakes, depending on the size of the company and the scope of the assignment. Still, she shouldn't start off with a lame attempt at justification or an apology for the amount. One simple sentence, "My fee is twenty-five thousand dollars," sets an appropriate tone.

Peter's reaction—a sharp intake of breath, followed by rapid side-to-side shaking of the head—is predictable. "That's awfully steep," he says. "I'm just a small businessman, not one of those big-city outfits." The issue is joined. How should Connie handle this situation?

First, she has to walk a fine line between not appearing too rigid, which runs the risk of blowing the deal, and not seeming to pull numbers out of the air. One technique is to hint that movement is possible, without actually moving. "Look, Peter, if you want to use my services, I have the feeling we'll be able to work out the price. Let's talk first about some of these other items." Perhaps the other items will furnish tradeoff material. In any event, the ultimate price will be a function of the scope of the assignment, which remains to be worked out.

On a pliant issue, I'll often send an implicit signal that I'm prepared to negotiate, as a way of sharpening the distinction between it and a blue chip. So, for example, when Connie replies that she would be happy to come back after six months if she were paid for her time, Peter could say almost playfully, "But, Connie, you're *too* well paid up-front. I need to figure out a way to get more for my money."

WHEN YOU'RE BLUFFING

Now we move from candor to fiction. Your "this is it" posture, after all, could be bogus. And the question that you and every negotiator has to face is whether you should bluff.

Bluffs are clearly a staple of bargaining. When they relate to your position on an issue (as contrasted with when they involve misrepresentations of fact), they're not ethically repugnant. And they can be effective. Still, I don't usually like to bluff. The reason is that a bluff has three possible outcomes, two of which are adverse to the bluffer—not good odds, in my book.

Let's say that Connie takes a "firm" position that $25,000 is the minimum she's willing to accept for the job. In fact, she would do it for $20,000, if necessary. The positive outcome for Connie is that Peter believes her, acquiesces, and signs up at $25,000. But assume he calls her bluff, stating firmly, "In that case, we have no deal." If he's believable, and Connie realizes she won't get the job for $25,000, she'll be forced to lower her price. Although she can try to put the best face on this (linking the reduction to a diminution in the scope of the assignment, for example), her credibility may be impaired for the balance of the negotiation.

Now if that were the only risk to bluffing, I might favor it as a technique. At least in a situation where the bluffer is credible and the other side has few options, the prospect of prevailing could outweigh the potential loss of credibility. But there's another possibility, too: namely, that Peter will, in fact, *believe* Connie's bluff. However, because he's unwilling to pay that much, he will simply decide not to use her services, without giving Connie a chance to reduce her price.

The classic case here is the buyer who bluffs on his "top price" only to wake up the next day with the property having been sold to a third party at a somewhat higher price—but one that the bluffer would have been willing to pay. It's this fear of *succeeding* with the bluff but then having it blow up in your face that makes me consider the risks of bluffing generally unacceptable. There is, however, one situation in which a bluff makes good sense. I'll tell you about it in chapter 10.

If you decide to ignore my counsel and bluff anyway, here are a few thoughts that might be of help.

- Save your bluff for a significant issue. Once exposed as a bluffer, you're unlikely to have another chance, so don't squander it on something unimportant.
- Bluff at the end of the process, rather than at the start where it presumptively lacks credibility.
- Make your bluff appear consistent with something you've been saying all along.
- Try to come up with a plausible explanation for why there's no give in your position.
- If possible, couple your bluff with a show of flexibility on some other issue. It's a good way to highlight that your firm position is something special.
- Execute your bluff in such a manner that if the other side believes you but *isn't* willing to go along, you'll have a shot at backing down before the deal is aborted.
- If you're forced to back down, have a "changed circumstances" story ready to go in order to mitigate any harm to your credibility.

DEALING WITH WHAT MIGHT BE A BLUFF

Now let's look at a "this is it" position from the other side of the table. How can you tell if *your counterpart* is bluffing? Should you accept his "final" position as final? If he threatens that dire consequences will flow from your nonacquiescence (a subject we'll discuss in chapter 13), does he mean it?

Pretend, for these purposes, that you're Connie, and it's Peter's position on exclusivity that's at issue. You can live with his insistence that you not go after the business of the other pizza chains. Still, you would much rather have that flexibility, if the point isn't as important to Peter as he's making it sound.

There's no surefire answer to dealing with a possible bluff, which is just why negotiating is such a tantalizing occupation. Basically you're making an educated guess, the kind you constantly rely on in other areas of life. Afterward there will be plenty of time for self-congratulation or serious second-guessing. And sometimes, when you *don't* call the bluff, you'll never know whether it was real or not.

Here's the threshold question to ask yourself in this kind of situation: *If Peter's not bluffing, will I give in on the point?* If—unlike the case here—this occurs over an issue on which you are *unwilling* to accept Peter's position, then you wouldn't have to fret over whether he's bluffing or not. You *must* call the bluff, since the only chance of a deal occurring is for Peter to retreat. When this is the case, I prefer to do it quietly, with conviction but without any fuss or acrimony. Connie might say, "If this is your final position on the matter, Peter, which I sincerely hope it's not, then we're just not going to be able to do business." Peter should be under no illusion that Connie might later soften her stance.

It's a lot tougher, of course, when your answer to the threshold question is that if Peter *isn't* bluffing, you're prepared to *yield* the point, albeit reluctantly. That's the case here; and were you then to take that "sorry, no deal" posture, *you* would be bluffing. If it then turns out that Peter's position is genuine, you may lose everything. That's a chance I seldom want to take.

The technique I advise using here turns on your answer to a second question to ask yourself: *Do I* think *that Peter is bluffing?* Granted, you can't be sure, but you should be able to make an educated guess. If necessary, call a time out in the negotiations, in order to try to develop further information that bears on the credibility of Peter's position.

Let's say you *don't* think Peter is bluffing. You might then test the rigidity of his position by nibbling around the edges. Suggest various compromise formulations that if rejected still leave you positioned for ultimate acquiescence, without fear of losing the deal. For example, you can say that you "assume" Peter wouldn't mind your consulting for the other chains several years down the road, after he has had his head start. If you can get Peter to buy this exclusion, then you might try out a concept that frees you sooner, as long as you don't provide the other chains with advice similar to what you'll be giving to Peter. In such ways, you may be able to erode Peter's position, even though a frontal assault would have proved unavailing.

This method, however, fails to transmit a signal of your *own* resolve, which is the key ingredient needed to overcome a bluff. So if you suspect that Peter *is* bluffing, you should try to convey firmness coupled with some receptivity to an honorable compromise (but not capitulation). You can't, however, go as far as in the "sorry, no deal" scenario, which ought to be reserved for when that's really the case. It's a middle-of-the-road stance, with a slightly greater risk of losing the deal than in the prior formulation, but a risk you're willing to run because you believe Peter is bluffing.

So your posture might run along the following lines: "Peter, I'm simply not going to forgo forever the ability to take on any assignment from the other pizza chains. You wouldn't want to pay the amount of fee I'd have to charge to justify that! On the other hand, I fully understand the point you're making about wanting to gain an advantage over the competition as a result of my efforts. Let's see if we can come up with a formulation that protects your legitimate business interests, but doesn't unnecessarily restrict my freedom of action."

CREDIBILITY WRAP-UP

Keynote

The third basic skill of the smart negotiator centers around credibility—the ability to make his counterpart believe that he means what he says. At the same time, you have to make an accurate assessment of your counterpart's credibility. If you suspect that the other side is bluffing on an important point, you must send a signal of your own resolve in order to test the bluff, even if your actual level of resolve isn't quite so absolute. If your counterpart is bold enough to bluff, anything less on your part will only encourage his pretense.

Blunder

My candidate here is the bluff that's *so* effective it causes the other side (which isn't negotiating under the pressure of necessity) to call off the deal, even though the bluffer would have been willing to agree to the other's side's final terms. Only take a chance bluffing about an issue when, if the bluff doesn't work, you'll have the opportunity to pull it off the table.

Lapse

Too often we take our own credibility for granted and don't make any buttressing effort. It's almost as if we assume that everyone will consider us as honest and straightforward as we know we are! But a safer assumption for you to make is that your counterpart will be just as concerned with whether you're bluffing as you are with whether he is. Don't forget, in these environs, a certain amount of suspicion and doubt come with the territory.

5 JUDGMENT—THE ABILITY TO STRIKE THE RIGHT BALANCE BETWEEN VYING AND COMPROMISE

The final skill I want to discuss involves that most elusive of qualities—good judgment. As a negotiator you're called upon to make many difficult judgments:

- Should I stick on this point or fold?
- On another issue, can I press ahead, or am I better off easing up?
- What can I swap for what?
- Should I be the one to open the bidding, or do I wait for the other side to take the lead?
- If I don't want to wait, what should my opening offer be?

And so on. Loads of tough decisions, calling for lots of good judgment.

Experience is one important ingredient, but good judgment also requires the knack of analyzing situations, the courage to make concessions when they're called for and to stick with an unpopular position when it's necessary, the creativity to invent, the persuasiveness to sell effective compromises, and a dash of negotiating philosophy to season it all.

THE PRINCIPLE OF BALANCE

Good judgment in negotiating often comes down to keeping things in balance. The secret of effective negotiating is to achieve a functional balance between what you do to gain an advantage at your counterpart's expense and what you do to move the two of you closer to an eventual compromise.

If all your efforts are directed toward getting an edge on your adversary, the danger is that you'll come on too strong. Unless the leverage is completely skewed in your favor, this can cause irreparable harm, up to and including loss of the deal. On the other hand, if you don't push a little, if you never strive for advantages or stake out positions that invite rebuttal, then you're unlikely to attain what's within your reach. By seeking to avoid conflict, you simply whet your counterpart's appetite, inviting a flock of bold positions that can prove costly to satisfy.

So stay in balance. Recognize that there's a time to go for the jugular and a time to relax the grip, a time to stand firm and a time to yield gracefully, a time to wrap things up and a time to keep them dangling. This does *not* mean, however, that the balance between what you do for yourself and what you do for "the deal" always has to be fifty-fifty. Leverage and other factors dictate where to draw any particular line. Still, even when you're totally in the driver's seat—or deep behind the eight ball—you should attempt to strike a balance, albeit one that doesn't ignore the realities.

Carried to its extreme, the "nonnegotiable" style of bargaining flunks my principle of balance. *Some* movement is usually feasible—at least cosmetic, if not substantive. Refusal to negotiate around the periphery of a complex point is less a valid technique than the absence of technique. A little flexibility along the fringes aids you in retaining the core—and with less bruised feelings left in the wake of the bargaining.

The pace of a negotiation also ought to reflect a sense of equilibrium. There won't be a quick fix in a tough deal. The process has to run its course. People get nervous when things move too fast; they step back to reassess the situation. But too slow a pace creates its own problems, the delay exacerbating the obstacles and providing the parties with additional time to change their minds. Every negotiation should have a sense of movement, however sluggish, in a positive direction.

PERSEVERANCE AND ITS PROGENY

A good example of this principle is the balance that ought to be struck between *perseverance* on the one hand and *perspective* on the other. Good negotiators are patient, exercising a healthy dose of self-control. Sprinkle in some difficulties or obstacles to overcome, and the patient effort becomes "perseverance." When it takes on a more activist role, we have "persistence." At some point, however, this "tenacity" becomes relentless and translates into "obstinacy" and "intransigence." Perseverance with a dash of persistence strikes the balance I find to be most effective.

Perseverance may be the plainest of virtues, but don't underestimate it. When bargaining sessions drag on into the wee hours, points are often conceded that wouldn't have been if the parties had been fresh. Those with the stamina to persist frequently come out on top.

Appearances play a role here, too. Say you've gone out of town to negotiate an important and complex contract. You arrive in the other city at night, check into a hotel, sleep, wake, check out of the hotel, and arrive at the office of your counterpart, garment bag in hand, airline ticket sticking out of your jacket pocket, sneaking little glances at your watch.

What's wrong? Everything! By arriving at the negotiations with a metaphorical clock ticking over your head, you're telegraphing to your counterpart, *Hey, I've got to wrap this up fast, so I can make my plane home.* He smiles inwardly and slows down the tempo. He knows that perseverance on his part will pay big dividends, especially as the scheduled time of departure nears and you begin conceding points in order to wrap things up before your exit. How much better it would have been for you to show up at your counterpart's office, looking as if you had *all the time in the world* to remain there, seated at the bargaining table, making sure you get *everything* you deserve.

Why is patience so effective in negotiating? It has many attributes, such as revealing your counterpart's real level of desire: does *he* try to hurry things along? Or if you've made a complex proposal, your counterpart may need some time to become comfortable with the terms. But to my mind, the most significant virtue of patience is what it conveys to the other side.

Let's face it, your counterpart will usually be somewhat skeptical about your commitment to the positions you take. Patient adherence to a position provides you with gradually increasing credibility to supplement the rationale supporting your stance. Your counterpart is forced to think about what compromise to offer in order to resolve the point. And the same process occurs with regard to your continued nonacquiescence to the other side's demands.

All this can be accomplished without bruising confrontation, serious threats, or nonnegotiable postures. In fact, patience and perseverance are most effective when clothed in a low-key style that emphasizes deliberateness rather than obstinacy. So learn how to insist on your point without being overbearing—and how to say "no" without seeming too negative.

THE NEED FOR PERSPECTIVE

Although persistence is a virtue, the failure to temper it with *perspective* cuts down on your effectiveness. You're not going to prevail on *all* the issues that arise in a negotiation, so save yourself for the significant ones. Let your counterpart take home a few trophies, too, especially on issues that aren't that important to you or where the point he is making is unassailable. Don't become mired in the pursuit of trivia, generating bad feelings that make it harder to obtain concessions or reach compromises in those areas that count. As Benjamin Disraeli put it, "Next to knowing when to seize an advantage, the most important thing in life is to know when to forgo an advantage."

I advocate perspective even if the leverage *and* the logic are on your side. Negotiating power should be exercised with restraint. And although reasoned positions and rational debate are important, you also have to recognize their limitations. That's not some computer sitting across the table; it's a human being. And humans are often guided by their emotions. Emerging victorious on a trivial debating point can cost you in the end, particularly if you've made your counterpart look bad. There are always more points to come and the same counterpart to deal with.

Now, in counseling perspective, I'm *not* urging you to be saintly. Use your judgment to select as the issues to "lose" those that the other side considers important but you don't. Of course, you don't want the other side to know how you feel about your concessions, but even this shouldn't be overdone. If you make each issue seem equally important, you'll end up demeaning your key points. Again, balance and perspective are important. "When everyone is somebody," laments the Grand Inquisitor in Gilbert & Sullivan's *The Gondoliers*, "then no one's anybody."

THE CASE OF THE KITCHEN RANGE

Here's an example of the balanced approach I advocate, which also touches on some other negotiating issues. You've decided to renovate your kitchen and contact Ralph Range, a reputable kitchen designer— halfway between an architect and an interior decorator. Range takes a look around, hears what you want to accomplish, tells you (with unbecoming immodesty) about himself and his qualifications, and concludes that he can be helpful. Well, you ask, what's the deal?

Ralph's proposal is that for $5,000 (his "regular" fee) plus reimbursement of expenses, he will produce detailed drawings of a redesigned kitchen, help you shop for the necessary appliances, keep an eye on things as construction progresses, and provide other specified services. It sounds a little high, so you decide to test just how "regular" his compensation is and whether the amount can be reduced if you don't need all the services offered. You start by proposing that he lower his base fee (which in your view should include his expenses) to $4,000, with a further reduction for eliminating Ralph's need to oversee the actual construction (which will be done by your own trusted contractor).

In addition, you don't want to commit for the whole program until you're satisfied with the direction Range is taking. So you ask him to sketch his concept of how the kitchen will look before doing the detailed drawings; this will enable you to decide whether or not to move ahead. Of course, Ralph will be entitled to something for his trouble if you then decide not to proceed. You suggest $500.

Skipping the repartee, Range's reply can be summarized as follows. The $5,000 fee is nonnegotiable; otherwise his other clients would be in revolt. It can, however, be reduced by omitting some of the usual services. So for eliminating the supervision function, he'll knock it down $750, to $4,250. His expenses, while few, are fully justified (and for this he cites chapter and verse); they should be paid in addition to the fee. He can't reveal his kitchen concept for a mere $500. That's the guts of his service, and too much work goes into the initial measuring and plotting of contours. And no offense, but Range is concerned that after seeing his proposal, you might dismiss him and have your trusted contractor execute his design.

You assess the situation. Range would clearly like to have your business, but from what you can tell, he has plenty of customers and isn't desperate. You probably won't get far arguing over his "regular" fee, but you may make further headway on the price by dropping other services. You'll also end up giving Ralph his expenses; he has to "win" something, and this item sounds both justifiable and inexpensive.

The central issue for you is your need to decide whether Range is heading down a fruitful path before you commit to the whole program. That's where you'll take your stand. In fact, unless Range is willing to accommodate you on this, you won't engage his services. You can be flexible, however, on the price for the sneak preview—up to, say, $1,000. And by the way, you have no intention of "stealing" Ralph's ideas. If they're good, you'll want his detailed blueprint; if not, you'll start over with someone else. But now that Ralph has raised the issue, you need a way to handle this red herring.

FORGING A BALANCED APPROACH

A little patience on your part will probably work wonders at this point, forcing Ralph to realize that you're not so entranced with the prospect of hiring him as to give in on all fronts. Then, after a few more rounds (which I'll omit for the sake of brevity), here's what you might propose to Range:

"Ralph, I would like you take on this job, but I'm going to insist that you provide me with an early look at your plans. I'm simply not prepared to pay the full amount for your services if the project is heading in a direction I don't like.

"You've told me at length about your capabilities, about all the plaudits you've received. You really should have enough self-confidence to believe that I'll want to proceed after seeing your sketch. As for the notion that I might 'steal' your idea, I'm shocked you could think I'd do such a thing. In any event, you can protect yourself on this score by keeping the hard copy.

"I agree with your point, however, that there's more to the preliminary work than meets the eye. So I'll raise the amount payable, if I don't proceed beyond the initial look, to seven hundred and fifty. With respect to the overall price, I'd like to omit the service you ordinarily provide in helping the customer shop for appliances—since I know exactly what I want—and lower the fee to thirty-five hundred.

I'm willing, however, to reimburse you for the kind of reasonable expenses you've outlined."

Now let's analyze what you did here. You staked out your firm position on having a first look in forceful, but not threatening, tones. Although previously this was the last issue discussed, you decided now to lead with it—a shrewd move, since the placement emphasizes its importance. Ralph has to realize you mean business on this one. On the other hand, you've shown flexibility around the periphery of the point by increasing the price for a preview. In effect, you're inviting Ralph to come back on that aspect rather than challenge the concept of a first look.

Your attempt to persuade Ralph to see things your way embraced several useful approaches. First was indignation ("I'm shocked . . ."), designed to blunt his "stealing" paranoia. This kind of "How dare you?" technique is de rigueur when someone questions your honesty, good faith, or ethics. Don't use it, however, to protest normal disputes arising over the terms of the deal.

You then pointed out that Ralph's reluctance implied a lack of self-confidence, a tried-and-true tactic to use against someone who's pitching for your business. And you managed to throw his own words of self-promotion back in his face, a gambit that can often be effective, as we'll see later on. You also included a face-saving device (letting him keep the hard copy), which gave Ralph a painless route along which to retreat.

At the same time, you proposed a reduction in the overall price. By coupling it to a further reduction in service, however, you made it an easier pill for Ralph to swallow, since you weren't directly questioning his "regular" fee. You were also accommodating on the minor issue of Ralph's expenses, to which he seemed to attach much importance.

All in all, this was a nice, balanced approach. If Range wants the assignment, he'll accept your proposal. Of course, he might come back at $1,000 for the look and $4,000 for the job. You could then package a $900 look with a $3,750 fee, and the deal would be sealed.

If you were to hold out at $750 and $3,500, however, would Ralph eventually come around? He probably would, but think of it this way: don't you want the guy who's doing your kitchen to *feel good* about it? That's much better than to have Range sulking over the undervaluation of his services, for which he retaliates by doing a halfhearted job.

THE ELEMENTS OF STYLE

We've been discussing balance and judgment in terms of *substance;* now let's switch to *form.* All good negotiators have their own styles. Some favor a combative approach—tough positions, threats, ridicule—in a style that fairly bristles. Others try to catch their flies with honey, masking their aspirations under a sugar-coated or mock bewildered guise. Still others are in between or off to the side. And some negotiators adapt their manner to each situation. Thus it would be presumptuous of me to recommend one all-purpose style. I will, however, suggest a few significant stylistic elements.

For openers you have to feel natural. You'll be uncomfortable adopting a style that doesn't ring true, a situation in which you're constantly thinking *What* should *I say now?* instead of trusting your instincts. I'm also a great believer in consistency. I realize that some negotiators deliberately adopt a posture of inconsistency, painting themselves as eccentric or whimsical to keep the other side off balance. But for most of us, that's tough to pull off. Your goal, after all, is to be persuasive to those on the other side. You want them to trust you, to accept what you say as credible. It just doesn't work when they have trouble figuring out what you're up to.

Your style should deliver the particular message you wish to convey. An accommodating approach, for example, may be all right when you have lots of room to maneuver and the other side lacks the leverage to push you to the wall. It's not so good, however, when you're trying to underscore a firm position or have little room to retreat. And it's especially vulnerable when your counterpart's oversize appetite has been whetted by your prior accommodations.

THE HAIRY-CHESTED SCHOOL OF NEGOTIATING

There is one style that most of us find offensive. I call it the "hairy-chested school of negotiating." Here, the level of discourse exceeds the limits of civilized behavior. Every contravened position is taken as a personal affront. Emotion displaces reason; brinksmanship is all. The hairy one's favorite ploy is to rise from his seat, face purple with rage, make a great display of packing up his papers and yellow pads, and stalk out of the room, threatening to call off the deal unless he has his way.

My objections to this style are both aesthetic and practical. You only demean yourself by such theatrics, while making it unpleasant for all concerned. Bullying is just out of place in ordinary commercial negotiations. These are, after all, matters of voluntary agreement. If the parties can't agree, it may be discouraging, but the world isn't coming to an end, no one's life or liberty is threatened, and another deal will come along tomorrow.

It's also self-defeating on a practical plane. You're trying to persuade your counterpart to come around, to do business with you; but who wants to do business with a maniac? I find that brute efforts at intimidation seldom work. They just raise your counterpart's hackles, causing him to dig in deeper.

When I want to take a really tough position, I often *lower* my voice and speak more deliberately than before. The somber style highlights the seriousness of the message. If my client is prepared to lose the deal over this point, then I may get ready to walk out of the negotiations, but more in sorrow than in anger ("I'm afraid this isn't going anywhere, and as you know, the issue is crucial to us"). I'm also very slow about putting away my papers and rising from the chair, giving my counterpart plenty of time to halt my exit by putting something meaningful on the table.

Having said this, I must add that *controlled emotion* does play a definite role in negotiating. There are times when I consider a momentary flare-up to be requisite, as a narrowly focused expression of disapproval over the other party's misbehavior. I'm *not* talking about a situation where your counterpart has been reiterating the same point or position ad nauseam. True, this might leave you feeling terribly frustrated, but you shouldn't blow up. However misguided, he's entitled to his position. If you don't like it, and the issue is serious enough, your remedy is to call things off—but not to explode.

On the other hand, when your counterpart tries to retract a concession previously granted, or suffers a convenient loss of memory, or purposely misquotes something you said, that's another matter. This conduct warrants a dramatic warning; and a brief but convincing display of your indignation signals him that he's heading down a dangerous road. In fact, if you *don't* get a little hot under the collar, if your mild protest can be interpreted as taking things in stride, you may be inviting your counterpart to try more of the same later on. My preference is to make clear immediately how intolerable I find such a display of bad faith.

Now, I know what you're thinking. Okay, I won't be obstinate. I won't take nonnegotiable positions unless they really are nonnegotiable. I won't rant, rave, and stalk from the room. But what about when I run into one of those birds who *does* that stuff, hurling threats at me from across the table? What do I do then? Good question, and I'll try to answer it in chapter 13.

JUDGMENT WRAP-UP

Keynote

Good judgment is the fourth basic skill in smart negotiating, and it should permeate such other aspects as applying leverage and establishing credibility. The key to good negotiating judgment is the ability to keep yourself in balance, acting in moderation and avoiding far-out positions. Try to measure any proposed course of action by such a yardstick. If you decide to deviate from this standard and climb out on a limb, make sure you have a compelling reason for doing so—not to mention a safe way back if it's sawed out from under you.

Blunder

The most common mistake I observe (and am guilty of myself on occasion) is giving in to a sense of impatience, satisfying the need many of us feel for instant gratification. "Let's wrap it up" becomes the byword, and we find ourselves settling on terms that could have been improved with a little more patience. Admittedly there are times when you're better off grabbing what's on the table than holding out for small additional gains that put the deal in jeopardy. But where the reward outweighs the risk, *slow down*.

Lapse

This one is easy: it's the failure to put things in perspective. You can't prevail on all issues, so save your fire for what's significant. Don't fuss with minutiae. Let your counterpart take home some trinkets, *even* where both the leverage and the logic are on your side.

PART II

The Negotiator's Game Plan

6 AN OVERVIEW OF THE GAME PLAN APPROACH

Imagine you're about to take a step that's likely to involve some bargaining. This makes you a bit uneasy—a feeling many people share on the eve of negotiations. It's not just the prospect of confrontation; it's that you lack a plan of action. And that's not like you, because in other situations related to your work or area of expertise, you know exactly what you're doing.

Why is this? Perhaps it's fear of the unknown. You don't know in advance what your counterpart is going to say or do, so it's tough to predict the direction the negotiations will take or the risks involved. Or your apprehension might stem from the realization that a compromise is likely to be required. In the past you've never been comfortable about how to compromise, or when, or whether you're ending up in the right place.

So there you are, on the eve of this encounter, assailed by self-doubts. Let's make it more specific. Imagine you are a midlevel executive in a midsize company who feels undercompensated and has decided to approach the boss for a long-deferred raise.

ASKING THE BOSS FOR A RAISE

Asking for a raise is an elementary negotiation with a single dominant issue—your paycheck. But no matter how complex the deal, the main issue you face is how to go about it. What's required is a logical approach to conducting and concluding the negotiations. In short, you need a game plan.

Such a plan, in order to function effectively, should be

- readily grasped;
- adaptable to your personal style;
- applicable to a broad variety of situations (including dispute resolution);
- not dependent on guile or superior knowledge, or even on experience (although it helps);
- viable whatever the balance of leverage (although responsive to it);
- effective against any bargaining style;
- designed to reach agreement where the parties' realistic expectations overlap, while nixing deals that are not in your best interests.

The game plan I recommend meets all these conditions. It contains four steps, commencing prior to the bargaining and continuing during its entire course. Each step addresses a major question for the negotiator:

- *What* do I want?
- *Where* do I start?
- *When* do I move?
- *How* do I close?

Stated affirmatively, these four steps will help you—on significant issues such as price—to

- assess your realistic expectations;
- determine an appropriate starting point;
- devise a constructive concession pattern;
- arrange the ultimate compromise.

The four steps are interrelated. You can't select an intelligent starting point on an issue without knowing where you want to end up. If your initial position isn't well chosen, you'll have trouble with the journey toward your realistic expectation. And you won't be able to clinch the deal on favorable terms when that trip has been mishandled.

Let's see how this plays out in the case of asking for a salary increase, keeping things simple for the moment. You'll find a more detailed analysis in the next four chapters, each of which focuses on one step of the game plan approach.

WHAT DO YOU WANT?

Assume you're currently earning $40,000 a year, a level you've been at for several years now. You begin—*before* starting the talks—by figuring out what you can *realistically* expect to achieve from the negotiations. This expectation is the beacon by which to guide your course. If you don't have one, you won't know how close you are to achieving it. Maybe that's why many people ignore this step; they don't want to have to face up to a shortfall! But that's simply myopic. If you ultimately do fall short of your realistic expectation—as sometimes happens—you should be in a position to make a sensible decision at that time whether to accept what's been offered or to chart an alternative route, such as, in this example, leaving the company.

Actually, where feasible, you should try to make this kind of decision *in advance*. Your ability to exert leverage without bluffing often turns on identifying your *second choice* outcome, in case your goal remains elusive. In this situation, for instance, if you won't stay with the company unless you get your desired raise, and assuming the prospect of your leaving would upset your boss, you should devise a non-threatening way to telegraph the likelihood of your departure *before* the boss has turned you down. Knowing what he's up against will give him an extra incentive to accommodate you. If, on the other hand, your second choice outcome were to swallow hard and remain with the company, then you wouldn't dwell on your prospective departure—fearing, and justifiably so, that such a bluff could be turned into a self-fulfilling prophecy.

Your realistic expectation is a blend of aspiration and feasibility. The *aspiration* is what you would reasonably hope to achieve from the negotiation—a combination of objective elements of value and where you'll feel good about the outcome. The *feasibility* is a combination of what you think your counterpart wants to achieve (in other words, *his* expectation) and the relative weight of the various leverage factors present. You may lack good information on the feasibility of your expectation at the outset. Still, an imperfect determination is better than none; and you'll be able to revise your expectation as you learn more during the negotiations.

So in deciding what to reach for in terms of your raise, you take into account a number of factors:

- Pay scales and typical percentage increases, both within your organization and at comparable companies;
- Where you think you fit on the scale, considering your performance;
- The size of the raise your boss, Ross, will be willing, or able, to offer;
- Your assessment of the relative leverage, including the answers to such questions as

1. Is this a good time to be asking for a raise?
2. What's the current job market for your specialty?
3. How has the company fared lately, and what's likely to lie ahead?

Let's say, after reflection, you conclude that a 15 percent pay hike from $40,000 up to $46,000 is a realistic expectation.

WHERE DO YOU START?

The next question is where to start. Should you walk in and put your $46,000 number on the table immediately? If you do, there's always the chance that Ross will smile and say, "As a matter of fact, I've been thinking about a raise for you. Based on your performance, you certainly deserve one. And what you've proposed sounds fine to me. Congratulations."

Tell me the truth, how would that make you feel? After your immediate sense of relief, don't you think those nagging second thoughts would set in? Could I have gotten *more?* The boss accepted my number so readily; would he also have swallowed $48,000—or as much as $50,000?

That's one scenario, and probably wishful thinking—even with the second thoughts. Ross's more usual reaction will be that you are entitled to a raise, but times are hard, profits are down, the wolf is at the door—so how about $2,000? Then, no matter how well you negotiate from that point forward, you're likely to end up short of your expectation. In fact, the only way you can achieve it is to stand your ground, refusing to deviate one dollar from your opening proposal, and hope that Ross so fears losing your services that he's willing to swallow his pride and capitulate.

In many quarters, however, your conduct would be viewed as almost un-American! What's more, at least in the circles I travel in, your firm stance is unlikely to be believed. In addition, a boss who is forced to capitulate won't be much fun to live with in the months ahead.

So you decide to pick a more ambitious starting point, which makes sense if you're wise about the selection. Starting out, for instance, at $60,000—a 50 percent increase over current salary—would *not* be well advised. You can't justify it, you won't appear to be bargaining in good faith, and it's likely to provoke a sour reaction from your boss. In fact, in order to counter your big appetite, Ross may adopt the position that you're not entitled to *any* raise, justifying it on the basis of the company's rotten condition.

The starting point you select should always be defensible. I think that either $48,000 (a 20 percent raise) or $50,000 (25 percent) would be appropriate, depending on what kind of objective support you can develop to back them up. The $48,000 is a more reasonable number, one that Ross might even accept gracefully. The $50,000, a little riskier in that it might invite confrontation, gives you more playing room and sends a very positive view of your self-worth. (Some negotiators, for psychological reasons, would advise limiting your high end to a number beginning with a "4"—say, $49,500).

I would probably advise reaching a little here, assuming you can justify the higher level as a fair one because it's comparable to the salaries of similar executives in other companies. I would feel even stronger about my advice if you sensed there was little practical risk of the boss adopting a "no raise" posture.

How about going in to ask for a raise without specifying the amount, leaving it up to Ross to suggest a figure? Many people say they want to hear what the other side has to offer before committing themselves. And under certain circumstances, I agree. Here, however, where *you* have the sizable ambition and are raising the subject, I think you should put your number on the table first. So let's say you start with the $50,000 figure. Ross's reply is that you're

entitled to a raise, but times are tough, and so forth, and he thinks
something in the vicinity of $43,000 (7.5 percent) would be appro-
priate.

WHEN DO YOU MOVE?

Now how do you go about achieving—or at least getting within hail-
ing distance of—your $46,000 expectation? Should you creep to-
ward it in hundred-dollar increments? Should you offer, right off
the bat, to split the difference (which, for a fifty-fifty split, works
out to $46,500)?

This can be an intricate process, and there's no single answer—
except that I don't think either of *those* two ways is worth a damn.
The process begins with how you react to your boss's counterproposal. You can't let him infer from your reaction that his $43,000
might be acceptable. The more you can objectify your response—
"But that would put me well below the level of the comparable executives I mentioned"—the better your chances of keeping the
negotiations alive.

Then there's the delicate issue of dropping your asking price. You
want to do this in a way that both preserves your flexibility for a
further move and inspires reciprocal movement from Ross. I would
think a drop to the $48,000 level is in order here, which should get
Ross to go up at least to $44,000.

The dance goes on from there, as we'll see, with various steps
designed to transmit messages and keep up the momentum. At the
same time, you're alert to any clues Ross sends your way, while using
your knowledge of his negotiating style—gleaned from your daily
experience with him—to your advantage.

HOW DO YOU CLOSE?

Let's assume now that after some more bargaining, you're at $47,000
and Ross is mired at $45,000. How do you close the final gap? At this
point it's more tempting—although not without risk—to offer to split
the difference. But if rigor mortis has started to set in, your compromise may have to be more creative. The key here might lie in dis-

covering *why* Ross refuses to go higher. If it's money, that's one thing; but often the *real* reason is something else entirely.

For instance, assume you find out that the percentage increase of a raise to $45,000—12.5 percent—is the same the boss gave another executive a month ago, after telling her that this was as high as he could go. Ross may be afraid that if he grants the higher increase you're seeking, the other executive will hear about it and be angry at him.

Now that you know what's causing the blockage, perhaps there's a different way to latch on to that last $1,000. How about through a car allowance? After all, you've been using your car a lot recently on company business. That way your boss can preserve his 12.5 percent ceiling on salary, but you end up with the full $6,000 compensation increase you're seeking.

Your game plan helped you achieve, or at least come close to, the raise you think you deserve. It also gave you a strategic framework for the negotiations to overcome the sense of apprehension and uncertainty that often accompanies such a confrontation. And its deft execution should have earned you Ross's respect as an able negotiator.

7 ASSESSING YOUR REALISTIC EXPECTATIONS

Now that you've had an overview of the game plan approach, let's examine each step in the process in greater detail. Step one, and a vital element, is the need to assess your realistic expectations with respect to price and other key issues that are likely to be negotiated— *before* the negotiations begin.

WHY EXPECTATIONS ARE IMPORTANT

Too many people enter into negotiations without determining in advance the outcome they want to achieve. Without a realistic expectation, however, you don't know where to start the bidding, you'll have trouble figuring out what steps to take along the way, and—most important of all—you won't know where to stop!

Sometimes, when embroiled in the heat of the bargaining, you may lose your bearings temporarily. Rising tensions can make you unnecessarily tightfisted; conversely, in a lively bidding contest your reach may exceed your grasp. But with your realistic expectation serving as a prominent—although not inflexible—compass point, you have a better chance of avoiding these pitfalls.

Some people back into their expectation instead of determining it beforehand. A buyer, for instance, will often focus totally on his opening bid, a figure that, were he able to buy at that price, would startle him into worrying that he was getting damaged goods! But undue emphasis on his opener can tantalize the buyer into wanting to end up in that vicinity. I always stress to my clients the need to come at it the other way: by first determining their realistic expectation and then working backward to the appropriate opening bid.

Certain negotiators determine their price expectation but neglect the other key issues. They're inclined to wait for the other side's position or reaction, or they say, "We'll deal with that once the price is determined." That's just wrong. Many issues, masquerading under other guises, ultimately translate into dollars and have to be evaluated up-front along with the price. On those blue chip issues that you'll want to raise early to emphasize their importance, you can't take a prudent initial position until you've formed your expectation. And there's always the risk your counterpart will bring up the issues you won't be raising, at which point your expectation becomes central to devising the most suitable response.

I see a person's realistic expectation as a *good* outcome of the negotiations, the price (or other terms) that you would be agreeable to pay or receive and that your counterpart could well accept. And your efforts to achieve that outcome should reflect a hardheaded determination. It's neither the best price (or terms) that you might get if your counterpart caves in, nor the worst that you may be forced to pay or take if he hangs tough and you're dying to do the deal.

The ideal outcome, of course, would be to cut a better deal than your realistic expectation. But in my game plan approach, you don't get there by revising your expectation. Rather, you take your shot by a more aggressive initial position. And you neither count on getting a bargain nor let that possibility dictate your overall strategy.

THE PERIODIC NEED TO STRETCH

Your realistic expectation is *not* a bottom line. At the outset of a negotiation, before all the information is available and prior to your necessary investment of time and effort, you often don't know how far you'll be willing to reach. My experience is that lurking beneath the surface of most realistic expectations is some *less* favorable outcome that you may find yourself willing to accept, if necessary.

I call this the "stretch." It's not a first-class outcome of the negotiation, but it's still satisfactory, in the sense that you've decided it's better to do the deal on these terms than not do it. Phrased another way, as you near the end of a negotiation, you often have to pose yourself this key question: If I stick on *my* terms and thereby lose the deal, will I then regret not having paid (or accepted) my counterpart's higher (or lower) price?

Frequently this is the key to deal making: not how far you've had to travel in the negotiations, or whether you're irritated by your counterpart, but how much you're willing to stretch. Most of the time there aren't any magical solutions just waiting around for cooperating parties to discover. Rather, *there are satisfactory outcomes, which have to be ground out inch by inch.* If, ultimately, you're willing to stretch, it's usually because either necessity, time pressure, or strong desire is motivating *you* (more than your counterpart) to make the deal.

Naturally, however, you'll try to get the other side to believe that your realistic expectation—and perhaps even some positions you take before your retreat to that point—represent a real stretch. But since your credibility is important, it shouldn't be squandered on unrealistic postures. You're also out to persuade your counterpart that his own expectation won't swing the deal, that he should start thinking seriously about his own stretch. And, of course, the real or apparent leverage you bring to bear will carry considerable weight.

To illustrate why having a realistic expectation is a necessary first step in the negotiating process, let's start with the price a *buyer* is willing to pay for an item (or a recipient for services). Later we'll deal with expectations in terms of other significant issues, as well as look at expectations from the vantage point of the *seller* of goods (or provider of services).

The model to keep in mind here is of a purchase of property that is *not* being held out for sale in the ordinary course of a seller's business. It could be real estate, a business (or some segment of it), or any valued item. This is *not* fungible merchandise bearing a price tag. Rather, it's a single item, the price of which will be determined through the bargaining process.

THE CASE OF THE CAUTIOUS CATERER

Ms. Fingerfood, who operates a catering business specializing in residential parties, is introduced to Mr. Edison by a mutual friend. Edison has a patented invention, a special device called "the Gizmo," which allows a caterer, who prepares certain foods in advance, to warm and freshen them at the customer's home. Food passed through the Gizmo comes out tasting as good as if it had been cooked on the premises. Edison offers to sell all rights to the patented invention to Ms. Fingerfood for $20,000. She is intrigued by the Gizmo and, after observing a "road test," decides to pursue this opportunity. Pretend you're Ms. Fingerfood. What should you take into account, even before any real negotiation has taken place, in arriving at your realistic expectation on price? I consider the following factors significant.

First and foremost is your *aspiration*: where *you* would like to come out, not in a perfect world, but in the realistic one we inhabit. This represents an amalgam of objective value and subjective worth to you. Basically it's an outcome that will make you feel good. (Or, as one wag defined it, price is value, plus a reasonable sum for the wear and tear of conscience in demanding it.) Later on, we'll be leavening your aspiration with a dose of *feasibility*, based on what the other side's views are likely to be and the leverage that's present.

In determining your expectation as a buyer, I urge you to be utterly realistic. In the world of business, real bargains are a scarce commodity unless the leverage tips way over in your direction. Most people end up paying a full, fair price for something that's desirable. They pay the price because that's what it takes to make the purchase. If you're *not* prepared to pay a realistic price, you can still go through the exercise on the outside chance that you'll get serendipitous. But my advice is not to get too wrapped up in the process, because you're likely to be disappointed.

Those of you who are willing to pay a realistic price shouldn't set your expectations at the bargain level, because then you may blow the deal without ever putting your realistic price on the table. On the other hand, you needn't bother to think about stretching at this point, before the process has even had a chance to operate.

EVALUATING YOUR ASPIRATION

To determine your realistic price expectation, you ought to be familiar with comparable values and methods of evaluation in your field of activity. Make a candid assessment of your own expertise; if it's lacking, get some expert advice. This is nothing to be embarrassed about. Huge companies, whose payrolls bulge with graduates of the nation's finest business schools, routinely reach out to investment banking firms to help them value what they're buying or selling, paying enormous fees for sophisticated evaluation advice.

And by the way, *don't* take advice on how much to pay for something from a lawyer, unless he has independent knowledge of the market in question. We attorneys can be helpful in devising negotiating strategy, including the selection of a good starting point once we know your expectation. But most of us aren't much help on value—and if we pretend to be, watch out!

As Ms. Fingerfood, you should try to get a handle on the Gizmo's value in the marketplace. You need answers to several questions: What's the size of the potential market? Can the Gizmo be licensed to third parties? Are there similar products already being offered? How well does it work? What's involved in the manufacturing process? I won't dwell on this evaluation process, but it's central to the task of defining your realistic expectation.

Although abstract concepts of value are important, the real question for any buyer is what the property is worth to *you*. If you find *the* beautiful plate in an antique shop, which just happens to fill your twelve-piece dinner set—replacing the piece (no longer being made) that broke last winter—it's worth a lot more to you than its underlying value. There are other pertinent considerations as well: At what price can you afford or finance the purchase? Can you pass the cost on to a third party? What are the risks, and are they manageable within your limits?

Where (unlike this case) the transaction is part of a continuing relationship, you may decide to pay more than the lowest price at which you could force a deal. Keep the principle of balance in mind; for the negotiation to be successful and the relationship to prosper, the other side has to end up feeling that they've received something meaningful.

All these considerations should coalesce in a range of values, representing what the Gizmo is worth to you. Let's say this range turns out to be $12,000–$15,000. You would, of course, rather end up at the bottom of the range than the top, although this will be determined by other factors.

THE ROLE PLAYED BY FEASIBILITY

The other prime consideration in determining your realistic expectation is what it's *feasible* to expect. This is an amalgam of what your counterpart is really looking for and how the leverage operates. But put aside the leverage aspect for now and let's concentrate on assessing where you think Mr. Edison, who is asking $20,000, wants to come out. We'll assume, for the moment, that he's proceeding on a realistic basis. Reliable information on this assessment may not be available up-front, before you've had a chance to feel Edison out, do your probing, and observe how the process unfolds. So this factor often becomes more significant as negotiations proceed. Take care, however, to avoid being fooled by the positions he takes or by words he utters that lack credibility.

Still, you can often get a sense of your counterpart's expectations at the outset. Try to put yourself in Edison's position. For instance, knowing how much money he had spent in developing the Gizmo might furnish a clue to his state of mind. In the same vein, if you're dealing with someone who's selling an item that he previously *purchased*, the amount that *he* paid for it, adjusted for market changes in the intervening years and taken in conjunction with his initial asking price, might provide solid evidence of his expectation on resale. Likewise, a real tip-off might be an awareness of specific cash needs that a seller like Edison may have.

COMBATING THE THREE FACES OF UNREALITY

But now, what if Edison is *unrealistic* in his expectations? Since the premise we operate on is ultimate rationality, it's your job to introduce reality into the picture. First, you have to determine just what it is that makes Edison's attitude unrealistic. Basically there are three prime possibilities: his view of the intrinsic *value* of what he's selling, his view of what *you* will be willing to pay for it, or his view of what *third parties* would be willing to pay if you fizzle out.

If Edison is off on value, you have to provide him with outside valuation data in order to educate him as to the real worth of his product.

Don't rely just on trying to undercut *his* rationale. Show him some responsible independent views. You don't have to persuade him that your opinion is right; it's enough to leave the matter unsettled in his mind.

If Edison is off on what *you* are ultimately willing to pay, once again you have to bring him back to reality. You'll want to make him aware of your limits, be sure that he appreciates the leverage involved, and so forth.

The third level of your counterpart's unreality—who *else* is out there?—presents you with the daunting task of proving a negative. I'd be willing to bet that sellers' unreality on this score causes more deals to be blown than anything else. You can issue dire warnings ("I'm your only real buyer, Edison; those other guys will all prove to be apparitions"); but since you don't *know* this for a fact, it's tough to be convincing.

A buyer with nerves of steel can tell the seller, "Go ahead and test the market; you'll see what I mean. But when you come back, don't expect me to be here at the same price." Most buyers, however, would hate the idea of the seller taking them up on this bit of bravado, actually breaking off the negotiations to sample the competition. Perhaps the best you can manage are innovative variations on that same old theme ("I'm a plump bird in the hand, Edison—don't hold out for two skinny ones in that illusory bush").

Let's assume here, however, that you decide Edison *is* realistic and likely to be willing to accept something less than his asking price. Still, you don't know enough about him yet to predict where he wants to end up.

FACTORING IN THE LEVERAGE

The other aspect of feasibility is evaluating the leverage that exists in the situation and then using that know-how to help determine your realistic expectation. Leverage factors always inject a sharp dose of reality into the negotiating process, discouraging pipe dreams and wish lists. The factors, however, aren't always sitting there. Sometimes leverage needs to be *created,* as when a seller brings in a competitor for the buyer who's acting too cocky. And remember, what's significant is the *perception* of leverage, which can be massaged to some extent.

Although you'll acquire additional input as the deal proceeds, as a *buyer* you can make a fair assessment of the four main leverage factors right from the outset.

- Is the seller under any *necessity* to sell?
- If not, how badly does the seller seem to *want* to sell? How badly do you want to buy?
- Is there any apparent *competition*?
- How significant is *time*?

Here's where information can be valuable. As Fingerfood, what's the key fact you want to know? I'll tell you what would interest me the most: Just *why* does Edison want to sell his invention? How come he's not attempting to market the Gizmo himself? If this also interests you, how should you go about getting information that bears on his motive? I recommend asking Edison a direct question. And let's say that Edison, to his credit (if not his negotiating acumen), is quite candid: he needs the money and can't afford to develop the Gizmo himself.

Here's another direct question I would ask Edison: How much did it cost to develop the Gizmo? If his answer is "A lot more than I'm asking for it," this reinforces the atmosphere of desperation. And if his demeanor suggests that he just wants to get this process over with, even if it doesn't yield the highest possible price, he may be experiencing some time pressure.

Other leverage points may not be clear yet. For example, are there any competitive buyers? (You have a hunch that prospective purchasers aren't exactly pounding down Edison's door.) As for yourself, although the Gizmo seems like a good idea, you're far from committed. If the price isn't right, you'll pass it up.

So after factoring feasibility into your aspiration, you initially set your realistic expectation at the $12,000 low end of your valuation range. From here on you'll predicate your opening offer and your subsequent negotiating strategy on that determination—unless and until it turns out to be off-base.

FROM THE SELLER'S VANTAGE POINT

Now let's look at the same process from the viewpoint of the *seller*. Pretend that you're Edison, assessing your realistic expectation. I have a theory—more anecdotal than scientific—that buyers and sellers approach this process a little differently. A buyer starts out by determining what the object of his desire is worth and then shifts to what he can buy it for, using worth as a prime measure of how good a deal he's getting. Sellers, however, are generally less hung up on the concept of worth—at least where there's a strong impetus to sell—and more focused on how much the object can be sold for.

This distinction makes sense. The typical buyer not only has the alternative of not buying—rarely does a *purchaser* act out of necessity—but often has a choice of similar objects he could acquire. Since no two objects are the same, he needs to introduce elements of worth or value to test whether he's making the right purchase at a particular price.

For the seller, however, there's only one choice: whether or not to sell *this* object. Where he's indifferent on that score, the notion of worth may enter the picture. If he can't get a price reflecting reasonable value, he can take the object off the market—unless, of course, he senses that the market is heading even lower, in which case he may decide to take his hit right now. But when he has *decided* to sell, he's usually more interested in "How much can I get for it?" than in abstract concepts of value.

As Edison, you may consider the Gizmo to be worth considerably more than the $20,000 you're asking from Fingerfood. Still, you recognize that something south of $20,000 is the best you can hope to sell it for. You're painfully aware of some information that Ms. Fingerfood doesn't know but may have surmised—namely, that you've struck out in trying to interest any of the established appliance manufacturers. Now you're reduced to approaching a caterer with limited funds, for whom the Gizmo's broader applications may indeed be murky.

Another buyer-seller difference turns on who approached whom. When the seller makes the contact, as in our example, the buyer can afford to be coy: "I'm not sure I'm interested; something like this never occurred to me until you called." This posture is effective to conceal desire.

By contrast, the initiating seller obviously can't be as diffident.

Some do try, however, by pretending that they haven't decided to sell but are merely "testing the market" to assess receptivity. But this seldom rings true. And the buyer's effective retort—"Why don't you decide whether you want to sell and *then* come see me again? I'm not interested in spending a lot of time on something so iffy"—alerts the seller that he can't get away with that kind of posturing. On the other hand, where the initial contact is made by the *buyer*—"Would you *consider* selling that property?"—the seller is in a better position to be coy, and the buyer can't be casual at all.

Let's assume that, based on a variety of considerations—not the least of which is the pride you take in your invention—you would like to get at least $16,000 for the Gizmo. Now you have to check your aspiration against what's feasible under the circumstances. What do you think Ms. Fingerfood is willing to pay, and how does the leverage shape up? She may have financial limitations—an obviously crucial consideration in many negotiations—although she's probably not pressed at these levels. You sense her fascination with the Gizmo—not surprising, given your active promotion of its virtues. You're also touting the dollar potential of licensing the Gizmo, although this is a tougher point to establish (because, if it's so easy, why aren't *you* doing it?).

Buyers, by contrast, engage more in *negative* selling, downgrading the product to lower the price. I'll never forget, when I represented E. F. Hutton, how Peter Cohen and his Shearson colleagues attempted to disparage the value of each of Hutton's assets in order to justify Shearson's disappointingly low initial bid. Listening to them, I understood the purpose behind the exercise—vintage bargaining strategy for a buyer—but I kept thinking: If they believe things are *this* bad, would these guys still be sitting here across the table from us? And ultimately Peter Ueberroth and the rest of our Hutton team were able to negotiate an increase in price to a decent level.

In the final analysis, the combined negative leverage of your needing the money from the sale of the Gizmo to pay debts, the time pressure you feel, and the present lack of competitive alternatives makes you realize that Fingerfood's best price is likely to be less than the $16,000 you desire. So you arrive at an initial realistic expectation of $14,000.

Given Fingerfood's expectation to buy at $12,000, and Edison's to sell for $2,000 more, there may be no deal. But in my experience this is the kind of disparity that stands a good chance of being resolved *if* the buyer wants the property. Why? Because as the process unfolds, new information becomes available, the leverage can shift, and one or both parties may be willing to stretch enough to close the original gap.

REASSESSING EXPECTATIONS AS THE NEGOTIATIONS DEVELOP

When the negotiations begin, let's assume that Ms. Fingerfood counters Edison's $20,000 asking price with an initial offer of $9,000. Although Edison doesn't stalk out of the room, this doesn't fill him with confidence that even his pared-down expectation will be realized. But then, as the negotiations proceed, *two* developments occur that affect each side's expectations. First, a third party who manufacturers hardware appliances ("Hardy") becomes aware of the Gizmo, approaches Edison, and proposes a joint venture to develop the invention, which Hardy would finance.

Now Edison finally has a competitive alternative. But it's not quite the same as a competitive *buyer*; Hardy is offering a different type of deal in which the payoff will be in the future. So Edison has to make sure it fulfills his requirements, the main one being his present need for cash. This is a delicate point for him to raise in the Edison-Hardy negotiations, since it provides Hardy with valuable leverage information. But Edison balances it by revealing to Hardy the presence of Fingerfood as a prospective buyer. Hardy, realizing that cash is necessary to solve Edison's immediate problem, confirms his willingness to lend Edison funds on favorable terms tied into the joint venture.

The new development poses a tough valuation issue for Edison, who has to measure one potential deal against the other—apples and oranges. (This kind of thing can also happen to *buyers* when they're simultaneously bidding on two properties with differing characteristics but are interested in buying only one.) Let's say Edison determines that at prices from Fingerfood below $16,000, he would prefer Hardy's joint venture proposition. The leverage factor of competition has caused Edison to increase his expectation from $14,000 to $16,000. This will make it harder to reach a deal with Ms. Fingerfood.

Edison tells Fingerfood about the offer from Hardy that he's "tempted to pursue," especially at the kind of purchase price Fingerfood has offered. This is smart negotiating on Edison's part. He's making Fingerfood feel the hot breath of competition. She now has to reassess the feasibility built into her realistic expectation. As a result she concludes that she probably won't be able to buy the Gizmo at the $12,000 low end of her aspiration range.

The second development is that the more Fingerfood sees of the Gizmo, the more she's drawn to its licensing potential. (Could it be that Hardy's interest has whetted Fingerfood's appetite?) Putting her increased desire together with the decrease in feasibility causes Fingerfood to revise her realistic expectation upward to the high end of her range, or $15,000.

Now we have the makings of a deal. Fingerfood may eventually stretch up to the $16,000 that Edison feels he needs to surpass Hardy's proposal. Or Edison may stretch down to $15,000, if he ultimately prefers the idea of a sale over a joint venture. Or they might even meet somewhere in the middle.

On the other hand, if Hardy had come into the picture but Ms. Fingerfood's interest in the Gizmo had *waned* over time, the two leverage factors—competition and desire—would have been working at cross purposes. Under those circumstances it's unlikely she would have been willing to pay Edison's price. As I've said before, in a rational world not every deal deserves to be done.

At any rate, you can see that determining your expectations isn't a static exercise. Don't let yourself become fossilized into sticking with your original assessment. There's nothing wrong with this kind of change of heart when it's based on developments involving bona fide leverage factors. I distinguish this, however, from changes based on such emotional factors as your being caught up in the excitement of an auction ("deal heat," we call it) and overpaying; or, conversely, becoming so upset that you refuse to move when you should and thereby lose the deal.

EXPECTATIONS ON NONPRICE ISSUES

Now let's apply these principles to the myriad nonprice issues that arise in a sale or other transaction. In order to determine your realistic expectations here, in addition to assessing the factors previously discussed, you should also take into account the characteristics of the issue involved. To illustrate this, put yourself in Ms. Fingerfood's shoes once more and we'll examine three issues that arise *before* Hardy comes into the picture:

- *Noncompete.* If you buy the Gizmo, you want protection against Edison subsequently inventing a similar device that's better or cheaper than the original.
- *Indemnity.* You've asked Edison to indemnify you for your expenses if someone else shows up with a competitive product—one that was developed prior to this deal and is based on the same technology—and you decide to sue them for infringing Gizmo's patent.
- *Obligations.* Edison is requiring that you assume certain unpaid obligations relating to the Gizmo, totaling about $1,500.

To you, the principal difference between the first two issues is that the *noncompete* is a *blue chip*—more of the *immovable* than the *staunch* variety (as we discussed in chapter 4). If Edison is unwilling to provide you with the requisite assurance, it's a deal breaker. The *indemnity* issue, by contrast, is more of *bargaining chip,* your attitude on it ranging somewhere between the *malleable* and *pliant* categories. You consider it unlikely that such a competing product will appear. You don't know whether, if it did, you would bother with litigation. And there's a real question as to whether Edison should be responsible for your defense of Gizmo's patent once he has sold you the rights.

On the *noncompete* issue—and on blue chips generally—you should set your realistic expectation at a high level. This is true even if you suspect that Edison will be opposed to supplying the protection sought, or if the leverage favors him. You *need* this safeguard. If, as here, you're immovable, then you're not going to do the deal without it, although you'll be willing to discuss the period of time and geographic areas. And you're unlikely to change your expectations much during the negotiations, unless you learn something that suggests you don't need the protection.

On the other hand, with the *indemnity* issue, as with most bargaining chips, you have to give more weight to *feasibility*—to Edison's likely expectations and to the leverage inherent in the situation. For instance, Edison may have given strong indications from the outset that he doesn't want anything hanging over his head once the deal is closed. When Hardy then comes into the picture, the resulting shift in leverage might dictate that you won't be able to have your way on the indemnity. So you set your expectation at something less than complete protection on this score—for example, that you're entitled to be indemnified only if Edison actually *knows* of such a competitive product and has kept the information from you. And remember, on bargaining chips like this, what happens as the negotiations proceed can greatly affect your expectations. For example, were Hardy not to show up and the leverage began to point more in *your* direction, then you might get tougher on this point.

The *obligations* issue has a different characteristic. It's really a dollar item, as so many nonprice issues turn out to be. If you were to pay $15,000 for the Gizmo and assume the $1,500 of obligations, your real purchase price could be viewed as $16,500. So in determining your expectation, you need to assess this in conjunction with the price. At $14,000 you may be willing to pick up the obligations; at $16,000 you would probably be unwilling; at $15,000 you might be receptive to splitting them with Edison.

Too often, however, dollar items like this are left to be dealt with in a vacuum, *after* the price has already been negotiated. That's not wise. If Edison wants to negotiate the price first before turning to other issues, make it clear to him that in discussing price, you're operating on the assumption that you won't have to assume *any* obligations. If that's *not* the case, you should point out, then it will definitely change the price you're willing to pay.

EXPECTATIONS WRAP-UP

Keynote

As a first step in the game plan approach to smart negotiating, you have to formulate realistic expectations on price and other key issues, *before* the negotiations begin. That way you will know where to start out, what steps to take as you go along, and where to stop.

Blunder

The big mistake here is making an opening proposal on an issue without having determined your realistic expectation, with the result that you find yourself too close, or too far away, to achieve your eventual goal.

Lapse

The lapse in this instance consists of being unrealistic, failing to temper your glossy aspirations with a cold dose of feasibility—both in terms of what your counterpart wants and how the leverage tilts.

8 DETERMINING THE APPROPRIATE STARTING POINT

Once you've determined realistic expectations on price and other key issues, your next concern is where to start the bargaining. Here's the way I look at this second important step in my game plan approach. On significant issues like price, where the differing objectives of the two parties outweigh any common interests, you'll undoubtedly have to change your position during the course of the negotiations in order to reach agreement. That being the case, prudence dictates that you leave yourself enough room to do so and still realize your expectations.

Of course, some people label their opening stance as a final position: "I don't negotiate. Here's my offer. Take it or leave it." But in my experience, bargainers who adopt that posture are unlikely to be believed, even if they exude sincerity. They're stuck with the baggage of the trade—the perception, reinforced in countless other deals, that *some* movement will occur. You can't expect your counterpart to take what he's first offered, especially when the offer doesn't meet *his* expectations.

In addition, I'm convinced there's a vital psychological dimension here. Each party needs to experience the satisfaction of seeing the other side move, in order to feel that the resulting agreement has been adequately bargained. Your refusal to budge will leave your counterpart with a nagging sense of having failed as a negotiator, an ominous mind-set that is potentially hazardous to the deal.

STARTING OUT IN SPORTING GOODS

Stan, who owns a sporting goods store ("Good Sport") in a small northeastern city, decides on his sixty-fifth birthday to sell the business and move to Florida. Beth, a lifelong sports fan mired in a prosaic family business, is attracted by Stan's newspaper advertisement: "Successful sporting goods store for sale—reasonable price." They get together. Beth tours Good Sport, reviews some pertinent information, and announces that she's definitely interested.

WHO GOES FIRST ON PRICE?

So who goes first in terms of price: Stan the seller or Beth the buyer? *Inside* Stan's store, *he* goes first; that pair of skis on display carries a price tag of $250. But how does this play out when Stan is selling *the entire store*? There's no price tag hanging on the front door. Do you think Stan would be wise to have an asking price? If he doesn't, should Beth insist on hearing one before she makes an offer? The answers to these questions can shape the course of the bargaining.

The conventional wisdom is to let the other side make the first proposal, to see where your counterpart is coming from before committing yourself. The premise is logical enough. If you're the seller, the buyer might propose a higher price than you would have sought. If you're the buyer, the seller may value his property below what you would have offered. And if *you* go first, you'll never know. Besides, even if you don't get lucky, you'll pick up valuable information before having to bid.

At times I go along with the conventional wisdom. A buyer who lacks enough data to make an intelligent bid, for example, should hold his fire. The seller who wants to preserve the posture (whether true or fictional) that he hasn't made up his mind whether or not to sell, may do better letting the buyer go first, underscoring the message that it will take a blockbuster offer to move the seller off the fence. Nevertheless, when there's a choice in the matter, I frequently counsel my clients to put their number on the table *first*. I advise sellers to let the buyer know what price they're looking to receive; I advise buyers to tell the seller what they consider an appropriate price to pay.

Why do I often go against the conventional wisdom? Because I think it makes good sense for a negotiator to *take control* of the price issue. For instance, put yourself in the shoes of a *knowledgeable buyer* (unlike Beth). You want the seller negotiating off *your* opening number, not his own. Your bid sends a message to your counterpart:

if he wants to play ball, here's the ballpark where the action will occur. Or, to change (and mix) metaphors, think of this as a first-strike deterrent against the seller shooting for the moon.

In my experience the chances of a seller asking for less than the buyer would dare offer are slim. In the real world, negotiators worry about just the opposite: a seller who trots out an exorbitant figure and goes to great pains to support it, thereby digging a hole that's tough to climb out of. This makes for rough sledding in the resulting negotiations.

How about when you're a *seller*? The last thing you need is a lowball offer, requiring lots of energy to elevate the buyer into the realm of reason. True, you can't eliminate this risk, even if your asking price is reasonable. But you increase the chance of it occurring when you invite the buyer to put the first number on the table without any guidance.

Just one note of caution, however: *Don't go first unless you know value* (or are well advised on that score) *and have formulated a realistic expectation to guide your negotiating strategy.*

Now how does this play out in the purchase of Good Sport? If you're Stan, I think you should have an asking price, a figure supportable by independent criteria. Beth, who isn't in the business of buying companies, is likely to bid cautiously. Inviting her to go first runs a real risk of receiving a lowball bid that she'll defend to the death.

If you're Beth, I think you should insist on knowing what price Stan has in mind and his basis for it. Stan knows much more about what he's selling than you know about what you're buying. You'll learn a lot from Stan's initial asking price, the justifications offered in support, the accompanying body language. You may even pick up helpful information touching on such matters as Stan's need to sell, his timing, whether there are competitive buyers, and how close his opening price is to his expectation—all before you've committed to anything.

WHO GOES FIRST ON NONPRICE ISSUES?

Turning now to *nonprice issues*, my general rule of thumb on going first is this: If it's important for the issue to come out your way, then *you* should raise it. For example, say that the Good Sport store lease, which is on terms favorable to the tenant, has less than two years to run. For Beth, what happens at the end of the term is significant. Will she be able to keep the space? Will the landlord seek a hefty increase in the rental? What renewal options might be obtainable now? Beth has to press Stan on this issue. By contrast, from Stan's perspective, once has sold the business and moved to Florida, he couldn't care less. So this is an item he's not anxious to flag.

I can think of two exceptions to this general rule. The first occurs when you don't want your counterpart to realize the importance to you of a particular issue *and* it's one that's likely to come up anyway during the course of the negotiations. The other involves the kind of issue that, if nothing is said about it in the agreement, would come out your way by operation of law. Here, silence is golden—since any discussion may lead to confrontation. But if the law goes the other way, then you ignore the issue at your peril.

WHEN TO RAISE THE ISSUE

Once you've decided to raise a certain issue, the question becomes *when* to do so. Your timing on this can affect the outcome. In most deals of any consequence, there is an initial period of bargaining that, if successful, culminates in a meeting of the minds on key issues such as price. (We'll call this the "price negotiations.") Then, a second round of bargaining takes place concerning other details to be reflected in a written contract (the "contract negotiations"). For each nonprice issue, you have to decide whether to put it on the table *before* or *after* the parties' minds have initially met. Should the bargaining over this issue be part of the price negotiations or be saved for the contract negotiations?

Let's assume, for example, that Good Sport—like most companies—has a few skeletons in the closet. Stan, realizing he will ultimately have to reveal these to Beth, must decide whether to do so before agreement is reached on price. Early disclosure carries the risk of scaring Beth away before she has invested much time and effort in the deal. It may also lower the price she'll be willing to pay. Fearing such consequences, many sellers refrain from broadcasting the bad news until later in the negotiations.

The problem with waiting is that it risks a different adverse reaction from Beth: "Why wasn't I told about this horror *before* we agreed on price?" This carries an imputation of sharp dealing on Stan's part. And with the contract negotiations still unresolved, Beth isn't bound to go through with the deal. So Stan has to worry that she'll use this new revelation as an excuse for walking away or renegotiating the price.

To test this, put yourself in Stan's position. Let's say that George Grip, an ex-salesman for Good Sport whom you terminated earlier this year, has threatened a lawsuit against the company for money he claims is due him. You've denied the obligation, but the outcome of the case, if it's ultimately litigated, isn't clear. You know you'll have to tell Beth about Grip's claim at some point. Should you do it during the price negotiations or wait until the contract negotiations?

As a general proposition, a seller is better off bringing up bad news *voluntarily* than having the buyer discover it. A buyer who unearths a skeleton is likely to infer that the seller was trying to avoid disclosure, despite the latter's belated protest that he was "just about to raise the issue." So if Beth is preparing to review certain company files that contain references to Grip, you should definitely tell her about the claim before she spots it herself.

But assume that Beth is unlikely to learn of Grip's claim on her own during the price negotiations. What then? I can see you making a rational decision *not* to bring this subject up just yet. After all, the claim hasn't gone to litigation, the outcome is uncertain, and it's not clear who will ultimately bear the burden: will it pass with the business, or will you be asked to hold Beth harmless against any adverse impact?

More important, you don't want to have to deal with the "side effects" of the Grip affair up front. It will be harder to sell Beth on the deal if she is forced to ponder such questions as: Am I buying into a lawsuit? Has Stan been doing things that will produce litigation in other areas? How often has he refused to honor his obligations? Are there other unhappy employees? Is Grip bad-mouthing Good Sport in the community? So you conclude that it's best to bring this up after the parties have reached an agreement in principle, although before Beth discovers it on her own. And, ideally, you'll be able to keep the matter in perspective at that point.

But now change the facts slightly. Say that Grip's case isn't very good, although he's claiming a large sum of money. Assume further that you don't want anything hanging over your head once the sale has taken place. You may then elect to raise *l'affaire Grip* with Beth early on, before any deal is struck. Your aim here is to persuade her that the claim has no merit. "Be sure to have your own lawyer evaluate it, Beth," you say, "because this will be *your* responsibility after the closing."

Such forthrightness on your part may help Beth decide that this is an acceptable risk for her to run, without the claim having any effect on the price negotiations. By contrast, raising it later—with possible overtones of concealment that suggest concern on your part over the outcome of the lawsuit—might give her a lot more trouble. Beth may then wonder whether the facts you've provided her are the truth, the whole truth, and nothing but the truth.

HOW MUCH ROOM TO GIVE YOURSELF ON PRICE

Now let's go back to the issue of price. If you're going to take the first crack at it, the key is to *choose a starting point that neither appears to overreach nor manages to underachieve.*

I'm aware that some self-styled experts advise you to begin the negotiations with a truly outrageous opening offer. If you're the seller, they say, ask twice what you're willing to sell the property for. When you're the buyer, tell the seller you'll be willing to take over the debts of his business, but that's about as far as you're prepared to go.

Well, to each his own, but I don't buy it. My worry is that your counterpart will feel compelled to counter your outlandish opener with an outrage of his own, resulting in a longer, harder road to reach your realistic expectation. Even worse, the other party may simply refuse to make a counterproposal, forcing you to bid against yourself to get something going. Insulting offers can also give rise to severe disappointment and even anger, getting the negotiations off to a terrible start from which they never recover. I find these risks unacceptable.

At the other pole are those who pride themselves on opening with truly modest ambitions, thereby demonstrating a cooperative attitude and showing their trustworthiness. They hope to induce the other side to come back with an equally moderate response, thus reducing the prospective differences between the parties. This approach has its place, but generally speaking, I don't favor it. You can't trust the other side to be as reasonable as you've been. As a result, the initial bid and asked boundaries are likely to be skewed in the wrong direction, with your counterpart reluctant to make the longer trip to *your* expectation and looking for more movement on your part than you're prepared to deliver.

So in most cases, if there's a rational basis for giving yourself some room, I think it's wise to do so. The main exception to this advice is when your realistic expectation is based on an independent principle that you want to make the lodestar for the price negotiations. For instance, say you're selling a house in a development. A similar house next door sold last week at a favorable price, and you want to hitch yourself to those coattails, using that prior sale price as the basis for your own. It would be self-defeating to conjure up an asking price which violates the "fair" principle that you're vigorously espousing to the potential buyer. You may, however, be able to make a little room for yourself without doing violence to the principle—for example, by contending that the better upkeep on your home entitles you to a 5 percent premium over your neighbor's shabby abode.

In any event, my general approach to the opening proposal lies well between the extremes of outrage and undue moderation. I advise making a first offer that is sufficiently reasonable to be viewed constructively by the other side and thus to evoke a positive response. On the other hand, it should give you enough room to move deliberately to your expectation without being forced to stretch.

The precise amount of room depends on many factors: the other side's likely goal, the information you possess, the relative leverage of the parties, and so on. It also hinges on an item we'll discuss shortly: the rationale you're able to bring to bear. Without it, your number lacks backbone. I always caution my clients against putting a figure on the table that they can't back up with a plausible rationale.

To quantify that advice—exactly *how much* room you should leave yourself—as a general rule of thumb in a sale transaction, I recommend an opening offer that's not less than 10 percent nor more than one-third away from my client's realistic expectation. My preferred starting point is in the 15–25 percent range, but obviously particular circumstances can render this rule of thumb inappropriate.

Now let's apply this to the Good Sport situation. Say that Stan, whose realistic expectation is $100,000, begins by asking $120,000 for the business. Beth, with a realistic expectation in the $90,000–$95,000 area, counters at $75,000. Although the resulting gap of $45,000 isn't paltry, this strikes me as an achievable deal, provided the parties exhibit flexibility and engage in a constructive concession pattern.

On the other hand, if Stan had initially asked $150,000, which Beth felt had forced her to counter at $50,000—leaving a hefty gap equal to Stan's entire expectation—then I hold out little hope for the negotiations. You might be able to close a gap of that magnitude in a Turkish bazaar, but seldom in the kind of real-world business situations you're likely to encounter.

IS USING A RANGE HELPFUL?

Some people like to express their price thinking in terms of a range. The potential buyer of a business, for instance, might say to the seller (who hasn't stated an asking price), "I'm thinking of paying something in the seventy thousand to eighty thousand range." The reasoning is that the $80,000 number will whet the seller's appetite without the buyer actually having made a firm bid at that figure. Then, when the buyer eventually does make an $80,000 offer, it will represent a concession on his part, since it's at the summit of his previously stated range.

Astute negotiators receiving this kind of proposal, however, routinely deem it an offer at the top of the range. Their premise is that the buyer would never have trotted out the $80,000 number if he weren't signaling his willingness to go that high. Accordingly they give him little or no credit for the subsequent journey there. As a matter of fact, when I'm representing the seller, I'll often emphasize this point by subsequently characterizing the buyer's proposal as "your $80,000 offer," neglecting the range aspect entirely. Needless to say, this is why it's clearly folly for a buyer to suggest a range whose upper limit exceeds his expectation.

Still, there are times when using a range can be helpful. For instance, you may want to propose the range and indicate that where you end up within it will depend on certain factors, such as the results of a physical inspection of the seller's equipment. Using a range is also consistent with a posture of not having thought the matter through entirely, a pose that can sometimes be desirable in the early going. On the other hand, a range detracts from the cloak of definitiveness in which many negotiators seek to wrap their intentions and may undercut the finely tuned rationale developed in support of a bid.

BARGAINING ROOM ON NONPRICE ISSUES

Since most *nonprice* issues lend themselves to positional bargaining, it makes good sense to leave yourself some maneuvering room here, too—particularly with issues that translate into dollars. The main problem in giving yourself sufficient room on nonprice issues is in finding a supporting rationale that will stand up to scrutiny.

Let's say, for instance, that Good Sport had previously carried a line of weight-lifting equipment that proved unsuccessful. Last year the whole line, inventory and all, was sold to a merchant named Pecs for a $10,000 promissory note. Pecs subsequently defaulted on the note, forcing Good Sport to bring a lawsuit to compel payment. Beth, who considers Pecs to be a deadbeat, has taken the position that she's not including any possible recovery on the note in her price calculation. Stan understands this but nevertheless maintains that the claim should be pursued, to which Beth is agreeable.

Now, if nothing further is said, any recovery on the Pecs claim occurring after Beth takes over Good Sport will benefit her. Therefore, Stan contends—with some justice—that *he* should be entitled to the benefit if there's a recovery, since she hasn't "paid" for it. But can Stan take the position that he ought to get *100* percent of any gross recovery? After all, some effort on the part of Good Sport, including payment of legal fees, will be required to collect on the Pecs note. It would be hard for Stan to fashion a rationale to support such a position.

Therefore I don't think Stan should go to this extreme, even though it would give him more room in the resulting negotiation. A better opener is that he's entitled to any recovery on the Pecs note, *net* of the postdeal expenses incurred in connection with collecting the claim. This is rationally defensible as a means for Stan to realize on this contingent asset of the business. It provides him with a shot at this good result, while still leaving him room for a satisfactory compromise—perhaps through giving Beth a percentage of the net recovery as an incentive for her to pursue the Pecs claim.

Many nonprice issues don't provide a lot of room for maneuver. Often your desired result is rooted in a principle that you're anxious for your counterpart to adopt. A number of issues have a single customary outcome in similar transactions or possess only one rational resolution, in which case selecting a much tougher starting point just doesn't sit right. A buyer like Beth, for instance, invariably bears whatever expenses *she* incurs in the transaction, such as legal fees. (By contrast, the buyer will sometimes pay the *seller's* expenses or allow them to be paid out of the business.) Beth's insistence on Stan paying her expenses runs the risk of being badly received, of poisoning the air; she's better off not trying to vary the usual outcome.

Finally, on an issue that's important to you but not to the other side—and where your counterpart is unaware of the imbalance—you're well advised not to seek much more than you need. If you get greedy here, your counterpart may feel the need to cross swords. With a more modest request, the issue may slip by quietly.

BUTTRESSING YOUR POSITION WITH RATIONALE

In most of the negotiations I participate in, the parties adopt an attitude of reasonableness, striving in a spirit of give and take to resolve the difficult issues facing them. Naked power displays are much more the exception than the rule. In this reasonable atmosphere, you have to be able to support the positions you take with a credible and persuasive rationale. When asking for something, you have to show why you're entitled to it. Your counterpart may dispute your views. But if *your* reasons are more logical, your chances of success increase sharply—unless, of course, the leverage runs so much in favor of the other side that reason won't prevail.

A good rationale is particularly vital—yet, surprisingly, often neglected—with regard to price. When you're trying to acquire a property or business, an opening bid unaccompanied by any indication of how you *arrived* at that figure lacks real substance. Even if it doesn't persuade your counterpart, it forces him to take issue with your *rationale*, rather than just trotting out another figure miles away from your own. Disputes over rationale can be a lot more constructive than arguments over numbers.

Making a plausible case for your opening bid—using whatever objective-sounding touchstone may be available—is particularly important when your offer is much less than what the seller expected. It lessens the risk of the seller walking out of the room, disillusioned and angry. Rather, it forces him to come back at you with his own rationale, which is just what you're trying to accomplish in order to get serious negotiations underway. And it's equally applicable when the *seller* is going first, as a means of enticing the buyer into the bidding. A rationale is also important for nonprice issues, where a lot of time is spent disputing the most equitable resolution. I can report, from painful experience, that when your counterpart has all the good arguments and expresses them cogently and forcefully, it's very difficult to resist going along—at least part of the way. Savvy negotiators can often come up with compelling reasons for their positions on the spot, but advance preparation makes a lot of sense here. This is especially true when you're unwilling to expose the *real* reason behind your position—because, presumably, it would cause the other side to refuse your request.

There are times when you may have to "back in" to a rationale. If you sense instinctively where you should start out in order to realize your expectation, then you have to come up with some plausible reasons for *that* starting point, as opposed to having arrived at the number by way of the reasons. Still, whichever way your private journey proceeds, you should present the reasoning as if it were irresistible.

Rationale also works for you in another, quieter way. In the last analysis, the issue of where to start out is quite judgmental. It has to *feel* right. The harder it is to come up with logic to support your position—the more you have to back into reasons that leave you feeling uncomfortable—the more concerned you should be that your counterpart will perceive your position as overreaching. So developing a rationale furnishes a useful litmus test to determine whether the position you're taking is defensible.

GIVING YOUR FIRST OFFER THE PROPER EMPHASIS

In addition to providing the rationale, you should support your first offer with appropriate words and demeanor. Here again the extremes are untenable. Don't tout your opening number as "nonnegotiable," or as your "best" or "final" offer, when those descriptions amount to a fabrication that the other side will soon discover. On the other hand, you needn't apologize for your bid, whatever it is. Every so often I observe a negotiator who fairly radiates concern over how the other side will react to his initial proposal. He focuses on an ashtray, avoiding any semblance of eye contact with his counterpart. As he blurts out the offer, his fingers tremble, his voice stutters, his entire body language telegraphs contrition. Don't let this happen to you. If you're that uncomfortable, choose a more reasonable number; but never signal the other side that you're not making a serious proposal.

I favor a straightforward presentation, neither overblown nor humble. If you're a buyer like Beth and you're going first, a suitable phrase is "I think an appropriate price is seventy-five thousand dollars"—provided the number is then backed up with a supportive rationale. But when the other side has been eagerly awaiting your number, a better procedure may be to explain how you went about determining the price *before* you mention the actual figure. Then conclude by saying, "And *therefore,* the price I've arrived at is seventy-five thousand dollars."

I recommend this for two reasons. First, as soon as the other side has heard your number, their attention level drops off sharply. Thus it makes sense to present the rationale while they're still listening. Second, this approach points up that you arrived at your number via an objective process and didn't just back into the rationale—even if you did!

By the way, your first bid should be expressed as a round number, whether or not the underlying calculations produce that precise result. If you're the buyer, always round the figure *up,* thereby showing the seller that you're not trying to squeeze out the last penny. This can be even more effective if you round up by a meaningful amount, while still maintaining adequate room between the bid and your expectation. The words to accompany your largesse are, "I'm adding a substantial premium to the calculation in the interest of getting a deal done."

Some buyers, starting out low in anticipation of a long drawn-out negotiation, like to signal the seller not to be too discouraged. I can understand the concern, but I don't like to hear a buyer say, "Here's my opening bid, which I'm definitely prepared to negotiate." Never disparage your own offer. I prefer a more subtle approach, such as having the buyer's agent tell the seller's agent, "My client's opening offer is seventy-five thousand, and my sense is that there's some room in that number."

Let's switch over now to a seller like Stan. There are various formulations Stan can use in putting a first price on the table—all accompanied, of course, by an appropriate rationale. "I'm looking to get a hundred and twenty thousand" doesn't chill the bidding. "I think the right price is one hundred twenty thousand" invites the seller to state a different view of what's "right." "My asking price is one hundred and twenty thousand" is somewhat weaker, implying that the seller has plenty of room to move—although it may be suitable where the asking price is quite high. But *don't* say, "That's my asking price, which I realize is high, and I'm willing to come down."

If this is one of those situations where circumstances dictate an opening bid that's close to your expectation, you need to do something special to get that point across. For example, you might say, "That's my bid—and I want you to know, it's approaching my limits," while offering appropriate reasons for why this is so. But remember, credibility is crucial. If you're not that close, avoid the posturing. You don't want your counterpart to discover you didn't mean what you said, since it will undercut all the other points you're trying to make believable.

REACTING TO THE OTHER SIDE'S PRICE OFFER

Let's switch bases and assume that your counterpart has made the initial price proposal. Now it's your turn to take a responsive opening position. How should you go about it? The process begins with how you react when your counterpart makes his proposal. If he's any kind of a negotiator, he's watching your reaction, hoping for a genuine response that provides useful information.

If, for instance, your counterpart is a *buyer* who is making a lowball bid on your property, he'll anticipate a strong negative reaction from you. If you *don't* react that way, however, he may infer that the low price didn't strike you as so far out of line. If your counterpart is a *seller* who has just informed you of the absurdly high price he's asking for his property, he'll be looking to see whether you treat it as absurd or, unexpectedly, appear to be entering into serious negotiations on that basis. And the same considerations hold true for a nonprice issue.

So even if you've decided not to make the first proposal, always be ready to react to your counterpart's opener. Don't transmit the wrong signal or waste the opportunity to "send a message" to the other side, a message that can't be delivered as effectively later on because then it lacks spontaneity and carries the "manufactured" label.

I'm a strong believer in characterizing the proposal you receive from those on the other side in order to reduce their expectations and set the stage for your counterproposal. This is true even if your counterpart's opening price isn't preposterous. There's always *something* negative you can say about even the most forthcoming proposal! If you're the seller, for instance, and the buyer has gone first, here are some all-purpose retorts to pretty good offers: "I wouldn't be willing to sell at that price," or "I've turned down better offers"—if, in fact, you have—or "I expect to do much better along the way" (if it's early in the selling process).

Your verbal rejoinder is particularly important when your counterpart's opening proposal is wide of the mark. Here, in addition to letting him know he's out of range and to avoid having your silence misinterpreted, you may also want to get him bidding against himself. For instance, let's say that Stan starts out by asking $150,000 for the Good Sport business. Instead of bidding in response to this, Beth's reaction might be, "Oh, wow, that's a wild price! Tell me, Stan, what are you *really* looking for?" Her goal is to get Stan to reduce his asking price into a more reasonable range before she has to put her own number on the table.

Alternatively, if Beth were to kick off the bidding by offering $50,000 for the business, Stan might say, "Come on, Beth, that's not even a serious offer. Make me a serious offer and I might be willing to negotiate." His hope, of course, is that she'll come back with a higher number before he has to name his price. Whether you're the seller or the buyer, you lose nothing by these attempts; there's really no downside. Even if it doesn't work, the signal you're sending—that the other side is way out of line—might have a worthwhile impact on his or her thinking.

PUTTING YOUR RESPONSE ON THE TABLE

Now it's time for you to make your first counterproposal, taking into account what you've gleaned from the other side's initial offer. As we saw in the last chapter, trying to estimate what your counterpart would like to pay or receive—about which you now have a clue—is a basic element in determining your realistic expectation. This expectation, in turn, will serve as a major influence on your counteroffer.

Your response to the opening offer should serve three main functions:

- First, to set up a *bid-and-asked* range that will enable the two of you, through a well-managed concession pattern, to arrive in the vicinity of your realistic expectation;
- Second, to send your counterpart a *message* that will shape his expectation in a way that furthers your interests;
- Third, to induce your counterpart to make a *constructive second proposal* that represents meaningful movement from his initial offer.

Overlaying these three functions, however, is the need for you to provide a plausible rationale. Say that you have to choose between two counterproposals. The first is less ambitious but has a strong and reasonable basis. The second is more aggressive but relies on some arguments of the "backing in" variety. Here, the first proposal might be your better choice, the more convincing rationale overriding other considerations.

Put yourself in Beth's shoes. Stan has started out by asking $120,000 for the business, and now it's your turn to respond. Based on Stan's asking price, you refine your $90,000–$95,000 realistic expectation range to the $95,000 level. Stan's number is high, but not outrageous. What should you bid?

How about $50,000? In terms of the three functions, this provides you with a more than ample bid-and-asked range and sends a definite hard-nosed message. But it's not likely to induce a constructive responsive offer. Stan may even say "Come on, Beth, get serious" and refuse to drop his price until you sweeten the pot. And you'll probably be hard put to master any convincing rationale for such a bid.

How about $90,000? This will generate a constructive response, but it sets up skewed bid-and-asked boundaries for your route to $95,000. You're much too close to your expectation at this early stage, while Stan is still a good distance away.

A bid of $80,000 creates workable boundaries and is designed to induce a constructive response from Stan. The problem here is that it may send the wrong message—namely, that you're willing to pay $100,000, which is that nice round number halfway between the bid and the asked. I'm sorry, but that's the way people think, and it's tough to eradicate such an inference.

So to cover all three bases, your optimum bid is probably $70,000 or $75,000, provided you can muster up a good rationale for those numbers. Remember, however, if your best reasons fit $80,000 (or even $85,000), you might be well advised to override these other considerations and go with the higher number. But if you do, you should accompany the proposal with a brief warning message: you're not going to play negotiating games, you're putting a number on the table that's the right price for the business, and so on. It's vital for you to make Stan realize that you're nearer your top dollar than he might otherwise assume.

Now reverse the roles and play Stan. Assume that Beth made the initial offer of $80,000, and your realistic expectation is $100,000. A counter by you at the $150,000 level, which Beth will consider ridiculous, is unlikely to induce her to move. On the other hand, if you propose $105,000, you're left with an unattractive bid-and-asked range. A counteroffer of $120,000 does send the message that a $100,000 deal is in the cards. But I would recommend you come back with $125,000 in order to get a little edge and not look quite so pat—provided, of course, you have reasoning to support it. If the best rationale were to aim you at $115,000, however, I'd probably advise you to counter with that, while sending an appropriate message about not being too far from your sticking point.

REACTING AND RESPONDING ON NONPRICE ISSUES

How about nonprice issues? The process and considerations are basically similar. Make sure you develop your realistic expectations and initial positions on these issues early—even if you're not going first—so that when your counterpart's starting points are way off the mark, you can provide the appropriate response.

For instance, pretend you're Beth. Stan goes first and says, "I'm asking one hundred twenty thousand dollars, but I'm making no representations with regard to Good Sport, express or implied. You've got to take the business as is—caveat emptor."

Eyes bulging in disbelief, you step up and respond in kind: "That's absurd, Stan. This isn't the sale of an ersatz Rolex watch on the street corner. You've got to stand behind what you sell. And it's on that basis, and that basis alone, that I'm prepared to offer seventy-five thousand dollars, which I think is the right price for the following reasons . . ."

Now there may in fact be a number of compromises that you can make on this principle that Stan "stand behind" the business, specific items on which you'll ultimately be willing to bear the risk. Nevertheless, you need to establish the *principle* your way right at the outset. It would only detract from the force of your message if you were to start out by discussing the possible exceptions. As I find myself saying so often to my clients or colleagues, "Hey, let the *other guy* bring that one up." Don't ever feel you have to do his job for him.

STARTING POINT WRAP-UP

Keynote

The second step in my game plan approach to smart negotiating is deciding *where* to start the bargaining process, as well as *who* makes the first offer, and *how* to respond to that offer. The key to shaping the bargaining process lies in choosing a starting point that neither appears to overreach nor manages to underachieve. In this regard you should avoid the extremes of both unbridled ambition and undue moderation. You don't want to drive the other party away mad or get him counterbidding at absurd levels, but you need enough room to maneuver handily to your final destination.

Blunder

Too many negotiators wait for the other party to make the first proposal, only to have him trot out an exorbitant figure and then dig himself into a real hole supporting it. If you think there's a chance of this happening, take control of the negotiations with your own carefully considered first proposal.

Lapse

The major omission is the failure to back up initial positions (as well as those taken later on) with a credible and convincing rationale, in order to give them some semblance of backbone.

9 DEVISING A CONSTRUCTIVE CONCESSION PATTERN

Now that the opening positions are on the table, your next task is to choreograph the movements that will lead both parties into the general vicinity of your realistic expectation—close enough to enable you, using the techniques described in chapter 10, to reach a deal.

THE EMPHASIS IS ON THE PROCESS

Let's say Victor puts his business up for sale. Victoria offers $60,000. Victor says, "Sorry, I'm asking one hundred thousand dollars." Victoria replies, "That's way too high—too far away for me even to increase my bid." Victor says, "Okay, you've got a deal at sixty thousand." And now Victoria whirls around to her colleagues, aghast. "Hey, what's wrong here?" she sputters. "What does the seller *know* about the business that I'm not being told?"

Pardon the hyperbole, but there's a valid point to be made here. The $60,000 might well have been Victor's realistic expectation. Now, however, he could lose the deal entirely because his counterpart's suspicions have been raised. Believe me, Victoria would probably feel better paying $72,000 after a hard-fought negotiation than "succeeding" on her first nibble! A tight deal, featuring plenty of give and take, always makes the parties more comfortable with the end result.

It would be equally unwise, after Victoria's $60,000 bid and his $100,000 asked, for Victor to say, "Okay, let's split the difference at eighty thousand." And that's true even if $80,000 was precisely the number he was looking to achieve. The path a negotiator has to take to arrive at his destination is often more circuitous than abrupt.

I'm convinced that in negotiations over money, property, services, or contracts—as with so many other aspects of the business world—the *process* is what's important. Victoria needs to feel that she has done her job, that she has made Victor walk over some hot coals on the way to a deal. Too quick an agreement on what Victoria perceives to be tough issues can cause her to worry that (as a seller) she's not asking for enough, or (as a buyer) she's purchasing damaged goods. Compromise proposals, however ingenious, depend on timing and their manner of introduction. Spring one too early or impetuously and it's unlikely to work.

Knowing how to manage this process effectively in order to set things up for the final compromise is an essential element in a negotiating game plan. It's *not* a trip you should leave to chance. You can journey to Europe without hotel or travel reservations and hope things work out in each city on your itinerary. But it's much more reassuring to book ahead—with the caveat, of course (both in Europe and during negotiations), that you may want to linger longer in one place than previously planned or get out of town faster than anticipated.

The term commonly used to describe a typical step in this process is "concession," which may be an unfortunate choice of words. In other areas we think of a concession as yielding a right or privilege. It sounds as if you're giving something up, which is how many people approach the process, viewing each step as a tense, grudging struggle. To my mind this is the wrong attitude to take. The only *real* concession you make, in the sense of being deprived, occurs if and when you're forced to stretch beyond your realistic expectation. Everything else is simply part of the negotiating dance—tactical adjustments, if you will—designed to bring you and your counterpart to mutually satisfactory terms.

So if you ask $100,000 for a business you would be happy to sell for $80,000, *don't* think of that territory between $100,000 and $80,000 as *your* terrain. It's more like a no-man's-land. If you can end up occupying part of it by making a deal at $85,000, more power to you. But if holding out for a slight edge in your favor appreciably increases the risk of the deal aborting, then such intransigence isn't worth the candle. A deal at $80,000 accomplishes what you set out to do.

But don't get me wrong. This *isn't* how you should paint the picture to your counterpart. He should be under the impression that you're giving away the store to come down so low on price. If he thought your journey was painless, then he would push you to stretch beyond your expectation, down into the $75,000 area. So be mindful of the difference between the way you *actually* feel and how you *portray* the agony you're suffering.

To emphasize the need for an overall game plan in this important process, I'll use the term *concession pattern* to describe the path from starting point toward expectation. The concession pattern is easier to visualize when the issue is price or is otherwise measurable in dollars—$100,000, $90,000, $85,000, $82,500, and so on. But you should also try to calibrate nonprice issues along similar lines, devising intermediate positions that close the gap but still leave you some room to move.

SUBSTITUTING MOMENTUM FOR INTRANSIGENCE

The literature on negotiating bombards readers with pithy tidbits of advice about concessions. For example: Never concede without getting something for it; Don't concede near a deadline; Always let the other guy make the first concession; Keep your concessions small and infrequent; and so on. Much of this advice is of the "hanging tough" variety.

My problem with this is that although you clearly won't give anything away, you're equally unlikely to generate much in return from your counterpart (unless you possess overwhelming leverage). Reciprocity of movement is essential to negotiating. The hard-nosed approach doesn't help to whittle down a big bid-and-asked gap to the bite size needed for springing the final compromise.

So instead of waiting around for your counterpart to buckle, I recommend you follow a constructive pattern of concessions. Use the maneuvering room you've provided yourself. Don't let your first bid take on a life of its own; after all, it was just a place to start. Without belittling it, get off the mark—while also rousting your counterpart from *his* opening perch—and begin moving toward a deal.

Although you're usually looking to generate reciprocity with a concession, sometimes you concede without an explicit quid pro quo. Your best judgment may be not to prolong the agony on this particular issue but, rather, to wrap it up and move on to something else.

Concessions provide much needed momentum to a deal, a commodity that, unfortunately, the other side doesn't always supply. When things bog down, I'll sometimes suggest to a client that we proffer some meaningful movement on a minor point (or a symbolic gesture on a major one), without coupling the concession to any direct or indirect tradeoff.

On the other hand, when I'm trying to demonstrate firmness on a point of real significance, I feel it undercuts my stance to be fussing around with concessions on minor matters. It sends an implicit signal that suggests I eventually expect to compromise the major point. In those cases my preference is to express confidence that if and when the time comes, we'll be able to make progress on such details. But, I continue, it makes no sense to waste our efforts on little items until we agree on the biggie—"on which, as you know, our position is unshakable."

SENDING A MESSAGE

Every concession you make sends your counterpart a message. It can be explicit, given content by the words you use in describing the movement. But the message may also be *implicit*, with your actions speaking louder than your words. Always ask yourself: What does my counterpart infer from my concession—from its size, the timing, the point that's conceded, the pattern—regarding my state of mind and likely future conduct?

There's a three-part message I like to send—explicitly or implicitly—when making a concession: (1) *this one is meaningful, but* (2) *there may not be many more,* (3) *particularly if it's not reciprocated.* If movement on your side appears to come too easily, the other side doesn't give it full value. I'm not suggesting you pretend that each paltry concession is ripped out of your hide. Still, your counterpart should be made to understand that it's not entirely painless; it's costing you something. Otherwise you're unlikely to induce him to relinquish something of value in return.

The part of your message that suggests a limit on further concessions will grow stronger as you near your expectation. But the signal that the well dries up fast if your concessions aren't reciprocated should be consistent from day one. "In the interests of moving the deal ahead," you say, "here's what I'm willing to do; and I hope you'll take this in the right spirit and *be responsive.*"

Don't apologize for partial concessions. When price is the issue, furnish a rationale to justify why your latest move puts you at the right level. On a nonprice issue, try to characterize your partial concession as having been designed to satisfy your counterpart's *basic problem.* Admittedly it doesn't go all the way to the extreme position he has been taking. But such an extreme, you tell him, is something that he doesn't really need.

If your concession on one issue is contingent on your counterpart making a reciprocal concession on another issue, be explicit about the connection: "If you're willing to close before year end, I would be willing to drop my insistence on the audit." Then if the other side *isn't* willing to close this year, you're still in a position to insist on the audit. (By contrast, an attempt on your part to pull back an *unconditional* concession can generate considerable ill will.) To be sure, your counterpart now knows that, at least under certain circumstances, you're willing to close without the audit; and he will undoubtedly try to think of how to get you to give it up without his having to agree to an early closing.

My preferred way to concede a point when it's *not* part of a swap is on the basis of fairness. Assuming that my counterpart has advanced a plausible argument in support of the result, I tell him he has persuaded me it's the right outcome. This is not done to flatter him (and I wouldn't want him to interpret it that way), although the compliment can't hurt. Rather, I hope he will recognize that the rule of reason is alive and well in these negotiations. Then when *I* make a persuasive argument on a different point later on, he should treat it with the same respect that I just gave his.

GOOD SPORT REVISITED

To illustrate the concession pattern as a process, let's continue to follow the negotiations from the last chapter over Beth's possible acquisition of Stan's Good Sport business. Assume for these purposes that you are Beth, but now you happen to be quite knowledgeable about values in this marketplace. You would like to buy Good Sport at a price in the $90,000–$95,000 range, which you consider a realistic expectation. Before even hearing Stan's asking price, you've made an initial offer of $75,000, to preempt him from starting out with an outrageous number he would later have trouble disavowing. You have a hunch that Stan wants to end up getting at least $100,000 for Good Sport. As we join the talks, Stan is preparing to respond to you with his asking price.

REACTING TO A COUNTEROFFER

Let's focus first on your *reaction* to Stan's counteroffer. The principles involved are similar to those discussed in the last chapter on reacting to an opening bid and are equally applicable to either party's responses to subsequent proposals down the road.

Stan's asking price, in conjunction with your $75,000 initial offer, will provide the bid and asked boundaries for the negotiation. It's not unusual (but neither is it inevitable) for price negotiations to end up somewhere near the midpoint of the parties' opening positions. On that premise, you're hoping that Stan will start out asking less than $115,000. If he opens at $105,000, for instance, your chances of making the deal in your $90,000–$95,000 expectation range are excellent. At $125,000, however, things are much more difficult. And if his number is $145,000, your chances are slim. (In fact, if you could have known Stan was going to reach that high, it would have been better to discourage him from naming a price and to keep the bidding unilateral for the moment.)

Before receiving Stan's counteroffer, you should plan your reaction in advance. Don't leave this to chance. If Stan is a good negotiator, he'll be observing closely how you respond. If, for instance, your reaction to a $105,000 price is a self-satisfied smile, Stan may sense that you now consider your expectation attainable. You would *not* have smiled that way, he reasons, if your real objective were $85,000, because *that* result then wouldn't have seemed so achievable. Through your inadvertent reaction, Stan has surmised valuable information concerning the vicinity of your expectation, information you don't want him to know.

It's even worse when you unintentionally send the *wrong* signal. Say, for instance, that Stan comes back with $130,000, which you receive calmly and without immediate comment. (Some people negotiate that way, taking their misguided cue from the legendary poker face at the card table.) Stan, noting that his asking price didn't shock you too much—as it wouldn't, if your expectation was in the $105,000–$110,000 range—is likely to infer that you have more room to travel than you actually do.

How *should* you react in that case? If you consider prices above $115,000 to be unhelpful, then you ought to respond with some fervor (although never with temper) when you get one. "What are you talking about, Stan? How can you possibly justify a hundred and thirty thousand for Good Sport? Don't you have any interest in making a deal? We'll never get together at this rate!" This signals Stan that he shouldn't expect to end up anywhere near his asking price. You've got nothing to lose, because unless he climbs down from the clouds, there won't be a deal anyway.

Now let's say that Stan's counteroffer is $105,000. That's good news, and you're pretty sure you'll be able to make a favorable deal. But you don't want Stan to know that you're *pleased* by his number, or he might put on the brakes and never get down to your $90,000–$95,000 range. Still, you would like him to feel that his restraint is appreciated, in order to encourage more of the same later on.

My preferred means of handling this is to characterize the other side's proposal as "constructive," while at the same time making it clear that further significant movement is expected to be forthcoming. You might say, for example: "I think that's a constructive proposal, although a long way from home. I'd be interested in knowing how you justify that figure; maybe I've missed something." Or where the gap is even smaller, "We may eventually be able to work something out. Why don't we leave price for the moment and move on to some of the other issues."

The middle case is where Stan's asking price is $115,000—neither outrageous nor terrific, but adequate enough to continue the negotiations. You don't want to react with negative fervor, which could damage the negotiations, particularly if Stan thinks he has bent over backward to make a reasonable counteroffer. On the other hand, you correctly shy away from the "constructive" label. The point to get across here is that at this juncture it's uncertain whether a deal will result, given the gap that exists; but you're willing to stick with it a little longer to see if things work out.

So you might say, "Oh, come on, Stan, one hundred fifteen thousand dollars is a lot more than Good Sport is worth. You've got to be more realistic or we'll never be able to do business." Your tone casts no aspersions; your body language is neutral. The message you're transmitting is that you know he's "just negotiating"; and when he's had enough of the fun and games, you're ready to get serious.

THE FIRST CONCESSION AND BIDDING AGAINST YOURSELF

Once Stan counters and you react, the time has come for the next move. And the question is, who should make it? Some negotiating gurus advise you *not* to make the first concession on a major issue such as price. I've heard them invoke, in support of this postulate, research data that suggests the first conceder comes out on the short end of the final settlement.

I don't see it that way. It's helpful to have the other side make the first concession, but let's face it, there's a prevalent tit-for-tat mode to positional negotiations. After receiving the other party's counter, the initial proposer is usually expected to make a new proposal containing some element of concession. And violating this practical etiquette can be serious business.

So assuming you've given yourself enough room, don't be afraid of making the first concession when it's expected. (As for the research data, all it proves is that the first offerer—who is also likely to be the first conceder—generally gives himself *more leeway* in his opening bid than the respondent.) To this advice, however, I offer one caveat and one exception.

First, the caveat. If Stan presents his counteroffer at the same meeting at which you made your initial offer, don't retreat from your price *at that session.* It undermines the force of your initial proposal, particularly if you've gone to some lengths—as you should have—to develop a rationale that supports the amount of your offer. Keep talking, by all means. Find out whatever you can about Stan's needs. Discuss other issues. You may even suggest that you have some price flexibility, as by saying, "I'll go back to the drawing board and see if

I can make the numbers work at higher prices, although certainly not at what you seem to have in mind." But for that day, at least, don't back off your proposal.

The exception to making the first concession occurs in a situation where Stan has gotten greedy in his counteroffer, reaching for, let's say, $130,000. Here it probably makes sense to refuse to increase your bid, by way of emphasizing how out of line Stan is. Your goal is to get Stan to "bid against himself"—that is, to reduce his asking price to a more reasonable level before you'll deign to continue the negotiations. As contrasted with the use of this tactic by the *recipient* of an initial bid (which we discussed previously), it's sometimes easier for the *first* bidder to accomplish this, after the second party has countered—when, says the first bidder with some heat, "Notwithstanding my reasonable proposal, you deliberately chose to ignore it and lob in a ridiculous reply."

Remember, however, no one likes to bid against himself. There's an element of surrender involved, an implicit admission that the bidder's previous offer was overreaching. This doesn't sit well with most folks. As a result, insisting that your counterpart suffer this indignity can introduce real tension into the negotiations.

So I advise limiting this tactic to where it's clearly warranted. If, for instance, Stan counters at $105,000, you shouldn't try it. If you do, Stan will probably refuse to bid against himself. You'll then have to resume the conventional back-and-forth mode of bidding, which at this level you would be crazy *not* to do. And you will have suffered a needless bargaining setback that could adversely affect other aspects of the negotiation. Let me give you a general rule of thumb here: *Don't insist that your counterpart bid against himself, unless the midpoint of the bid-and-asked range created by his last bid is a lot worse than your realistic expectation.*

MANAGING THE CONCESSION PATTERN

Some negotiating pundits advise that any concessions you make be both small and infrequent. I would agree that you should shun the opposite extreme of making them large and frequent, but I find it difficult to be *both* chintzy *and* sporadic, particularly since the goal is to inspire reciprocity.

Take the situation where, after your $75,000 opener, Stan sets his offering price at $115,000. What about now inching your way up to $76,000? This will probably inspire Stan to drop his asking price to $114,000! In my book this kind of bargaining makes no sense, unless you're marooned on a desert island with nothing else to do until a rescue vessel appears. Of course, it's *possible* that you'll reach a deal by this method eventually; but in the real world the likelihood of the negotiations aborting along the way is simply too great. Constant small changes encourage the other side to wait for next week's version. There's no credibility, no finality, to any particular offer. So if it's a choice between multiple moves in small gradations or a few bolder strokes, I invariably opt for the latter. After all, it takes a substantial move to induce real reciprocity.

In the Good Sport negotiation, the concessions should be in multiples of $5,000, at least until the parties get close. It's tough to claim significance for anything smaller. I can't express this in terms of an invariable percentage, but beginning the concession pattern with something much less than a 5 percent change will not be likely to generate meaningful movement on the other side.

Price negotiators tend to think much more in dollar terms than in percentages. But in doing so, *buyers* often penalize themselves while overlooking real bargaining opportunities. Remember, *equivalent dollar concessions always represent a greater percentage shift for the buyer than for the seller.* The reason, of course, is that the buyer is working off a lower base.

Let's take an example. Say that Stan is asking $125,000 and you offer $75,000. Stan now drops $15,000 to $110,000, while you go up $15,000 to $90,000. Have you each made equal concessions? In dollar terms, yes; but in *percentage* terms, not by a long shot. Your increase represents a 20 percent bump over your initial counteroffer, but Stan's decrease constitutes only a 12 percent drop from his original offer. And a percentage differential remains as the bidding continues, although it decreases as the gap between the parties narrows.

How do you as a buyer use this knowledge? When Stan drops down $15,000 to $110,000, you're perfectly justified in saying something like this: "Okay, Stan, I'll match your move. You decreased your price by twelve percent. I'll increase mine by the same twelve percent, or nine thousand dollars, and accordingly bid eighty-four thousand."

Or if you had gone first and increased your bid by $15,000 to $90,000, your reaction to Stan's subsequent $15,000 decrease to $110,000 could be: "Come on, Stan, that's only a twelve percent decrease, compared to my twenty percent increase. To match me, you should come down twenty-five thousand to one hundred thousand dollars"— hoping that this will get Stan to bid against himself.

How about where you're the seller? The short answer is to steer clear of percentages; they won't do you any good, and in most cases the buyer will overlook the point. But if some buyer does give you the "matching percentage" speech, my advice is to shake your head sadly from side to side and say, "Hey, that's all well and good, but if we ever reach a deal, you're going to pay me in *dollars*, not percentages. That's the only currency that fits in my wallet. What's significant is how far we're apart. So let's keep our eye on the ball—for purposes of closing the gap, fifteen thousand dollars is fifteen thousand dollars."

One piece of negotiating lore I do agree with is that the absolute size of your concessions should progressively *decrease*. This stands to reason. Increasing the size just tempts your counterpart to wait for what goodies may be yet to come, while level concessions signal a propensity for more of the same. Remember, the message you want to send is "I'm willing to give *some* ground here, but my tolerance is running out, and I'm getting down to real bedrock." So, depending on Stan's bidding, your path from $75,000 to the $90,000–$95,000 range could be first to $85,000, then to $90,000, and finally to a deal at $92,000.

You may be wondering whether you always have to match the other side's concessions dollar for dollar. The answer is absolutely not. But you should have a good rationale for *not* doing so. Your fallback reason is that your counterpart started too far out, which accounts for why he has farther to come.

To see how this works, switch over to being Stan for a minute. Your realistic expectation is to make a deal at $100,000. Let's say that Beth has begun the bidding at $75,000. You're afraid that setting your offering price too high will cause Beth to lose interest, so you counter at $110,000. Beth increases her bid by $10,000, up to $85,000. Your next move should be to $105,000, which is only a $5,000 decrease. Your rationale is that your initial asking price was quite reasonable, as contrasted with Beth's lowball first offer. So naturally she should have to dig a little deeper on the concessions.

By the way, since Beth is still $15,000 away from your expectation, while you have only another $5,000 to go, you should couple your move here with a strong indication that you're reaching the end of your string. If and when you descend to $100,000, you'll have to label it as your final move. It's prudent to lay the groundwork for that speech now, so that it won't come across as artificial.

Should you ever make a *larger* concession than your counterpart? Generally not; this can send a real signal of weakness and encourage the other side to continue its chintzy behavior. On occasion, however, if the other party is being particularly cheap and you've got bargaining room to spare, such a maneuver can snap your counterpart back to reality. For example, say that after Beth's initial bid of $75,000, you ask $125,000. Beth now inches up to $77,000. You could then make a big show of moving to $115,000, arguing that *this* is the kind of concession *both* sides need to make if a deal is to result. Your hope is to inspire Beth to make her next move into the high eighties.

One footnote to all this: It's unwise to adopt an invariable concession pattern that tells the other side exactly where you're headed. It gives away too much of an advantage. Pretend, rather, that you're leading a wartime convoy, steering a zigzag course to prevent the enemy submarine captain from predicting where you'll be at any moment. Don't telegraph your intentions. Keep your counterpart guessing, and you may not have to go the whole distance to your expectation.

"GET OUT OF THE BUSINESS—AND STAY OUT"

Now I want to explore how the concession pattern works in terms of nonprice issues. Let's change the Good Sport facts slightly and assume that rather than retiring to Florida, Stan—still a vigorous fifty-five—is planning to stay and work in the local area. It's just that he's tired of sporting goods and wants to try his hand at something else.

You're Beth, and this worries you. What if the "something else" doesn't work out and Stan wants to come back into the sporting goods business? He could be serious competition for you, given his customer and supplier contacts. You feel the need for real protection on this score: an agreement on Stan's part that once he has sold the business, he won't compete with Good Sport.

As a threshold matter—analogous to the skeleton-in-the-closet issue we discussed in the last chapter—you have to decide at what point in the negotiations to bring up the noncompete issue. (After all, *Stan* isn't going to raise it!) And you'll want to be alert to his reaction, which is likely to provide a clue to his intentions. In fact, if he treats it as significant, you should really begin to worry about the potential for competition. Remember, *a negotiator always learns something from the choice of issues on which the other side decides to lock horns.*

Some considerations may point the other way, but here I think you should introduce the subject of noncompetition up-front, to emphasize the significance you attach to it. And if Stan offers real resistance, the terms of the noncompete agreement should be negotiated right alongside the price. After all, it represents part of the value of the business you're buying.

Let's assume you raise the subject early, focusing on four elements of the noncompete agreement: the duration, the geographic reach, the business scope, and the hiring away of Good Sport employees. You should begin by assessing your realistic expectation on each element. Here's your initial thinking:

- *Duration.* You would like the agreement to last for at least three years, which is the time you need to get yourself firmly established.
- *Geography.* You want the restriction to extend to the entire metropolitan area surrounding the town where Good Sport is located, which you consider the real zone of potential competition.
- *Scope of Business.* Your desire is to prohibit Stan from competing in any retail enterprise primarily devoted to sporting goods. A business specializing in other products, which sells only a few sporting goods, isn't a problem—although you're not sure just where to draw the line. A special concern of yours is sportswear for active people, which is now a small segment of the existing business, but one you hope to expand.
- *Employees.* You don't want Stan soliciting your employees—at least the present employees who have worked for Stan over the

years. You recognize, however, that it's sometimes hard to decide
what constitutes solicitation and what doesn't.

So now you stake out your opening positions, trying to give yourself
some room for the upcoming negotiations, but without wanting to
appear unreasonable.

- On duration, you ask for five years.
- On geography, you opt for the county in which the town is located, a substantially larger territory than the metropolitan area,
  but not excessive on the surface.
- On the scope of business covered, your opening posture em-
  braces anything to do with sporting goods *and* sportswear.
- And you don't want Stan *hiring* (let alone soliciting) *any* of Good
  Sport's employees, either those employed at the time of the sale
  or later hires ("There are plenty of other good people out there;
  stay away from mine").

You accompany your positions with an appropriate rationale, along
these lines: "Stan, you're asking me to pay a steep price for Good
Sport. The value of this business is, to a large extent, the result of
your personal efforts. If, in the near future, you can move next door
and set up shop in competition with Good Sport—and even recruit
some of its employees—the value of what I'm buying would be substantially diminished." And, by the way, you're entirely correct. Every purchaser of a business is entitled to this kind of protection. The
only question is how much.

Assume that Stan makes a comprehensive counterproposal: one
year; just the town; only stores that sell nothing but sporting goods;
and no solicitation of preexisting employees, but he can hire them if
they leave of their own volition.

THE ANATOMY OF A CONCESSION PATTERN

Now what concession pattern should occur here in order to get the
parties close to final agreement on noncompetition? Should *you* make
the first concessions? If so, what might they be? Or should you

disparage Stan's proposal, trying to get him to bid against himself? What are some of the intermediate stops along the way to your destination? Should each of the four elements be negotiated separately, or are they better off being "packaged"?

A good way to start is by rating each of the elements in terms of their relative importance to you. Then figure out their likely significance to Stan, a subject on which you may have gotten helpful information through questioning him on his post-sale intentions *before* the noncompetition issue ever arose. Next, evaluate the positions Stan has taken in terms of how unreasonable you consider them to be. Finally, determine what intermediate steps exist between your opening positions and your expectations.

Let's see how this might play out on the various points:

Duration. This is important to you, because of your need to get established without interference from Stan. Your three-year expectation is halfway between the opening positions of one and five years. Stan's offer is much too short, but you can't jump right to three ("Let's split the difference") without the risk that you'll end up closer to two.

There's an important factor working for you on this issue, one that comes up often in business negotiations. At this point in the proceedings, when he's trying to encourage you to pay a fair price for the business, a savvy Stan wouldn't want to alarm you with the possibility that he's planning a rapid return to sporting goods. Yet his harping on the one-year duration could give rise to just that suspicion. Thus Stan's hands may be somewhat tied. You should exploit this by disparaging his proposal, questioning his intentions, and trying to get him to bump the period up to two years (that is, to bid against himself) *before* you concede anything.

The pattern could run as follows. You disparage. Stan goes to two years. You say, "That's better, but still much too short"; however, you're "prepared to live with" four years. He goes up to two and a half. You reduce to three and a half, with a speech that suggests you're running out of room. (Admittedly it's hard to say that an odd number like three and a half is *completely* nonnegotiable.) My hunch is you'll get to your three-year expectation.

Alternatively, when you drop to four (with Stan at two), *he* may offer to split the difference at three. If he does, and even though three is your number, you should *not* accept the split, for several reasons.

First, now that you know he's prepared to give three, while you're still at four, you may be able to get three and a half. Second, even if you don't get the three and a half, some further bargaining will make Stan feel that he hasn't given anything away, thus helping to lock in the agreement at three. Finally, if and when you ultimately agree to three years, you may be able to use your final six-month concession to extract something from Stan on a different element of the noncompete agreement.

One footnote on the general subject of negotiating the *duration* of a contractual provision. As contrasted with dollars, which have a certain inherent rationale in terms of their relationship to value, periods of time seldom possess intrinsic logic. Listening to negotiators battle over whether something should last for two or three years sometimes reminds me of a couple of kids in nursery school, beating up on each other over the possession of wooden blocks. That's why, whenever possible, I try to relate the time periods or dates to more meaningful criteria—for example, the date of the next annual meeting of shareholders, or upon completion of the first independent audit after an acquisition.

Geography. Here you have an excellent business argument for your metropolitan area expectation, since the shopping centers outside town present real competition for downtown stores like Good Sport. Since there may be few handholds between your respective positions, you might choose to go right from your countywide opener to your expectation, while stressing that you consider the metropolitan area to be an absolute sine qua non. If your logic is persuasive and your will appears unshakable, Stan will probably concede the point, although you may have to pay a price for it elsewhere.

I prefer, however, to approach this a different way—provided you're able to develop a respectable business reason to support your countywide position. Because the geography element interacts with the scope-of-business issue, you could condition your willingness to retreat (from the "sensible" county line to the "barely tolerable" metropolitan area) on Stan's reciprocal concession that sportswear is within the scope of the protected business. *Always be alert for opportunities to make your concessions do double duty, not only resolving the matter in question, but furnishing trading bait for some other issue.*

Scope of business. Restricting Stan outside the sporting goods line may prove difficult, because he can afford to take a stronger position without scaring you away. In fact, he could argue in good conscience that he may well *want* to go into sportswear, if that's where opportunity beckons. And since the sportswear line at Good Sport has always been ancillary, he shouldn't be barred.

This is one of those issues that often results in an unwieldy compromise, creating difficult interpretative questions down the line. You do have plenty of stopping points along the way, using such concepts as the type of sportswear carried, whether it really competes with what Good Sport has been selling, if it's the primary product of the new business, and so on. Just where you end up here may well be a function of the outcomes you reach on the other issues.

Employees. Good Sport has a fine group of employees, and you would like to keep them together. You have a good equitable case to bar Stan from *soliciting* them to leave. The argument is less compelling, however, when applied to the concept of Stan hiring someone who leaves Good Sport on his own and then seeks a position in Stan's new venture. So you want to steer clear of this distinction.

My suggestion is to use an argument that negotiators typically employ to avoid the merits when their counterpart's position is the more logical one. You simply point to the difficulty of *proving* in the future whether or not Stan induced a particular employee's departure. That's something, you say, you're not anxious to squabble over later on. If you couple this with a willingness to exclude *future* Good Sport employees from the restriction, you can probably resolve this issue.

One feature here that can provide the parties with additional bargaining room is that the prohibition on hiring employees doesn't have to last as long as the basic noncompete provision. You might, in fact, begin your concession pattern by disengaging their respective durations. Assume that you would be satisfied with a two-year restriction on hiring employees—by which time you'll either have their loyalty or not—but you still want at least three-year restrictions on the other points. You could drop down to three years on employees—ignoring, for the moment, the distinction between old and new hires—while temporarily staying at five years for the balance.

This concession may soften Stan up, although he'll probably press for an ever shorter hiring freeze—not too short, however, because once again he doesn't want to signal that he's out to raid his old employees. So he may propose *eighteen months* of not *soliciting old* employees. You could then concede on excluding the *new* employees but at *three years* of no *hiring*. This concession pattern may eventually lead to no *hiring* for the first year, with a second year limited to no *solicitation*. You can see the many possibilities.

When the dust settles, some points may still be open on several sub-issues. In the next chapter we'll examine how to package these for a final settlement.

THE USE AND MISUSE OF DEADLINES

The second worst predicament you can face—ranked just below having your counterpart walk away from the table, never to return—is to come up against someone who negotiates endlessly in hopes of improving his position. Unfortunately, the ability to filibuster offers a real temptation to a negotiator who's not getting his way. One of the few methods to apply some discipline to this bird is through the use of a deadline, either imposed by events or crafted for the occasion.

Remaining rigid or inertial is feasible when there's no time pressure; maintaining the same posture as an important deadline nears is much tougher. We see this frequently in collective bargaining negotiations. As the strike deadline approaches, with serious consequences to both sides, more progress is made suddenly in the final hours than in all the prior sluggish weeks. In commercial negotiations where one party needs the deal signed by year end, it's easier to pry concessions out of that party during the week after Christmas than the week before.

Now, of course, there are deadlines and there are deadlines. An agreement between the parties to finish the negotiations by a certain arbitrary time carries little weight, since each party knows it can be extended. On the other hand, a final date imposed by outside events—one that both sides acknowledge as significant and that has sanctions behind it—can prove a strong impetus to reaching agreement.

The deadline I have in mind, however, is the kind that affects one party more than the other, setting up *leverage* based on *time* (as discussed in chapter 2). The justifiable premise here is that the party who's worried about the consequences (should agreement not be reached by a certain date) will be tempted to concede more as the deadline nears.

In my experience the most unforgettable examples of this occurred in the takeover wars, centered around the deadline imposed by the raider's unilateral tender offer. I remember when Triangle Industries made such an offer for the shares of my client, National Can. Twenty business days later Triangle was entitled to buy all shares tendered to it, which would have given Triangle control of National Can. When my client, having failed to find a "white knight," finally approached Triangle a few days before the deadline to try to negotiate the best deal possible, it wasn't possible to negotiate the best deal! Lacking leverage, we had to settle for the skimpy price increase that was all Triangle was willing to pay for a negotiated agreement.

If the *other side* is facing the deadline, you can use this to your advantage, provided you know of its existence. Never assume that there aren't real time pressures at work on your counterpart just because he appears unruffled. You can't expect the other side to be forthcoming on this score, and accurate information may not be available.

Sometimes your best clue comes when the other side increases the pressure to move things along. Provided the deal isn't otherwise in jeopardy—as it would be if you were only one of several viable buyers for a desirable property—you can test this out by slowing things down yourself, in order to see whether the pressure increases. You might never discover just what is causing the urgency, but its existence may nevertheless work in your favor.

How about time pressure on *you?* You might have a personal deadline, unknown to the other side and unrelated to the deal you're negotiating, which makes it crucial for you to know by a certain date whether you have an agreement. If your counterpart knows about this, he might be tempted to stall until near the deadline, holding out for concessions you would yield in order to get the deal done on time. So you don't want him to find out about it. But your conduct, as the deadline nears, might be a giveaway: pushing things along, conceding points you had formerly prized, and so forth. Don't let this happen. Plan ahead. Keep the negotiations moving at a good pace earlier, so that your behavior appears to be unaffected as the deadline nears.

I find that many self-imposed deadlines appear more rigid than they actually are. When you feel time pressure is affecting your conduct, stop and assess how important the deadline is. Force yourself to think about the unthinkable: What will happen if you don't make the deadline? The probable consequences may not seem so onerous and might be outweighed by the desirability of recovering your freedom of action.

How about a deadline that one side tries to use affirmatively against the other in the bargaining? Sometimes this takes the form of a threat (which we'll be discussing in chapter 13): "This offer is good only for twenty-four hours." Other deadlines are more in the nature of a warning: "On May 15, we're instituting a general price revision, which will affect the terms of our deal if it hasn't been signed prior to that date." Still others represent a simple recital of fact: "If we don't agree by March 15, I won't be in a position to make delivery of the item by March 31, which you've told me is the date you need to have it in hand." Or "This deal has to be approved by our board of directors, which is meeting on October 15. If we haven't signed by then, the next board meeting isn't until January 14."

If you're setting the deadline, make it seem that you have a good reason for doing so, that you're not just being arbitrary. The reason will not only make the deadline more credible but will also lessen the appearance of intimidation.

If the other side tries to impose such a deadline on you, your first task is to determine whether the date is real or just a ruse. One way to do this is through confrontation. If the deadline is unreasonable, you can label it as unrealistic and refuse to conform. Even if the deadline is realistic, it may not be *necessary*, prompting you to respond that you don't feel bound to comply. Your counterpart's reaction to your response will help you decide whether the date is real or simply intended to manipulate. Another way of handling a deadline is for you to acknowledge its existence but tell the other side not to expect that its brooding presence will cause you to change your position. This takes the sting out of your counterpart's maneuver and may dampen any illusions he might have held about its efficacy.

Still another possibility is to counter the ploy with a deadline of your own. "I'm in complete accord; we *both* have to know where we stand by the twentieth, because, in *my* case . . ." And then you proceed to explain your own reason for needing to know by that time. Better still, name an even earlier date! If the leverage in the deal is otherwise even, this should keep the other side's purported deadline from unbalancing it.

CONCESSIONS WRAP-UP

Keynote

The third step in my game plan approach to smart negotiating is to devise—and follow—a constructive concession pattern. It takes movement to generate movement. Use the room provided by your opening offer as bait to lure your counterpart to negotiate in a constructive direction. You must manage this concession process wisely in order to bring the parties close enough to spring the final compromise.

Blunder

Overly tough bargaining is the culprit here, making concessions that are either too few in number or too small in size. You have to give in order to get.

Lapse

The problem here is in sending the wrong implicit signal—however inadvertently—by the way you react (or *fail* to react) to your counterpart's newly stated position. Be prepared—let him know what you think on the spot.

10 ARRANGING THE ULTIMATE COMPROMISE

Now we're down to what chess players call "the endgame." After determining your realistic expectations and staking out initial positions, you've engaged in some constructive bargaining, making and receiving concessions, keeping alert for valuable information, periodically assessing the relative leverage, exuding credibility, and perhaps even reappraising your original expectations. Still, there's a gap between you and your counterpart on price or some other weighty issue. And the movement that characterized the earlier bargaining has lately slowed to an occasional twitch as both sides dig in.

At this point, to oversimplify, there are four possible outcomes to the negotiations:

1. The two of you will fail to reach agreement and go home.
2. You will agree to your counterpart's position and strike a deal on those terms.
3. Your counterpart will acquiesce to your position as the basis for agreement.
4. The two of you will settle on a compromise at a point somewhere between your two positions.

The good news for you is that in three out of four possible outcomes, a deal gets made. The bad news is that except in number three, it may not be the best deal that you could have negotiated.

WARM BODIES: A PIECE OF THE ACTION

Sally wants to sell her successful employment agency business ("Warm Bodies") in order to pursue her hobby of portrait painting on a full-time basis. She believes Warm Bodies is worth between $500,000 and $1 million, but she has no idea whom to sell it to. A mutual acquaintance introduces her to Felix, who works as a finder, locating buyers for businesses. Sally and Felix begin negotiations over the terms on which he would undertake the assignment to find a buyer for Warm Bodies. The principal issue to be negotiated is Felix's fee, which is ordinarily contingent on an actual sale of the business and based on a percentage of the purchase price received.

FACING UP TO "NO DEAL"

We'll begin by addressing the first of the four possibilities—no deal. Assume that Felix holds out for a fee based on a straight 5 percent commission, which he considers his standard charge for a company of this size. Sally, who has located other finders willing to work on a 3 percent basis, is unwilling to pay Felix any more than that, even though she thinks he would do a first-rate job. Felix won't go to Sally's 3 percent, Sally won't go to Felix's 5 percent, and neither of them is willing to compromise.

Sometimes failing to reach a deal is the correct result under the circumstances. Here, Sally refuses to pay Felix what he thinks his services are worth, since cheaper competitors are available who can do the job. Felix, who believes he can fill his book with other assignments at his regular rate, is unwilling to compromise on the fee.

This is basic to negotiating: the realization that no matter how skillfully you manage the process or how creative you are at devising compromises, you may not get all the way home. Not every deal is made in heaven. When the issues dividing the parties are significant—such as price or, in this case, payment for services to be rendered—and their respective expectations aren't even close to overlapping, then it's time to move on. Don't waste further energy on the project.

In other cases, however, the parties may fail to reach agreement on a deal that *should* have been made. Perhaps one party is bluffing; when his bluff is called, he refuses to back down, fearing the loss of face. Felix, who could be bluffing on his fee, may have become so committed to the 5 percent figure that he can't lower his sights, even when he realizes it's not in the cards.

Another possibility is that there's an intermediate position agreeable to each side, but neither is willing to take the first step in that direction. Here a 4 percent compromise seems obvious, but Felix and Sally are each waiting for the other to move. And sometimes, where the intermediate formula that could serve as a compromise is less visible, neither party is able to see it.

I'm willing to accept a busted deal when there's no basis on which the parties can get together. It bothers me, however, when the basis does exist but the parties don't get there. And it's no solace to blame everything on the other guy. The real question is, could *you* have done something differently to produce a meeting of the minds?

SHOULD YOU COMPROMISE OR HOLD FIRM?

Assume you're negotiating one of those deals that should be made. But the question is *where*: at the whittled-down position you're now espousing, at your counterpart's present level, or at a compromise formula somewhere in between?

Let's approach the issue analytically. Your first assessment should relate to *yourself*. Are you firm at your position, or willing to compromise, or even willing, if necessary, to go all the way to the other side's position? The second assessment for you to make concerns *your counterpart*. After processing the information available, the relative leverage, and your counterpart's credibility, do you think that the other side is willing to compromise or even to come all the way to your position?

The real problem here is that you seldom can be sure about your counterpart's bottom line. If you were certain that he was amenable to a compromise, you would never go all the way to his position, even if you were willing to. If you knew he was prepared to come all the way to your position, you would only compromise if it otherwise suited your purposes in the negotiation or if you wanted his goodwill. But you *don't* know. All you can do is make an educated guess.

Let's try this out on Warm Bodies. Put yourself in Felix's place. Although your 5 percent regular fee is clearly preferable, you're willing to take on the assignment for 4 percent; and you believe that Sally, who is still at 3 percent, would sign up on that basis. If you hold firm at 5 percent, but she's unwilling to go that far, the deal may well be lost. You certainly can't count on Sally to suggest the 4 percent compromise, particularly if you've stated your 5 percent position so strongly that she thinks *you* are unlikely to agree to a compromise. And there's always the risk that one day soon you'll receive a phone call from Sally, informing you that she has signed up with one of your cut-rate competitors.

This same problem might exist, by the way, even if Sally was willing to go all the way to your 5 percent but believed that by holding firm, *you* would eventually suggest a compromise. Both of you are then standing around, each waiting for the other to capitulate or offer a compromise. Needless to say, the deal is in real jeopardy.

THE RIGHT PLACE FOR A BLUFF

Alternatively, assume that you're willing to take on the job for as little as 3 percent; you really need the work. You're convinced that Sally won't go all the way up to 5 percent; she'll either stay at 3 percent or, at best, compromise at 4 percent. After trying unsuccessfully to get Sally to move, you're then forced to propose a compromise yourself. But you have to do it in a way that indicates you're *not* willing (even though you are) to undertake the assignment for the same 3 percent the other finders charge. Even if Sally is willing to compromise, she won't accept the 4 percent if she thinks you're likely to accede eventually to her 3 percent position.

Remember back in chapter 4 when I counseled against bluffing but noted there was one exception to my advice? Well, this is the exception. It comes up when you're the one who's proposing a compromise to resolve an issue once and for all, but there exists another possible resolution of the issue, *less* favorable to you, that the other side may suspect you would be willing to accept. And in fact, the other side is right: if pressed, you would cave in and make the stretch. When that's the case, and you really want *your* compromise to be the end of it, you must try to eliminate the stretch possibility from your counterpart's mind. And this requires you to bluff.

The way to handle such a situation is to deal explicitly with the stretch possibility, get it right out there on the table. Try to develop some persuasive rationale as to why you would *not* be willing to accept it. The fact that you're simultaneously making a move to compromise the issue—look, you're *trying*, after all—should provide a more receptive audience for your pitch.

So, for instance, you might accompany your 4 percent compromise proposal with a little speech along these lines: "Look, Sally, if the size of the fee percentage is the only thing that's important to you, then I suggest you hire one of those guys who's willing to try his luck at finding you a buyer for three percent. I can't match that kind of cut-rate fee. My practice is to take on only a limited number of clients, and I have a much higher cost of doing business than those other guys do. But in my opinion, you would then be taking a very narrow view of the situation. The real question should be, who's going to do the *best job* for you? If I can find you someone who pays one hundred thousand dollars more for Warm Bodies than any buyer produced by one of these other finders, ninety-six thousand of that still goes straight into your pocket."

The bluff is not without risk, however, and I don't recommend it unequivocally. After all, Sally could decide that the size of the fee percentage *is* the most important thing in her mind and thus end up with one of the 3 percent finders. In that case you will have lost out on business that you could have had. So if the difference between your resolution and the stretch alternative isn't really so important to you—or if you're faint of heart—you might not want to attempt the bluff. But, otherwise, I feel that under the particular set of circumstances I've outlined, the odds of the bluff working are good enough to justify the residual risk.

PUTTING IN A GOOD WORD FOR COMPROMISES

Now let's switch from the analytical framework to the *practical* side of compromise. Most deals don't get done unless you can find accommodative solutions to divisive issues. Ambrose Bierce defines "compromise" cynically in the *Devil's Dictionary*: "Such an adjustment of conflicting interests as gives each adversary the satisfaction of thinking he has got what he ought not to have, and is deprived of nothing except what was justly his due." I prefer to think of compromise as the search for a favorable common ground.

It's unfortunate that the word used to describe this process also appears in the phrase "He compromised his principles." In the sphere of negotiating, this negative connotation is quite undeserved. In my book a compromise—however messy or inelegant—that satisfies both parties sufficiently to do the deal is one hell of an accomplishment.

To pull it off, your attitude has to be that you and your counterpart are in this thing together. In the kind of voluntary two-party transactions we've been considering, you don't have the luxury of dismissing an obstacle by saying "That's *his* problem." In most cases your counterpart doesn't have to do the deal. If, for example, his tax problems appear insurmountable—every twist and turn in the negotiation results in a whopping tax bill that he refuses to pay—then he may just walk away from the table. Thus *his tax* problem is *your deal* problem. Unless you can figure out a way to make the transaction palatable to him, kiss it good-bye.

Each compromise has two key aspects. The *first* is finding the precise number or formulation that does the trick: not giving away more than you have to, while satisfying the other side's often rapacious appetite. The *second*, frequently neglected, is how and when to introduce the compromise so that it's viewed as a solution to the problem, not just another of your positions that becomes subject to further negotiating. There's a window of time you have to aim for that's neither premature nor too late to keep the deal from aborting. Let's start with this second aspect.

GIVE THE PROCESS TIME TO WORK

The best way to appreciate prematurity is to examine a fully ripened compromise negotiation and then work backward. Let's return to the Warm Bodies saga and see how a deal might develop.

Felix starts out asking for a 5 percent fee. This means that on a $500,000 sale price for the business—the bottom of Sally's anticipated range—Felix will make $25,000. This amount, he tells her, is the minimum he's willing to consider for the assignment. Sally, for her part, opens by offering him 2.5 percent. At that rate Felix would have to find a buyer willing to pay $1,000,000 for Warm Bodies in order to receive his $25,000—not impossible, perhaps, but highly unlikely. Felix then comes down to 4 percent. His premise is that he's likely to come up with a buyer willing to pay at least $600,000, which would result in a commission close to his target figure.

Sally has something else in mind. Her offer introduces the concept of a differential fee: 3 percent on the first $750,000 of proceeds and 4 percent on all amounts received over $750,000. Her notion is to give Felix an incentive to find her a high price. Felix replies that he's willing to consider a differential basis but thinks it ought to be 4 percent on the first $600,000, 3 percent on anything over that up to $800,000, and 2 percent on sums over $800,000. Sally protests; that runs the *wrong* way, she says, "rewarding pedestrian performance." And the chase is on.

I won't go through the various twists and turns, but assume that the parties craft a compromise that builds on the twin pillars of Felix's desired minimum and Sally's differential percentages. Sally will guarantee Felix a minimum fee of $25,000 on a completed deal, which covers her for all purchase prices up to $800,000. That means the effective percentage ranges from 5 percent at the $500,000 level to around 3 percent at $800,000. Above $800,000 he gets 3 percent of each dollar as an incentive to strive for a higher price.

This is an imaginative solution, but one that had to evolve out of the bargaining. It just wouldn't have worked if either party had proposed it at the outset. The gap between Felix's 5 percent and Sally's 2.5 percent had to begin to close. The differential percentage concept had to be introduced. The parties had to present their conflicting views of the direction the percentages should take. Sally had to grasp that Felix's major interest lay in being assured of receiving his minimum number if he produced a buyer. And she had to be satisfied that he would be sufficiently motivated to get the highest price for her business.

In other words, it was essential to give the process *time to work.* Time—and what evolves in its wake—has a singular way of clarifying the real objectives of both parties in a negotiation, allowing them to craft compromises that address those aims with some degree of precision.

SPLITTING THE DIFFERENCE

A prime example of prematurity is the haste with which some impatient bargainers rush to "split the difference." If Felix starts out by asking for 5 percent and Sally counters at 1 percent, then even if Felix were willing to perform at 3 percent, he would be foolish to say "Let's split the difference." It puts him, in effect, at 3 percent, while Sally is still at 1 percent; and the deal (*if* one is made) will probably end up somewhere near 2 percent.

Splitting the difference also involves problems other than prematurity. Take the more typical situation in which Sally has moved up from her initial 2.5 percent position to 3.8 percent and Felix has come down from 5 percent to 4.2 percent. The movement has become increasingly painful, however; and now there's a hardening of the bargaining arteries, with each party characterizing the last position taken as "final." To make it more vivid, we'll assume that Sally wants to engage Felix, he would like to have the assignment, and all other issues have been resolved.

Now we can all see that the deal is virtually begging to be done at the rational compromise level of 4 percent—in other words, simply by splitting the difference. In the privacy of their offices, both Felix and Sally realize this, and each is willing to make a final move to that compromise—but not an inch farther! Pride and emotion have taken over the field. Felix is absolutely unwilling to go down to 3.9 percent, while Sally wouldn't be caught dead at 4.1 percent. (Believe me, this *happens*!) So how do they go about making the deal at 4 percent?

The tactical decision here usually involves *who* is going to suggest splitting it down the middle. If you wait for the other side to move, it might never happen. If you do it yourself, you run a risk. Say that Felix suggests splitting the difference at 4 percent. If Sally doesn't accept, then regardless of the caveats he attaches to the proposal, the 4 percent becomes, de facto, Felix's new position. Sally now knows Felix is prepared to go to that level. Meanwhile she's still at 3.8 percent and could use these elements as the basis to press for a compromise at 3.9 percent, a deal Felix won't accept.

This wouldn't happen if the compromise could be suggested by a neutral observer; then neither side would have changed position before acceptance. Unfortunately, however, someone fitting that description is seldom available. Lawyers and other agents can be helpful—"I could try to sell my client on the four percent if you would work on yours"—but the other side usually infers from the agent's identification with his principal that the proposal has been precleared, so the damage may still occur.

At this late stage of the negotiations, it's clear that splitting the difference can constitute a first-rate solution to this kind of problem, one that leaves both sides feeling relatively upbeat about the outcome. But it has to be handled right to avoid the negative baggage. So here are my suggestions with regard to splitting:

- Don't split with someone who has created a favorable "middle" for himself by starting the bargaining at an extreme position.
- Don't jump prematurely to the middle. Splitting works best on small gaps that have required hard work to narrow.
- Try to keep your counterpart from hardening his position to the point where he says "This far and no farther."
- Be patient. If *you* made the last concession, give your counterpart a chance to accept those terms, or at least to introduce the split, before suggesting it yourself.
- If *your counterpart* proposes splitting, don't go for it right away, even though you're favorably disposed. Make this final movement seem like a real wrench, a violation of your basic principles. It will help cement the deal.
- If your counterpart makes no move, leaving you the task of breaking the logjam, make sure all other issues of significance are resolved so that the split you propose can make the deal *happen*.
- Introduce the subject with this kind of caveat: [Felix to Sally] "Look, my position is still that 4.2 percent is the right place to do the deal, and what I'm about to say shouldn't be deemed to change that at all. . . ."
- Never say "Let's split the difference," which amounts to an offer that's capable of being rejected. Rather, pose the question: "Would *you* be willing to split the difference?" If your counterpart says "Yes," then shake on it immediately. If he says "No," then reply, "Neither would I." (If your counterpart poses the same question initially to you, your best reply is "I don't know. Would you?")
- Alternatively, you might try something like this: [Felix to Sally] "A lot of people in our position would resolve this impasse by splitting the difference. Now that's not usually my style, and I happen to think 4.2 percent is the right number for this deal, but I'd be interested in your views on the subject."

One other thing: the assumption throughout has been that the split offered is exactly 50 percent of the way between the parties' respective positions. But it doesn't have to be, particularly if there's a handy reference point closer to your position than to your counterpart's. For example, if Felix was at 4.1 percent and Sally at 3.8 percent, Felix might offer—"in the interest of getting this impasse behind us and moving on"—to split his fee at a nice round 4 percent. Since Felix broke the ice, Sally might just go for it. Of course, if you were Sally, you would counter by agreeing that a split makes sense, but you think that 3.9 percent is the appropriate place. Then when the dust clears after this dialogue, you'll probably have a deal in the vicinity of a true 3.95 percent split.

I once wrote an article suggesting—only semifacetiously—that this type of impasse over purchase price might be resolved by a roll of the dice. The theory was that each of the possible rolls (the numbers two through twelve) would be assigned an increment of the price between the parties' last positions. The more likely rolls (five through nine) were matched with the more intermediate (and thus more acceptable) compromise prices. But even this solution wasn't without its own problems. Who would propose it? What signal would *that* send to the other side? Should it be portrayed as bolt from the blue or made to appear more of a routine occurrence? How might the recipient of the proposal respond? So as you can see, there's more to splitting—even on a green felt table—than meets the eye.

REDUCING PRINCIPLES TO DOLLARS

When both parties strive jointly to accomplish a deal they want to see happen, most issues, even ones that appear deadlocked, are ultimately soluble. The trick is to cut through the rhetoric of sacred principles—your own as well as your counterpart's—and boil down the issues to dollars (or their practical equivalent), which can then be moved around. If the dollars don't quite do it, a face-saving device may be needed to provide hard-nosed or insecure bargainers the ability to back off without embarrassment.

Let me illustrate this with a variant of the Warm Bodies negotiation. Put yourself now in Sally's shoes. Assume that right from the beginning Felix's position has been that he should receive a minimum fixed fee of $10,000 for undertaking the assignment. This would be payable up-front and under all circumstances, no matter what purchase price is ultimately paid and even if he's unsuccessful in finding a buyer. In addition, he has asked for a contingent fee of 5 percent for every dollar of purchase price received over $200,000.

Your reaction to this is decidedly cool. Not only do you consider the percentage level inflated, but you're irked at the prospect of having to pay money to Felix before he accomplishes anything—and worse, *even* if he should ultimately fail. And you tell him so: "I'll compensate you well if you come up with a good buyer, and perhaps at an even better rate if we achieve a higher price. But I'll be damned if I'll pay for your failure."

Felix, not chastened in the least, retorts: "Look, Sally, I don't intend to fail. I'll produce a number of potential purchasers for Warm Bodies. But I can't force them to buy if they don't like what they see. I'm not a charitable institution. This will require a good deal of work on my part, and I want to make sure I'm compensated for it. I can, however, be more flexible on the contingent portion, either in terms of the percentage we use or the base level for the computation."

Now here's a negotiation that seems to be going nowhere, as you and Felix duel over the concept of whether the fee should be entirely contingent on the sale price or have a fixed component independent of a sale. And as long as those principles govern the dialogue, it may not get off the ground. So how might you attack the problem to resolve this impasse?

I'll tell you what I would do first: reduce the principles to *dollars*. What we're talking about here (in addition to any contingent percentage) is a possible outlay by you of $10,000 in a situation where you haven't achieved your objective. How likely is that to occur? Not likely, you say. You believe the business is quite salable; it's just the price that's in question. Given some assurance that Felix will do his job, you figure there's less than a 25 percent risk of no sale. Applying this percentage to the $10,000 possible outlay, your *practical* downside risk can be viewed as $2,500.

Now what can you *get* for taking that risk? One possibility is a commensurate reduction in the fee payable to Felix if a sale *does* occur. But first you have to lay the groundwork, so that your compromise isn't introduced prematurely. Here's a tack you might take: "Felix, let's set aside the issue of the fixed payment for the moment and discuss the *total* amount of your fee—fixed, contingent, what-ever—if you *do* produce a buyer. What you've proposed is way too high."

Now you proceed to negotiate Felix's fee for a successful sale down to a level you could live with if the fee was entirely contingent (which we'll call the "contingent formula," to contrast it with Felix's partly fixed "composite formula"). At this point you're ready to spring your compromise.

"Okay, Felix," you might say, "here's my proposal to you. I esti-mate the practical risk to me of having a fixed component in your composite formula at twenty-five hundred dollars," explaining to him how you arrived at that number. "I'd be willing to retain you on either of two bases, which you can elect between. The first is the contingent formula without any fixed component. The second is a different composite formula that saves me at least three thousand dollars from what I would have to pay under the contingent formula if a deal gets done. And here's one possible way in which that could be accomplished. . . ."

Of course, you have to make sure that under the composite for-mula, Felix is still sufficiently motivated to do his job. So, for in-stance, he might be required to produce a certain number of potential buyers for the property in order to earn his fixed fee. And there should be meaningful financial rewards to him for obtaining a high price, rewards that you would be happy to pay for the right deal.

If that compromise doesn't feel right to you, particularly if Felix were to elect the composite formula, perhaps it's because you need a face-saver. After all, you took a firm position against handing over any money to Felix *before* he proved what he could do.

Here's something that performs this function as well as serving as a further stimulus for Felix. He won't actually receive the fixed sum until either the deal is done or a fixed period (eighteen months, for example) elapses without a sale. That way you won't feel you're out of pocket; and Felix, who has to wait for his money, will be motivated to speed things up through a sale. As a final clincher you may have to add a small amount to the fixed fee in lieu of the interest Felix would have received on the funds or, alternatively, discount to present value the amount by which the contingent formula is reduced. My bet, however, is that you won't have to throw these into the pot, since Felix has no compelling argument for being paid in advance.

CREATIVITY I—DIVIDING UP ISSUES

The path to the ultimate compromise is not always clearly marked, and some creative ability may be required to discover the common ground. *The most important weapon in your compromise arsenal is the ability to divide up a seemingly indivisible issue, so that you satisfy your counterpart's* real *concerns* (which are generally narrower than those he has expressed) *while at the same time protecting your own* essential *interests* (which are usually more limited than those you've previously advanced).

Let's assume that Felix and Sally have agreed upon a straight 4 percent contingent fee. Felix's standard written contract stipulates that Sally is hiring him as her exclusive agent to sell Warm Bodies for an eighteen-month period. If the company is sold during that time, he gets his commission, whether or not his efforts actually produced the sale. The contract then goes on to state that although Sally can terminate the agency at any time, Felix would be entitled to his full fee if the business is sold within the two-year period after termination to anyone he originally introduced to her.

Sally bristles at this last point. "If our deal ends," she says to Felix, "it will be because I'm dissatisfied with your performance. Why should I have to pay you after that happens?"

Felix replies, "But you'll only have to pay me if my efforts, however unappreciated at the time, ultimately result in a sale."

"Well," says Sally, "maybe you would be entitled to *something*, but certainly not your full fee." And the dialogue goes back and forth, with no resolution.

Felix has a problem here that comes up often in negotiations: the inability to express his *real* concern. At a time when he's trying to persuade Sally to hire him, he can't very well convey his genuine fear that she will attempt to shaft him by temporarily "putting on ice" a hot deal that Felix has introduced, then terminating his services, and thereafter "de-icing" and clinching the deal. Her compromise suggestion to pay him at a lesser rate for a deal completed after termination doesn't completely solve his problem, because she would still have an incentive (albeit reduced in size) to do just that.

Now, in fact, Sally has no intention of trying anything underhanded; that's not her style. It's just that Felix's insistence on payment in full aggravates *her* real concern. She's worried that she'll have to hire someone else to complete the task after firing Felix for a job badly done, at which point she could be stuck with *two* full fees. She would find this particularly grating as time passes and Felix's role in the deal becomes more and more attenuated. He may have done the original finding but none of the essential wooing.

Felix also has a different concern, one that's typical for somebody engaged in business or likely to do other similar deals in the future. It's the *precedent value* of what he agrees to here. Subsequent clients who know the details of the Warm Bodies arrangement will want terms at least as favorable as Sally received. This creates a multiplier effect, which makes Felix less amenable to compromise with Sally than he might be if just this deal was at stake.

At least, this is what he contends. It's an argument that you hear (or may use!) frequently as a justification for inflexibility. But although the other side can't ignore it completely, it's by no means conclusive—especially if, as is often the case, the underlying facts are unlikely to become public knowledge. My frequent retort to someone offering this kind of rationale is, "We're negotiating *this* deal, not the one next month. If you want to make this deal, here's what it will take."

At any rate, to solve this particular problem, you have to grasp that the issue of post-termination compensation can be *divided into parts* in order to satisfy both parties. For instance, the formula could run along these lines: For some period after termination (Felix will argue for six months, Sally for two, and they'll settle at four), Felix will still get a full 4 percent fee for a deal with someone he introduced. After that his fee will be reduced to 2 percent for the next four months, 1 percent for the following four months, and nothing after that. This first four-month period at full rates is a practical solution to Felix's fear of being screwed—it's unlikely that Sally could keep a warm deal on ice for that long—while the decreasing scale thereafter satisfies Sally's desire to reduce his compensation for more attenuated services.

CREATIVITY II—EXPANDING THE PIE

Sometimes you can get very close to making a deal, but a gap remains that defies resolution. This is the time for some special creativity. For example, never underestimate the power of tax advantages. You may be able to structure a compromise so that Uncle Sam bears part of the burden, allowing the party with the tax break to stretch farther and satisfy the other side. If you're unskilled at tax planning, bring in an expert to help out.

Where the parties will have continuing commercial relations, you might include goods and services as part of the negotiated package, keeping in mind that their value to the recipient is always higher than their cost to the furnisher. The markup, in effect, enables the parties to bridge a troublesome gap.

The most elegant solutions to a negotiating impasse are those that expand the pie, adding some new element to the picture that permits one party, who now has more to gain, to surrender more than he was willing to consider previously. Let's go back to the Warm Bodies negotiation to illustrate the point. Assume now that an impasse has developed in the bargaining over the fee for a completed deal. Sally thinks Felix's price is too much to pay, even for success. Felix, who has come down considerably from his initial proposal, considers his present position as the absolute minimum to which he's entitled. Other formulations, such as different percentages for different purchase prices, haven't done the trick. How can the parties strike a deal?

One possible approach would be to provide Felix with the potential for making additional money from his relationship with Sally. He might then be willing to act as a finder for less. Conversely, if there were a source of funds flowing Sally's way, or if she received something else of value, she could then afford to "overpay" Felix on the finding assignment.

So, for instance, if Felix was also in business as an investment adviser, he might offer to invest and manage any proceeds Sally receives from the sale of Warm Bodies at a reduced rate from what he charges others for similar services. Or let's say that Sally needs to supply prospective buyers with an audit of the business by an independent accounting firm. The firm she has been using, however, is disqualified because of its day-to-day involvement with the company's books. Felix offers to introduce her to a firm that would provide competent audit services at a discounted price. This could be of real value to Sally, value that would help her pay Felix's asking price as a finder.

On the other side of the ledger, if Sally knows other owners of businesses who are interested in selling, she could offer to refer them to Felix. If one of these were to result in a relationship, then Felix would give Sally a credit for the referral against the full fee she ends up paying in this deal. Believe me, little touches like these can get you over that final hump.

COMPROMISING AMONG ISSUES

Up until now we've been concentrating on the compromise of individual issues. Commonly, however, such point-by-point bargaining will leave unresolved several issues of significance. We turn now to the task of swapping among them. Assume, for instance, that Sally and Felix have resolved all issues except the following four:

1. The *fee*. They've agreed on a straight 4 percent fee for a successful sale. They're also in agreement that if *no* deal occurs, Felix will receive $5,000 to cover his expenses. Where they differ is whether, if there *is* a deal, the $5,000 would be credited against the 4 percent fee (Sally's position) or would be paid in addition to it (Felix's position).

2. The *note*. It's possible that part of the purchase price for Warm Bodies will be paid by a note instead of in cash and that the note won't be worth its full face amount. The question is, should the note be discounted to fair market value for the purpose of determining the *real* "purchase price" against which Felix's 4 percent fee is applied? Sally says yes. Felix, arguing that it's too tough to measure the discount, holds out for valuing the note at face value.

3. The *term*. Felix wants his exclusive right to sell Warm Bodies to last for fifteen months (down from eighteen), while Sally is sticking at nine (up from six).

4. The *exclusive*. Is Felix entitled to his fee if, during his exclusive period, Sally sells Warm Bodies to a buyer she finds *herself*? Felix says "absolutely"—that's what an exclusive is all about. Sally has been resisting this but is now willing to pay him half a commission if it's her personal deal.

Now let's examine the dynamics of resolving these issues collectively, rather than one by one.

Sometimes, in trading among issues, the swap is logical. Whenever a promissory note is involved in a deal, for example, such features as its term and interest rate, as well as the collateral securing it, can be traded against each other and against the face value of the note. Each feature, in effect, represents a different index of value. Likewise, two unrelated issues, both of which are measurable in dollar terms, can readily be wrapped together: green is green.

Relationships among issues aren't limited to money. Felix might have gone along with a shorter period on the term issue if he had gotten the $10,000 minimum commission he originally tried for. Now, no matter how the $5,000 expense provision comes out, he needs a *longer* time to earn his success fee. In a similar vein, if Sally concedes on the exclusive issue, then she'll want the term of the agreement to be *shorter*.

It's tougher to swap as the issues become less related and don't translate into money. Some people might consider it cynical to offer to swap the resolutions of two unrelated nondollar issues. But it's only cynical if you assume there must be some *logical* relation in order for a trade to make sense. I don't assume that. Facilitating the deal is sufficient logic in and of itself.

Imagine that Felix says, "Look, Sally, in an effort to move things forward, you give me the fifteen months on the term issue and I'll give you the discounted value on the note issue." Now these two points have almost nothing to do with each other. On the other hand, their resolution doesn't cause either party to violate any deeply held principles; these aren't issues on which you can generate much heat. (The emotional high point so far occurred when Sally said, "If you like those notes so much, Felix, why don't you take a piece of them at face value in part payment of your fee?")

The signals Felix is sending with this offer are that the term issue is at least as important to him as the note issue—more so, presumably—and that he's willing to "lose" on the note. So this may tempt Sally to retort, in effect, "I'll take the note resolution you offered, which is the *less* valuable of the two, but let's *compromise* on the term at a year." Felix can refuse, of course, but he might have been better off not showing his true colors.

If Felix were completely indifferent between the note and term issues, he could say, "You take one, I'll take the other, and *you* can make the pick"—like someone cutting two equal slices of a cake and letting his companion choose the first portion. This is designed to show Sally that Felix values them about equally (unless she concludes that he values one more than the other but thinks *she* will jump in the wrong direction). It minimizes her ability to take what's offered on one and propose a compromise on the other.

THE PACKAGE DEAL

What if Felix were to say something like this: "In an effort to get the deal done, let me propose a resolution for each of the issues:

- On the note, your position is fair, and I accept it.
- On the term, let's split it at one year.
- On the fee, I should be entitled to the $5,000 for expenses in any event; but I'm willing to credit it if my total fee is $25,000 or above.
- On the exclusive, I consider this basic and won't agree to any exception during the exclusive period, even if you find a buyer yourself."

Now, obviously Felix would like this to become the solution for *all four* points. What he would *not* appreciate is for Sally to say "Fine" on his note concession but "No good" on one or more of the other issues. In order to prevent that, Felix should introduce his solution by labeling it a "package deal." The basis for his concession on the note is its link to his hard line on the exclusive and his proposed compromises on the term and the fee. He should tell Sally explicitly that she can't pick and choose her issues; either she accepts Felix's global solution or they go back to ground zero.

Now that kind of packaging isn't guaranteed to preclude Sally from reacting selectively. It does, however, allow Felix to reintroduce the note issue if, say, Sally was to insist on some exception to the exclusive. To be sure, she now knows that Felix is willing to concede on the note; it's not a deal breaker for him. But there's a *price* to be paid for giving it up. And the price is that the other issues be resolved in the way Felix has proposed.

Felix might emphasize this point, as well as heighten the sense of having offered a real concession, by placing a time limit on his package proposal. If it's not accepted by a certain date, he will withdraw the offer. Felix has to decide, however, whether any advantage he gains by such a deadline is offset by Sally's potentially adverse reaction to the pressure thus imposed.

Felix should not, however, characterize his proposal in "take it or leave it" terms, an attitude that creates unnecessary resistance. A better approach is, "I've given this a lot of thought and it's the best I can do. Any more and it's not worth it to me to do the deal." The message of firmness is still there, but it doesn't carry the same aura of intransigence.

Sally, for her part, shouldn't be cowed by Felix's package. If Felix gives one of those "all or nothing" speeches prior to making his offer, there's no need for her to accept that condition explicitly. On the other hand, she's unwise to reject it in advance, since that might discourage Felix from even making the proposal. (And after all, she *would* like to know what he has in mind.) If Sally feels the need to say something, she can just mumble something neutral like "I hear you."

But now, what if after hearing Felix's proposal, Sally is unwilling to accept the total package? Since she doesn't want to be accused of picking and choosing, her best bet is to formulate *her own* counterpackage on all four issues—and to attach the same warning label to the contents. "Here's *my* package resolution, Felix—and no picking and choosing, please:

- I'll take the note;
- I'll give you the exclusive;
- I want the term to stay at nine months; and
- I won't credit the expenses against the fee if you make less than $10,000 on the deal."

Although the result of this may be another temporary impasse, at least two of the issues (the note and the exclusive) can now be eliminated for practical purposes, by virtue of being similarly resolved in each party's package. Then they can get down to business on what's left, which appears to be quite manageable—perhaps using ten months and $17,500 as the numbers to be inserted. Taken together with any one of the compromise fee resolutions discussed previously, this should result in final agreement between Felix and Sally, so that they can now get on with the important business of trying to sell Warm Bodies.

THE END OF THE ROAD

Most deals get done because the parties end up hammering out a compromise resolution. If you're going to negotiate much, you have to learn to live with this reality. When the compromise you reach represents an outcome that's at least as favorable as your realistic expectation, then you've done well indeed. And that's true even if—with all the huffing and puffing and concessions and packages—it *feels* as if you've given up a hell of a lot. Just remember, all that territory reaching back to your opening position never *belonged* to you anyway. Presumably you've used it well to furnish the trading bait required to drag your counterpart, at times kicking and screaming, all the way to your expectation.

I've been emphasizing the *process* of bargaining, the virtues of perseverance, the search for advantages, and other such matters; but a smart negotiator also has to know when to stop the music and grab a chair. The opportunity that exists to make a deal today may be gone tomorrow. Agreements are reached between people, and people can change their minds, or new factors (such as competition) can intervene. Not infrequently, when I sense my client is close to reaching an accord he considers favorable, I find myself whispering to him, "If it takes all night, don't let this guy out of the room until you've shaken hands on a deal!" The resulting agreement may not be all you could hope to achieve by prolonging the process; but when the risk of losing the deal altogether doesn't justify the possible incremental advantage, that's the time to come to terms.

Investment banker Bruce Wasserstein understood this principle quite well the night he tried mightily, as Campeau's negotiator, to get Federated Department Stores to agree to sell to Campeau at a price that represented an increase over prior offers. But the obverse of the principle is equally important: Don't agree to a deal until you're satisfied it covers all the points you consider significant. Following that second tenet, our Federated team insisted that there couldn't be an agreement until all the substantial issues were hammered out and a contract signed. This required several days more of negotiations, which managed to give Macy's enough time to make its own offer topping Campeau's. As it turned out, Federated ultimately made a deal with Campeau, but at a price significantly above the one Wasserstein was urging us to accept that night.

The other side of the compromise coin, as anyone who negotiates regularly also knows, is that it's not always possible to do as well in the end as your realistic expectation. Sometimes, after exhausting all efforts to agree on better terms, the only compromise that will swing the deal represents a stretch on your part beyond the safety net of your expectation. When you're forced to face up to that stretch decision, try to isolate it from the emotions you're feeling, from the frustrations that have accompanied your journey thus far. Rather, phrase the issue for yourself in these simple terms: If the deal was good enough to do at the level of my realistic expectation, does it still make sense given the needed stretch? If it does, then shake hands, however reluctantly. If not, sayonara.

COMPROMISE WRAP-UP

Keynote

The fourth and final step in my game plan approach to smart negotiating is knowing how and when to arrange the ultimate compromise that will clinch the deal. You have to be willing to compromise in order to reach agreement. Don't think of it as surrendering, particularly when the solution meets or comes close enough to your realistic expectation. And don't depend on your counterpart to propose it, although by all means give him the opportunity if he happens to be so inclined.

Blunder

The bogeyman here is your compromise proposal that, because you haven't laid the necessary groundwork, *doesn't* end the bidding but merely becomes your new position—which your counterpart then proceeds to assail.

Lapse

Too many otherwise competent bargainers lack the creativity to fashion a good compromise when the resolution isn't readily apparent. The ability to find the common ground—reducing principles to dollars, dividing up seemingly indivisible issues, expanding the pie—is the hallmark of the smart negotiator.

PART III

Using Agents, Resolving Disputes, and Other Real-World Concerns

11 BARGAINING THROUGH, WITH, AND BETWEEN AGENTS

There's a wise old saw that says a lawyer who represents himself has a fool for a client. It's a lesson not limited to lawyers and courtrooms. Anyone approaching a significant negotiation should consider whether to go it alone or use an agent.

If you're like me, you're a much better negotiator for others than for yourself. That shouldn't be surprising. When your own property or interests aren't at stake, you can be more objective, more relaxed, even more creative. Conversely, if you're too anxious about the outcome, you may not trade wisely. And when you feel personally aggrieved, you often lack the necessary emotional detachment. Then, too, the ultimate negotiating decisions that only you can make—"yes" or "no," buy or pass, how much to pay—impose their own strain. Divorcing those decisions from the stress of confronting the other side directly can lighten your load.

In the business world negotiations are often conducted by representatives. Lawyers and investment bankers negotiate for corporate buyers and sellers; brokers abound in all facets of real estate; agents bargain over sports, publishing, and show business deals for their individual clients. And although the principals are the parties at risk, the agents can also have a personal stake in the negotiations, with the compensation for their services often tied to (or at least influenced by) the outcome.

THE PROS AND CONS OF USING AN AGENT

There are many good reasons to conduct negotiations through an agent:

- the agent's technical expertise or negotiating skills;
- the principal's emotional involvement in a high-stakes deal, which hampers his ability to negotiate effectively;
- the principal's desire to avoid having to answer certain questions or react to a new proposal on the spot;
- the agent's ability to float a trial balloon without implicating his principal;
- the principal's reluctance to cross swords directly with a counterpart who will be working closely with the principal once the relationship is established;
- the possible advantages obtainable through limiting the agent's authority.

The use of an agent isn't an unmixed blessing, however. It can involve such potential risks as

- faulty communication between principal and agent that harms the principal's cause;
- an agent with his own agenda or bias who doesn't faithfully represent his principal;
- a principal who won't level with his agent and thus impairs their dealings with the other side;
- a nitpicking agent who misses the big picture and thereby undermines the deal;
- the inability, due to interposed agents, of one principal to reach the other principal directly in order to be able to persuade, to pressure, or to extract a decision.

Still, these problems can be dealt with, and agents are all over the place, a constant feature of the negotiating landscape. The odds are you'll use (or be) one at some point; and it will add a distinct dimension to the negotiating process, both in terms of the principal-agent relationship and the interaction with the other side. So let's explore the terrain.

THE START-UP EMPLOYMENT CONTRACT

Phyllis, a successful fashion executive, has been approached by Consolidated, a major company, which wants her to head a newly formed

Consolidated division ("Start-up") in her area of expertise (Italian imports). She considers this a prime opportunity. But since she'll be leaving a comfortable position for a newly created one with an uncertain future, Phyllis realizes she needs a written employment contract, the first in her career. A mutual acquaintance refers her to Alan, a lawyer who specializes in executive compensation and employment matters. They hit it off well in the initial meeting, and Phyllis retains Alan's services to help her negotiate the contract. Let's focus first on the interaction between principal and agent, Phyllis and Alan. And from time to time we'll also look in on the other team, which consists of Conrad, the senior vice-president of Consolidated in charge of Start-up, and his lawyer, Larry.

UNDERSTANDING WHAT'S IMPORTANT TO THE PRINCIPAL

It goes without saying that an agent's primary obligation is to do what's best for the principal. That means finding out what the principal really wants, which may not be the same as what the agent *thinks* the principal wants or *ought to* want. An agent should never assume that his viewpoint necessarily coincides with that of the principal, even where such concurrence might seem self-evident. When you're the principal, make sure your agent fully understands this ground rule.

For instance, assume that Alan, negotiating with Larry, asks for a provision in the contract obligating Start-up to reimburse Phyllis for certain recurrent business-related expenditures she expects to be making. Larry responds by insisting on a "cap" that limits Start-up's aggregate obligation for such expenditures to a specific figure. Alan balks, and the two agents lock horns.

Since his position could save Start-up money, Larry considers the cap to be the kind of protection Conrad would endorse heartily. But Conrad, if asked, might surprise Larry by responding along these lines: "No, Larry, let's not press this point. I'm going to have to live with Phyllis as my division head for a number of years. If she's going to be irritated with me each time she makes an expenditure that's not reimbursable because it's over the limit, the heartburn isn't worth the dollars involved." If Larry has failed to coordinate with Conrad in advance, his insistence on the cap might actually *undermine* Conrad's real interests.

A good agent always spends time with his principal reviewing the likely bargaining issues in order to understand what's important to the principal. In the mergers and acquisitions business, we actually spend more time in caucus with our own clients than in jousting with the other side. If *your* agent isn't giving you enough attention, let him know how you feel about it.

As Phyllis's agent, Alan should begin by finding out what she considers most important in the contract. How critical is her salary level? Does she want part of her compensation to be directly dependent on her performance, a bonus for achieving certain targets? How significant to her are the "perks?" Is she worried about getting fired? About Start-up not succeeding? About restraints on her ability to compete if things don't work out? Phyllis, for her part, shouldn't be bashful. She has to tell Alan what she wants (as well as what's *not* important to her) in no uncertain terms—whether or not he bothers to ask.

THE AGENT'S INVOLVEMENT IN THE PRINCIPAL'S DECISIONS

Since negotiating strategy involves a series of decisions on the principal's part, the question arises as to how involved the agent should become in the principal's decision making. Clearly the agent needs to clarify issues, identify options, and predict consequences, but how about making a specific recommendation or even calling the shot?

I find it helpful to divide into three broad categories the situations that arise in this area. The *first* consists of matters lying squarely within the agent's area of expertise, about which the principal has little experience. Here the principal fully expects the agent to come out swinging; in fact, an agent who is reluctant to venture an opinion is often considered remiss.

For instance, when Phyllis and Alan discuss whether disputes that might arise under her contract should be resolved by a lawsuit or be subject to arbitration, she will lean heavily on Alan's expert recommendation for her ultimate decision. A top round draft choice who retains an experienced sports agent to negotiate a multiyear contract would be foolish not to rely on that agent's advice about what constitutes an appropriate performance bonus and other such matters. Principals should, however, be leery of the agent who dazzles instead of communicating. The jargon that lawyers and other professionals use in their dealings with each other may be as clear as mud to their clients. In order for the principal to make reasoned judgments on negotiating strategy—even when there's heavy agent input—the agent has to speak a language the principal can understand. The principal shouldn't pretend to grasp what's fuzzy but instead ought to seek suitable clarification.

The issues in the *second* category lie at the other extreme: where the agent has no special expertise and the principal is competent to decide. For lawyers, this often involves what are essentially business judgments: whether or not the client should make a particular acquisition, what price he should pay, and so forth. Assuming that Alan isn't an expert on financial statements in the fashion industry, it should be up to Phyllis to decide what operating performance of Start-up would constitute the base against which her incentive compensation is to be measured.

When I'm acting as an agent, I'm loath to offer my own viewpoint on matters about which I lack expertise. If the client needs specialized business or financial advice, he can obtain it from an expert source, such as an investment banker or management consultant. Even if I have a personal view, I'm often reluctant to express it, given the second-guessing that can occur if things don't turn out so well.

The *third* and largest category is composed of issues where the agent is qualified to proffer advice and the principal is also reasonably knowledgeable. Take, for instance, an issue we've examined elsewhere: the terms of the noncompete agreement that Conrad will undoubtedly ask Phyllis to sign. If things don't work out and Phyllis leaves (or is eased out of) Start-up, what restrictions will be imposed in terms of her future employment? Will she be precluded from hiring Start-up employees? From going after Start-up's customers? For what period? In what geographic area? And the question for us is how deeply should Alan (and Larry) get involved in advising Phyllis (and Conrad) on these issues?

The answer depends largely on what suits the principal's taste. Needless to say, tastes can differ. Conrad, for instance, may be the kind of client who wants his lawyer to stick to issues containing a heavy legal component, such as the *enforceability* of whatever noncompete agreement is reached. As long as the provision passes legal muster, however, Conrad prefers to sally forth on his own. Whether or not Phyllis is capable of inflicting harm by going after Start-up employees or customers down the road is a business question that Conrad feels quite comfortable handling. If Larry senses this is the case, he should refrain from volunteering obtrusive recommendations.

Phyllis, on the other hand, may very much want Alan's judgment on which noncompete provisions are typical and what can be done to limit their scope. If Alan suspects this to be the case, then—after identifying the various possible options she faces—he ought to recommend what Phyllis should be prepared to accept or resist. But as a principal, you always have to exercise judgment as to how much weight your agent's advice deserves. It's certainly not gospel; and if, after due rumination, the advice seems less than compelling, then don't follow it. I make it a practice, with issues falling into this third category, not to discourage my clients from coming out differently from the way I've recommended. I don't want my views to intimidate them—as might be the case with matters falling into that first "special expertise" category.

The one area in which agents—particularly (but not exclusively) lawyers—should never hesitate to express their views is where an ethical issue is involved. If the principal proposes an unethical course of action, the agent's voice ought to be heard loud and clear in opposition. This goes the other way, too; the principal must be equally alert to any potential ethical breach instigated by the agent.

THE RISK-REWARD ANALYSIS

Many negotiating issues involve a risk-reward analysis. Path A holds out the greater rewards but carries the greater risks; Path B, with lesser risks, offers lesser rewards. In this area it's the *principal* who should be the one to decide: "I'm a gambler—let's take Path A," or the converse. Say, for instance, that Consolidated is offering Phyllis a three-year contract and basing its compensation package on that duration. Phyllis, however, would like a five-year contract, providing her with two more years of security. Conrad is reluctant to go out that far but would be willing to do so at a lower annual salary level. The added-security-for-less-pay decision is clearly Phyllis's call.

The agent can be helpful in these situations in terms of focusing the principal on the relative risks and rewards at stake. But he also has to be sensitive to any differences in the risk-taking profiles of both the principal and himself. The issue is not whether the *agent* is or isn't a risk taker, or thinks the risk is worth taking in this particular instance; it's how the *principal* would react. So if Alan were to say, "Well, if I were in your shoes, this is how *I* would handle it," he should remember to add, "But I'm risk averse," making it clear that different strokes can apply for different folks. And Phyllis should understand that there's nothing wrong with her coming out the other way.

THE AGENT'S INVOLVEMENT IN THE PRINCIPAL'S GAME PLAN

The interaction between principal and agent often helps shape the course of the negotiating game plan. In terms of assessing *realistic expectations*, the agent's role can be central, although it depends on the type of issue and the kind of agent. For example, the price issue falls in the first "special expertise" category (featuring strong agent input) for an investment banker advising a company on the sale of certain hard-to-value assets. On the other hand, price would usually be in the second "no expertise" category for the typical lawyer and thus would be wholly the client's call. Conversely, on a nonprice issue with a hefty *legal* component—a contractual provision regarding indemnification, for example—the lawyer should be outspoken, the investment banker much less so. Many nonprice issues fall into the third category, in which the agent is generally heard but the principal makes up his own mind.

The agent who's an experienced bargainer should play a significant role in helping to determine the *starting point*, even when the assessment of expectation falls into the second "no expertise" category. The principal knows where he wants to end up. The agent should advise on how to get there, with regard to which the starting point is an essential feature. I seldom make a recommendation regarding a client's price expectation, but I almost always have a view on what price we should start out with or offer in response to the other side's proposal; the actual decision, however, remains with the principal.

An agent who participates actively in the negotiations should also play a key role in devising the *concession pattern*. Being on the front lines fosters a sense of what will work and what won't, what's likely to generate reciprocal concessions and what's not. It's a lot harder to judge this secondhand from the back room. Nevertheless, to make any meaningful concession the agent needs authority from the principal. Make sure your agent understands this when you retain him. Nothing will irk you more than to discover that the agent has ceded something significant without your say-so, even a point you would have yielded if asked!

As for the terms of the ultimate *compromise*—particularly one that involves a stretch—the decision is clearly the principal's, regardless of the agent's degree of expertise. Still, an agent who has been handling the negotiations is likely to have a good sense of *what it will take to get the deal done* (as contrasted with recommending *whether or not* the principal should stretch). This insight should be passed along to the principal, who has to decide whether to pay (or accept) the price the agent deems necessary or be willing to endure the consequences of losing the deal if the agent turns out to have been right.

The final stretch to compromise can often seem painful. But when viewed in the total context of the deal, divorced from the passion and effort expended to arrive at that point, the required movement may be relatively insignificant. As a potentially beleaguered principal, you may value the advice of a wise agent, who has retained the detachment needed to view such matters in reasonable perspective.

Agents also play a role in each of the other areas we've covered. In terms of the four essential bargaining skills, it's the agent who often communicates (as well as receives) signs of apparent leverage and who gathers and interprets information for the principal. Agents who lack credibility, or who sacrifice judgment in their zeal to bring home the bacon, can do considerable harm to their clients' cause. And as we will see in upcoming chapters, lawyer-agents will be central figures in resolving disputes and reducing agreements to writing.

"NEGOTIATIONS" BETWEEN PRINCIPAL AND AGENT

When the agent will be handling the negotiations and is seeking bargaining authority in advance, many a principal isn't forthcoming about how much he or she is ultimately willing to pay (or accept). Phyllis, for example, may fear that once Alan knows the least amount of money she's willing to accept in compensation from Start-up, he will promptly retreat to that minimum in his zeal to make a deal. (Clearly, an agent who bargains in this fashion shouldn't be allowed to conduct the negotiations.) So she keeps something in reserve, figuring that what Alan doesn't know won't hurt him and he'll be forced to bargain harder to achieve good terms. That doesn't sound too unreasonable, which is why principals often do it. But to negotiate effectively—to advise on such matters as the opening offer, appropriate concessions, and how to characterize each side's proposals—an agent really needs to know where the principal is heading. The principal's little game can lead to problems that could be avoided through greater candor.

The real risk in these situations occurs when the agent holds firm at the principal's ostensible limit, unaware that the latter would actually take less (or bid higher). All of a sudden the other side walks away from the deal. A seller sells to someone else (or takes the property off the market), a buyer finds something different to acquire, or, in this case, Consolidated locates a new head for the Start-up division.

If the other side could be relied upon to provide a clear warning before pulling out, the agent could then seek additional authority to make the higher payment or accept the lesser amount. But one thing I've learned over the years: you can never be sure *when* your counterpart will abort these negotiations and cut a separate deal with a third party. Worst of all, the agent may inadvertently have contributed to the problem by taking a convincing hard line at his principal's ostensible limit, causing the other side to figure that prospects for a deal were indeed dim.

An agent who suspects his principal of holding something back should emphasize the importance of candor. At the same time, a sensitive agent ought to reassure his principal that knowledge of the principal's *real* limit won't constitute a self-fulfilling prophecy. And even if you, as the principal, don't feel like 'fessing up to your real bottom line just yet, it may be enough to let the agent know that he's likely to have *some* leeway when push comes to shove.

DEALING WITH THE OTHER SIDE

Let's turn now to the dealings with the other side. First, of course, is the threshold issue: Who should initially conduct the negotiations? In the Start-up setting, for instance, should Phyllis deal with Conrad by herself, or should Alan meet with Larry alone, or should all four of them sit down together? This can make a difference, so it mustn't be left to chance—or, worse, to the other side's choice.

Imagine that you're Phyllis, faced with this decision. What are some of the pertinent factors to consider? First is your skill at negotiating, both in absolute terms and also relative to how you perceive the skills of Conrad and Alan. If you consider yourself deficient, while Conrad is renowned for his bargaining prowess and Alan appears tough as nails, you might prefer to have Alan conduct the negotiations with Larry. Conversely—and assuming he shares your view of the relative skills—Conrad might well opt to negotiate alone with you, keeping Alan a good distance away from the bargaining table.

On the other hand, if you're a skilled negotiator, Conrad has no notable reputation, and Alan is more of a technician specializing in compensation issues, then you might want to handle things yourself. This may be particularly appealing if you relish the opportunity to "strut your stuff" one on one with Conrad. Of course, the subject matter being negotiated is obviously relevant to your decision. You're in the best position to handle straightforward issues, like your salary. If certain pension questions or other technical matters become significant, there's more reason to involve Alan.

To digress for a moment, in complex numbers-oriented business deals, your side can often score points if the other side's negotiator (frequently a lawyer) and its financial expert aren't working well in tandem. If you suspect that the other side's lawyer doesn't grasp the significance of the figures, try to arrange for your lawyer to negotiate with his legal counterpart privately, without any financial or business people around to provide guidance. Conversely, if *your* lawyer looks bewildered, make sure to arrange the necessary technical support.

A factor worth considering (although often ignored) in determining the invitation list is which side will be raising the hard points. As Phyllis, most of the potentially confrontational issues will emanate from your end: compensation, perks, clarifying your responsibilities, and so on. Conrad may find it harder to resist your demands when they're presented to him one on one.

I've often observed that the farther an individual is from the bargaining table, the tougher he negotiates. I can picture Conrad sitting there, in the privacy of his office, pontificating to Larry: "Don't give in on this point" and "Make sure you get me that protection." If the principals come face to face, however, and Conrad hears the logic of your argument firsthand or senses your depth of feeling, his preconceived notions might go right out the window.

In circumstances where the principals will have to work closely together after the deal is made—as will be the case with you and Conrad—one or both may be concerned that the bargaining confrontation will damage the relationship before it gets off the ground. Conrad, in particular, may prefer to let the lawyers clash over the contract terms, while you and he take the more edifying path of developing Start-up's business plan.

Some things are just best handled agent to agent. Here's an example. Say that the bargaining over the issue of Phyllis's salary—which began with her initially asking $185,000 and Consolidated offering $115,000—has evolved, through a series of positional changes, to her asking $160,000 and Consolidated making the most recent move to $140,000. Now it's Phyllis's turn. She would be willing to shake hands at $150,000 but is leery about dropping to that level or, for reasons previously discussed, offering to split the difference.

Here's where an agent can be valuable. Alan tells Larry that Phyllis is prepared to go to $155,000. When Larry groans Alan says, "Look, Larry, Consolidated has three choices here. It can stick at a hundred and forty thousand, in which case I don't think there will be a deal. It can come up to a hundred and forty-five, which is constructive, but there's still a question whether the two sides will be able to close the gap. Or—and this is the course I think the wisest for all of us—you can come back to me, after talking with Conrad, and tell me that Consolidated would be willing to do a deal at a hundred and fifty thousand *if Phyllis* is agreeable. If you can do that, I think I can get Phyllis to buy that resolution. You understand, Larry, I'm not asking Consolidated to change its *position* to a hundred and fifty thousand; if Conrad is willing but Phyllis isn't, you'll still be at one sixty."

This question of who should handle the bargaining recurs throughout the course of the negotiations. Your views may change over time, and even from meeting to meeting, since the answer depends on such factors as where things currently stand and which items are on that day's agenda. Not surprisingly, the most crucial factor to consider may be what lineup has managed to produce the best (and worst) results in prior sessions.

"LET'S KILL ALL THE LAWYERS"

When the agents involved are lawyers, the client's attitude toward members of the legal profession is often a significant factor in deciding who's going to handle the negotiations. Let's face it, many business-people are more at ease without lawyers in the room, more confident about getting things accomplished while preserving the goodwill between the parties. They rail at the negative attitudes lawyers exhibit, seeing a problem behind every bush, overcompensating to avoid risk, generating conflict. (There's nothing new in this; even Shakespeare characterized lawyers as "poor breathing orators of miseries.") "Everything was fine until we brought in the lawyers" goes the familiar refrain, followed by the remark that lawyers are more likely to break deals than make them. As a result, many businesspeople avoid introducing lawyers into the early stages of a deal when, in their view, what's needed is nurturing—not disaster scenarios.

I can understand some of the frustration. Many well-meaning attorneys get overly technical or create roadblocks at sensitive moments. But in other ways it's a bum rap. Businesspeople who agree in principle on price and the date of closing often pass over a number of the potential issues lurking in most transactions. The lawyer comes in and poses some logical questions. As the parties then face off reflexively on opposite sides, the lawyer—like the messenger bearing bad tidings—becomes a convenient whipping boy. Or the parties may think their minds have met on a certain point, without considering one key aspect of it. The lawyer, seeking to eliminate this ambiguity, focuses on the unresolved aspect—and everyone bristles.

Keep in mind, too, that businesspeople who fail to consult with counsel until after they've shaken hands on a deal, and who then try to introduce new terms and conditions suggested by their lawyers, may find themselves accused of renegotiating the deal. Since the structure of the transaction (on which attorneys thrive) is often crucial, but seldom neutral, it makes sense to have a lawyer involved in this aspect from the outset. On the other hand, even if *your* lawyer is constructive and appreciates the business realities, his visible presence in the negotiations will trigger the other side to produce what may turn out to be a more antediluvian member of the profession. So my advice is to *consult* a lawyer early in the process. Depending on the circumstances, however, you may choose to limit the lawyer's initial role to advising you in private.

THE ISSUE OF LIMITED AUTHORITY

When you do your own bargaining and an issue comes up that calls for a response on your part, you have no place to hide. The other side knows that you're the decision maker. What's more, if you're like so many other principals who want to appear decisive, you don't relish having to reply, "I'd like to think this one over."

By contrast, if you use an agent and limit his authority, there's plenty of room to maneuver on any issue. The agent can claim he's powerless to move ("My client insists on this price and won't take a penny less"); or he can use his principal's absence to justify withholding a concession ("I'll have to see how my client reacts"); or he can indulge in various other forms of saying "no" without being directly confrontational. All the while the agent can be trying to wrest concessions from the other side. Many principals, intrigued by the possibilities of this imbalance, negotiate through agents whom they provide with drastically limited grants of authority.

I may be prejudiced here—a result, no doubt, of my usual status as agent—but I think it's ultimately self-defeating to send an agent off to do battle without any authority to deviate from the principal's stated position. If you're interested in making progress, it makes much more sense to give your negotiator some genuine flexibility, assuming that the other side's negotiator has authority to bargain. Remember, it takes movement to generate movement. You want your agent to be able to pounce on juicy opportunities as they arise at the bargaining table. He may have to make a few concessions to get something decent in return.

If your agent will be dealing with the other side's principal, it may be appropriate to advise your counterpart directly about your agent's authority. I'll never forget a particular moment in the sale of Seattle's Rainier Bank to Security Pacific. At one point the chief executive of Rainier (my client) was ailing and couldn't attend the negotiations. He summed up the situation to Security Pacific's top man in four words: "Jim speaks for me." This provided me with the necessary underpinning to be able to bargain effectively with Security Pacific's principals.

The story is quite different, however, when the other side's agent *lacks* the requisite authority and is there just to take, with nothing of significance to give. Larry, for example, might be dispatched by Conrad on such an expedition. He's instructed to find out all he can from Alan about Phyllis's requirements, to probe for useful information and signs of weakness, to suggest ways in which she ought to show more flexibility, and so on. Then, when Alan tries to get Larry to move off Consolidated's stated position, Larry simply shrugs and says, "I'll have to go back and talk it over with Conrad." Alan may be sitting there with all the authority he needs to cut a deal—but no one to trade with.

This isn't just frustrating for Alan; it's also dangerous for Phyllis. If the lawyers bargain and reach tentative accords that Larry has to take back to Conrad for approval, chances are—if Conrad is anything like lots of guys I run into daily—he'll have some conditions to insert or some additional concessions to extract, leaving Phyllis in an uncomfortable squeeze. So if it becomes clear that Larry is negotiating with an empty tank, Alan should give nothing further away. He may even have to call a halt to the proceedings, stating firmly: "Either get yourself some authority, Larry, or let's get Conrad and Phyllis together—because we're going *nowhere* as things now stand."

Nevertheless, in the later stages of a negotiation that has suffered hardening of the arteries, a brainstorming session between two agents—both of whom lack authority to bind—can sometimes be useful. I have in mind here a "trial balloon" type of strategy, in which one of the agents gingerly suggests a potential compromise that he "just thought up," along with an accompanying pitch to his counterpart: "If I can sell this to my principal—which may or may not be possible—do you think your guy might go along with it?"

WHEN BOTH PRINCIPAL AND AGENT ARE IN THE ROOM

In the kinds of business deals I'm involved in, the most frequent lineup is for each side to have both principal and agent together at the table. Agents acting alone often lack the authority or confidence to move ahead. Principals may feel uncomfortable making a deal without their advisers present, for fear of omitting some significant detail.

In an all-hands meeting, each side has its maximum firepower on the scene. As a result, real progress can occur.

From my viewpoint, one appealing feature of these meetings is the opportunity to make a pitch directly to the other side's decision maker. When an agent is forced to communicate through the other side's agent, he has no idea whether, and in what form, his message will get back to the other principal. My working assumption, however, is that it will be mutilated, with key parts omitted or misstated, and carrying the other agent's personalized spin!

Prior to an all-hands meeting, the principal and agent should, of course, discuss what's likely to arise, the positions they'll adopt (or avoid), and who will take the lead on various issues. Still, matters will come up at the meeting that haven't been anticipated. How should they be handled? Let's assume a Start-up bargaining session has been scheduled at which Alan will accompany Phyllis and Larry will be with Conrad. Most of the points will emanate from Phyllis's side. She and Alan have decided to split up the issues: on matters such as her compensation, Phyllis will take the lead; on others, such as the noncompetition agreement, Alan will take over.

Meanwhile Conrad should try—probably through a conversation between Larry and Alan—to get some advance intelligence as to the issues that will be raised. This enables him to formulate his responses beforehand, rather than having to improvise in the more pressured atmosphere of the meeting. If this isn't feasible, it might be wise for Conrad or Larry to make a general opening statement along these lines: "We're here to listen to all your points, after which we'll caucus and then get back to you on the whole lot." Now, Conrad's absence of reaction to a specific issue will lack the significance it might otherwise have if timely responses to each point were expected.

Alan is concerned because Phyllis, by her own admission, isn't experienced in these kinds of negotiations. She might not grasp the full import of a new point posed to her for response or be able to formulate the best reply on the spot. Alan will be hesitant to offer explanations in front of the other side or to react himself without first discussing the point with Phyllis privately. If they stand mute, however, they may compromise their credibility down the road, especially when they later attempt to plead outrage.

So if one of these points comes up, there's nothing wrong with Alan jumping in—before Phyllis is forced to reply—to say that this is a matter he would like to discuss privately with Phyllis before they respond. The agent, however, should take pains not to make the principal look like a simpleton who lacks understanding or judgment. For that reason, on the occasions when I do this, I may throw in a veiled reference to "certain technical aspects" of the question or its "linkage to other issues."

I'm a great believer in adjourning a negotiating session briefly to confer with my client in private, rather than winging it with the other side present. One word of caution here, however. If you're concerned about the ramifications of a certain issue that's under discussion, don't allow the *timing* of your call for a caucus (for example, on the heels of a particularly pointed remark by your counterpart) to arouse suspicion across the table. Instead, be patient and let the discussion pass on to other subjects before excusing yourself ("I think it's time for a short break"), thereby eliminating the risk of any raised eyebrows.

AGENT WRAP-UP

Keynote

When you're negotiating through an agent, make sure he knows just what you want to achieve, and develop a clear understanding of what role each of you will play to get there, both in terms of devising the strategy and of dealing with the other side.

Blunder

The major error here is to allow your agent to get into a negotiation where he has the authority to make concessions but his counterpart doesn't.

Lapse

A frequent pitfall is the failure to *consult* a knowledgeable agent early in the process, even if you're not going to use the agent to handle the first stages of the negotiations. The danger is that the agreement you reach, and only later discover works to your disadvantage, has by then passed the point of no return.

12 RESOLVING DISPUTES

In deal negotiations, the parties are usually starting fresh, with no prior history to bog them down. By contrast, the parties to a dispute share a common past but aren't exactly awash in nostalgia. In fact, at least one of them is mad as hell, blaming the other for some recent outrage and seeking financial recompense. The target of these aspersions is indignant at being unjustly accused. And the central question is whether they'll be able to resolve their dispute through negotiations or be forced to resort to the courts. The skills and strategies of *smart negotiating* remain applicable in such situations, but for a variety of reasons—including the looming specter of litigation, the emotions and other baggage that frustrate the bargaining, and the combative lawyers who dot the landscape—dispute resolution deserves closer examination.

THE OMNIPRESENT LITIGATION ALTERNATIVE

In deal making, if neither side is ultimately willing to break an impasse, one side can call a halt and head for home with nothing more than some bruised feelings and out-of-pocket expenses. When a dispute remains unresolved, however, there's seldom a neutral walkaway. The usual alternative to negotiating a settlement is a lawsuit, where the judge or jury decides the outcome. And since no one (including your lawyer) can be certain in advance what the outcome will be, it's hard to decide just where to settle.

The main problem is one of valuation. If the case is tried and the *plaintiff* (the party making the claim) prevails, he'll be awarded what he reasonably claims. If, however, the *defendant* (the party against whom the claim is being made) wins, the plaintiff will wind up with a goose egg, plus having to pay his own lawyer's fee. The judge can't just arbitrarily name a figure somewhere in between the dollars at issue, even though this is where the main jousting takes place when the parties try to settle. And if a jury is involved, the outlook is even more inscrutable. As a result, the negotiated settlement is almost bound to be at odds with the results of litigation.

Assume that litigation has actually begun. To oversimplify, for a settlement to occur at this point, the parties have to be in broad concurrence (at least tacitly) on a composite of two key variables: the likely outcome of the lawsuit and just how probable that outcome is. Take a case where the plaintiff has a reasonable claim of $100,000, plus some less worthy amounts of additional damage that he also alleges. If both sides concur that the likeliest outcome is a $100,000 judgment for the plaintiff, and that the odds of this happening are roughly 75 percent (failing which the plaintiff gets nothing), the settlement negotiations would hover in the vicinity of $75,000, with a fair chance of success. The ever-present risk of an adverse ruling, coupled with the high cost of litigation, frequently overcomes minor variances in viewpoint. But if, instead, the defendant thinks his chances of winning are at least fifty-fifty, and the likely damage award if he loses will be closer to $80,00, then the bargaining is a lot more strenuous. The defendant digs in at the $40,000 level, and the resulting gap may never be closed.

In contrast to deal making—which requires accommodation on a number of points—litigants can often resolve their dispute by agreeing on a single dollar figure. This might seem easier to accomplish than sorting out dozens of issues, but it isn't. The kind of progress on which deal makers thrive—as one issue after another is resolved or swapped—seldom exists in a dispute over money. There, nothing is settled until everything is settled, which puts much more pressure on the final breakthrough.

Some litigators claim that the choice between negotiation and litigation is not all that difficult; just try the winners, they say, and settle the losers! This reminds me of Will Rogers's advice on the stock market: "Don't gamble; take all your savings and buy some good stock and hold it till it goes up, then sell it. If it don't go up, don't buy it."

THE EMOTIONAL BAGGAGE

Human factors compound the difficulties. Messy disputes breed distrust. The plaintiff is aggrieved by the defendant's wrongdoing. The defendant, oozing self-righteousness, is outraged at being hauled into court. In this atmosphere mutual trust is a hard commodity to come by, yet it's a prime ingredient in successful negotiating. Has your adversary been truthful and forthcoming? Will he renege tomorrow on what was agreed to today? If the settlement involves future conduct—frequently a critical factor—can your adversary be trusted to perform as obligated?

In deal making, as we've seen, the prevalent attitude is that everything is ultimately soluble, that the other guy's problems are yours, too. In a dispute, this mood is conspicuously absent. The positions of the parties always seem irreconcilable—just read their legal briefs! With all that huffing and puffing, there's little disposition to solve the other side's problems. Each party is having enough trouble coping with his own.

The businesspeople and their agents who do deals want to get them done—preferably, yesterday. The emphasis is on being "constructive," on finding ways to resolve any impasse and move things along. The bête noir of all concerned is a busted deal. When two parties are at loggerheads in a dispute, however, the mood is quite different. Sometimes one of them prefers that the conflict remain unresolved, perhaps to keep pressure on a business competitor. But even the party who has more to gain from a negotiated settlement frequently appears ambivalent about settling. One minute he tells his lawyer to work something out; the next, like Napoleon's cavalry general, he's ready to "ride to the sound of the cannon."

Certain features of the cooperative approach to bargaining may work well to lower the emotional temperature of a dispute—for instance, trying to get both parties to see the situation from the other side's perspective and not to put the worst interpretation on what they say or do; telling your adversary how *you* feel while acknowledging *his* concerns; recognizing the need to save face; and so on. What I like to keep constantly in mind is the distinction between the confrontation at hand over how to resolve the dispute and the original clash that caused it. The more you can separate the current negotiations from what went on back then, the better your chances that reason will prevail.

The catch-22 here, however, is that it's often impossible to discuss a solution to a dispute without rehashing and interpreting the very facts that got you into this mess in the first place. The reason for this is that the true measure of any settlement is how it comports with the way a court, after considering the evidence, is likely to decide the case. Yet the more you dwell on history, the tougher it is to put the past behind you. I have no magic nostrum in such situations. But whenever I hear the talks relapsing into an angry reiteration of who did what to whom, I try my best to shift the emphasis to what can *we* do about this *now*.

THE SLOW DANCE TO INITIATE TALKS

There's often a lot of foot shuffling prior to initiating settlement talks, as each side—worried about displaying weakness—waits for the other to blink. I realize that timing can be important; and the day after your side gets licked in court on a preliminary legal motion may not be the best moment to hoist a white flag. In general, however, if settling is in your best interests, but the other side makes no conciliatory move, *you* should try to get a dialogue going.

A good lawyer knows how to convey confidence in his case, countering any implication of weakness. Some go one step better, suggesting that they're initiating talks because they know their adversary can't, since, given *his* lousy case, to do so would be a terrible sign of weakness! In light of the cost to both sides if the litigation continues, the best lawyer-to-lawyer pitch is simply, "I've got a suggestion. Before our clients make us rich, shouldn't we see if there's some way to settle this thing?"

A related question is whether your major effort to settle the dispute should occur *before* or *after* the lawsuit starts. Certainly the *timing* for beginning the talks is less of a problem before litigation begins. Few people are anxious to go to war, if it can be avoided. Other factors, however, cut both ways. For example, before the papers are served, neither party has invested too much time, effort, or expense in the dispute. The passions, animosity, and sheer momentum of the contest are yet to come. So score one for talking early. Still, while litigation may inflame the emotions, it can also serve to work off some of the venom. And as the parties see their legal bills mounting—with no trial date in sight—they may become more receptive to working things out.

Sometimes it takes a lawsuit to induce a recalcitrant adversary to come to the table. At other times it's the *threat* of litigation that carries force. Once the lawsuit has actually been filed, the pressure to settle dissipates as the parties dig in for a pitched battle. It may, however, begin to build up again, especially in more complex situations, during the pretrial discovery process that's an integral part of litigation—exchanging documents, deposing witnesses, and such. As each side gains a keener sense of its adversary's strengths and weaknesses, everyone has a better idea of what's likely to happen if the lawsuit goes to trial. As a result, settlement may become more (or, in some instances, less) feasible. On balance, at least where the relative merits of the dispute aren't too obscured, I favor trying to settle it early—before the arteries harden.

THE DECISION WHETHER TO HEAD OFF A COLLISION

Now take yourself back to a time before the dispute has even begun. Assume you're contemplating (but have not yet taken) an action that might be expected to raise someone's hackles—for instance, where it might be deemed to violate an existing contract between the two of you. Should you try to head off a collision before taking the action or just go ahead and let the chips fall where they may? And if you do approach your potential adversary beforehand, how should you handle it in order not to concede the violation implicitly? The actual facts of the controversy will dictate the answer in each instance, but here are two general rules of thumb that may prove helpful:

First, the clearer the violation, the more reason for you to approach your potential adversary *before* taking the step. Why burden the eventual negotiations with the residue of his irate reaction to your conduct? Besides, he might just sue first and ask questions later.

Second, where the violation is less clear-cut (but the other party's initial reaction is still likely to be negative), and you intend to proceed whether or not an accommodation is worked out, the better course may be to go ahead and take the action without prior discussion. My premise here is that the other party would take greater umbrage over your acting in defiance of his prior objection than if you were to proceed with your debatable activity in ignorance of his position.

If you do decide to talk first, what should you say? You don't want to concede the violation; on the other hand, pooh-poohing the problem sounds disingenuous—after all, why are you *there* talking? A better approach, assuming you can make a good argument that what you're proposing to do is valid, is to say that it's *not* a violation, but you're concerned it might *appear* to be. That's why you want to explain the circumstances before taking the action. Where the violation is pretty clear, however, and you're unlikely to proceed in the absence of prior agreement, then you may consider going so far as to acknowledge that the question "could go either way." This translates into "Let's negotiate." In any event, if you're *the other party*, you should view all such overtures skeptically and concede nothing until further investigation.

PROBLEMS RELATED TO LITIGATORS

With a lawsuit at hand or just around the corner, trial lawyers ("litigators") invariably become involved in the dispute. The litigators I know best—particularly my partners—are not only superb at their contentious craft, but also sensitive to the quite different skills needed to resolve disputes short of battle. I fear, however, that my experience isn't universal. So you may have to guard against ending up with a litigator who's more a part of the problem than a part of the solution.

If the lawsuit has started before the settlement talks begin, the litigator has been busy throwing his weight around. There he is, alleging fraud and depredation, seeking trebled damages, ridiculing his adversary's claims. In the litigation papers, everything is larger than life and choking on adverbs: the opponent's argument is "patently absurd," the simplest contractual phrase is "hopelessly ambiguous." And the litigators, who tend to be combative types, often reflect the indignation their clients feel.

To shift abruptly from all this bristling to a rational discussion of settlement possibilities requires a sizable psychological adjustment. And the real dilemma is that the litigators can't tell whether a settlement will ultimately be reached. So the left hand is negotiating, while the right prepares to resume the conflict. This uncertainty can deter trial lawyers from making conciliatory gestures or taking positions that imply vulnerability. They're reluctant to swap meaningful concessions for fear this will complicate their lives if they have to go back to the mat. Yet that very rigidity may be antithetical to the search for a workable compromise.

The litigator may also have trouble, of a more subtle variety, in his own camp. Clients like their gladiators to be tough, forceful advocates. Many successful trial lawyers respond by cultivating a hawkish image. It's hard for such a litigator—poised to defend his client's honor with gusto—to now prod his client in the direction of settlement. He runs the risk of being deemed a "softie," who's afraid to try the case and is ready to capitulate. Yet that prodding might be just what's needed, particularly with an irate client who wants his day in court but whose outlook at trial isn't rosy.

As the client, you have to determine whether your lawyer, who is presumably quite skilled in the courtroom, is equally well equipped to handle negotiations at the conference table. The qualities that make for a good litigator—the "winning" mentality, an instinct for the jugular—may not be conducive to compromise settlements. Conversely, qualities honed in negotiation, such as knowing when to adjust your sights or lower the temperature of the encounter, don't necessarily get sharpened in the skirmishes of a lawsuit. And even if your litigator is well equipped, you have to be concerned that the trial lawyer on the other side isn't up to the task.

Remember, it's *your* decision whether or not to settle. Listen to your lawyer's advice, but don't lose control of matters just because litigation is involved. If your gut tells you that this altercation should be settled, then *do* it—even if you and your adversary need to take over the negotiations from the gladiators to accomplish your purpose.

THE CASE OF THE FLAWED CONSULTATION

Now let's examine the dynamics of a sample dispute. Cory, a consultant, was retained by Alliance Inc., a diversified company, to do an extensive analysis of Alliance's existing employee benefit plans and to propose improvements. There was no written contract covering the engagement.

Cory had discussed with Alice, Alliance's vice-president of human resources, two possible methods of compensation: a flat fee of $100,000 or a fee based on the hourly charges of Cory and his associates, which, he estimated to her, would end up in that vicinity. Cory recalls having agreed with Alice that the fee would be the *greater* of $100,000 or the actual hourly charges. Alice remembers it as the *lesser* of the two—in other words, that the fee would not exceed $100,000 in any case. At any rate, Cory was paid $50,000 at the outset of the engagement, with the balance due upon delivery of his written report. Nothing was said one way or another about whether final payment was conditioned on Alliance's satisfaction with Cory's performance or recommendations.

Unfortunately this was one of those assignments in which nothing turned out right. Cory felt he didn't receive full cooperation from the Alliance employees who were supposed to provide him with information. The same employees complained to Alice about Cory's high-handedness and lack of sensitivity to their concerns. The work took longer to complete than Cory estimated: because of Alliance's non-cooperation, Cory claims; because of the incompetence of Cory's personnel, according to Alliance. As a result, the hourly charges ballooned to $125,000. Finally, when Cory turned in his report, Alice and her staff considered both the analysis and the specific recommendations to be woefully inadequate.

Cory submitted his final bill for $75,000 ($125,000 less the $50,000 down payment). Alliance refused to pay, citing the $100,000 upper limit; but Alice then went on to declare Cory's work so unsatisfactory that not only wasn't he owed another $50,000, but he should refund the original $50,000 paid on account. Cory reacted with some heat, and conversations broke off abruptly. As we join the proceedings, each side has now engaged counsel and is pondering the next step.

From Cory's perspective. Let's examine the situation first from Cory's point of view. He feels Alliance owes him another $75,000, although he recognizes that the outcome of litigation is never certain. Even if his case were a clear winner, however, he would rather not have to sue. He's aware of the vexations of a lawsuit, the long time it takes to get a judgment, the legal fees, and the potential harm to his reputation from any adverse publicity. On the other hand, he also knows that without a favorable court determination he's unlikely to receive payment in full from Alliance. He wonders how much less he should be willing to accept in settlement.

Here's a simplified version of the analysis Cory has to go through. If he sues, he might be awarded the additional $75,000. It will take time, however, and the legal fees he pays to achieve that result will reduce the net recovery. He has two legal hurdles to overcome: the uncertain dollar terms of the fee arrangement and Alliance's allegation that his work was so flawed, it doesn't merit payment. Cory's lawyer advises him that if his work product measures up professionally, then even though it didn't satisfy Alliance, his chances of prevailing on this second issue are quite good. Cory, who is convinced his work is wholly competent, thus gives little credence to Alliance's claim for refund of the first $50,000.

The terms of his fee pose more of a problem. Any agreement here was strictly oral. Since Alice will testify to a $100,000 maximum, the outcome will turn on which of them is a more credible witness—unless there's other evidence (such as a written record or the recollection of others) that sheds light on what the parties intended. Cory's initial estimate (which he admits making) that the hourly charges would come to around $100,000 doesn't help his cause, although he'll argue that the excess was caused by factors beyond his control. Alliance's dissatisfaction with the results of the assignment is also likely to work to his disadvantage in trying to convince the judge to award him the additional pay. Bottom line: Cory is worried that the judge will decide his fee should be limited to $100,000.

So here's Cory's rough computation of where he would be willing to settle. He begins by using $100,000 as the most likely judgment. He figures he has about a one-third chance of prevailing at the $125,000 level. On the other hand, there's a 10 percent possibility of his losing everything on the "flawed product" issue. So he treats these two "possibilities" as offsetting each other. He estimates $15,000 in legal fees to litigate. Accordingly, he is inclined to settle the case for a total consulting fee of around $85,000 (in other words, an additional $35,000 over what he has already received). In deal terms that's his realistic expectation.

Through Alice's looking glass. Alliance's lawyer advises Alice that if Cory's report is as deficient as she says it is, Alliance has a fighting chance of prevailing on a claim for refund of the entire fee. As for the deal terms, Alice has a clear memory of agreeing upon a $100,000 maximum, but there is one bothersome detail. In going through Alice's papers, Alliance's lawyer came across an internal memorandum concerning Cory's consulting assignment, on which this marginal note appears in Alice's handwriting: "100K (plus?)." It might have meant nothing more than that Cory was unsuccessfully trying to bargain for more than $100,000. But Alliance's lawyer knows it could also be interpreted as supporting Cory's $100,000-as-a-*minimum* argument and contradicting Alice's recollection.

Alice and Alliance have no desire to litigate. It will involve too much time, expense, bother, and uncertainty. The existence of this memo—which would have to be furnished to Cory in the discovery proceedings that go hand in hand with the lawsuit—makes such a course even less desirable. Alice also recognizes the difficulty of proving that the number of hours it took Cory to do the job was inherently wasteful. And the odds are against her prevailing on the "deficient report" theory. Putting these all together, she's worried that the judge would end up accepting Cory's $125,000 figure.

What's Alice's realistic expectation? For rough calculation purposes, she uses $125,000 as a measure of the likely judgment but shaves it down to $120,000 because of the lack of certainty. She then applies to that number Alliance's chance of success on the inadequate report issue, which (after questioning her lawyer) she estimates at 40 percent. She increases the result by $12,500 of estimated legal fees. When the dust clears she's in the same $85,000 settlement area as Cory.

Competing strategies. Thus, in the privacy of their own offices, Cory and Alice have roughly similar views as to where a reasonable resolution of this dispute could take place. Neither of them, however, knows the other's mind-set. Meanwhile, Cory's demanding the full $125,000, Alice is trying to get Alliance's initial $50,000 back, and the thermometer is rising. So the question is, how do they arrive at the compromise that's ripe for the picking?

The linchpin of Cory's strategy should be to persuade Alice that he's prepared to sue to enforce his claim. If Alice were to think that Cory might just go away mad with the $50,000 that's already in his pocket, she would be well advised to hang tough. That's a fine result for Alliance, since Alice isn't that serious about trying to recover the amount paid up-front. So Cory has to hire a litigator right off the bat—and not quietly, either. If Alice still isn't convinced that he will sue (failing a settlement), then he might actually have to bring the suit.

At the same time, Cory should make clear to Alice that in a settlement he would be willing to take less than his $125,000 claim. Demands for unconditional surrender don't advance the ball in dispute resolution. If Alice believes that Cory is going to stick at or around the amount of his claim, she has little reason to fear litigation. After all, that's the *worst* Alliance can do—and it might fare a lot better. So for example, Cory might say: "I'm sure neither of us *wants* a lawsuit. So while I believe a court would award me the full one hundred and twenty-five thousand dollars, I'm prepared to accept something less than that in settlement to avoid the time and expense of litigation."

As for Alice, of course, she has to appear undaunted by the prospect of litigation. If she seems apprehensive, Cory will push too hard a bargain on the settlement, thinking he holds all the cards. One way for Alice to show she's unfazed is to have Alliance's lawyer write Cory a letter demanding return of the $50,000 down payment, "failing which Alliance will be forced to take all appropriate action to enforce its rights."

But Alice also has to make it clear that in a settlement (as contrasted with a lawsuit), she won't press for return of the initial $50,000. Since settlement discussions aren't admissible in evidence, this wouldn't undercut her position if she has to go to court. And, in fact, she'll be willing to make *some* additional payment, although nothing like the amount that Cory is claiming.

Sue first? Now that both sides have engaged lawyers, should either of them commence a lawsuit *before* attempting to negotiate? This doesn't make sense from Alice's viewpoint, since she has too little to gain (given the uphill fight Alliance faces in getting back its initial $50,000) and more to lose from litigation. I also think that Cory (whose threat of litigation hovers overhead) is better off refraining from filing suit immediately, in order to give negotiation a chance. Once the lawsuit begins, Alice may be less inclined to sit down and talk. Her dander will be up over Cory's "audacity" in suing Alliance after turning in that "shoddy" report.

Of course, if Cory suspected the existence of Alice's damaging memo, he might sue to gain access to it. Some people have been known to commence litigation just to avail themselves of the discovery process—to mount a "fishing expedition" for any harmful documents that might exist. Any evidence *validating* Alliance's posture, by contrast, would no doubt have already been shown to him, in order to increase Alliance's bargaining leverage. For example, if the note had read "100K (*minus?*)," you can bet that Alice would have waved it in Cory's face at the first opportunity.

Who speaks? Assuming that negotiations will take place before suit is brought, who should conduct them—the principals or their lawyers? I'm assuming, for these purposes, that the lawyers for both sides are fully aware of what's going on and have consented to the talks, thereby eliminating any ethical problems that might otherwise be posed. Who conducts such talks can vary with the circumstances, but my sense here is that the negotiations are likely to be more productive if Cory and Alice start off by themselves. Certainly each of them should consult counsel behind the scenes. But it may be wise to keep the litigators, who might come on too strong in the initial sessions, out of the direct line of fire for the time being.

On the other hand, these talks are best conducted in an atmosphere free of rancor. Unfortunately, a sense of distrust is in the air. Alice probably feels that Cory lowballed the estimate, fudged the fee structure, screwed up on the staffing, and produced an inferior product. Cory, on the other hand, suspects that Alice is "misremembering" the fee arrangement in order to welsh on Alliance's obligation. These kinds of emotions aren't conducive to settling. At the very least they create in the parties a sense of ambivalence about whether to compromise or go to war. If Cory and Alice are so mad at each other that they can't carry on a rational conversation, the lawyers may have to get together.

Who initiates? Who should launch the talks? I don't think this matters, as long as it's handled appropriately. Of course, all things being equal, I usually prefer to have the initiative come from the *other* party—whichever side I find myself on. But I wouldn't wait forever before my side made the call. So, for example, if Cory wanted to initiate talks, he could telephone Alice and say, "Look, before we let the lawyers take over our lives here, why don't we get together and see if we can work out something that makes sense."

Or Alice could call Cory and say, with a little more bite, "Before I pay my lawyer a lot of money to keep me from having to pay you *any* money—and, in fact, to get what I've paid *back*—why don't we sit down and talk? Perhaps, if you can be reasonable about this unfortunate circumstance, we can work this out in a way that's satisfactory to both of us."

Content of talks. Once the talks commence, each party will trot out its strongest arguments. The operating premise, which makes sense, is that the more successfully a party can seize the high ground—emphasizing the equities favoring its position—the better it's likely to fare in the negotiations. In part this is because persuasiveness is always a strong card at the bargaining table. But when a dispute is involved, there's the added factor of acquainting the other side with how these equities will play out in the courthouse should talks break down.

The two big collateral issues here are the quality of Cory's report and the efficiency with which he went about preparing it. If I were Alice, those are the themes I would harp on, arguing along the following lines: "You estimated you could do the job for one hundred thousand dollars. I believed that was the maximum; but even if it wasn't, that was the inducement for me to go forward. I wouldn't have hired you if I thought it would cost a hundred and twenty-five thousand. You put junior people on the job, who were learning their trade at my expense. And your report reflects that. It's simply not usable. I hate paying *anything* for something that's worthless to me." And she should imply that were word to get around about how unhappy Alliance was with the quality and efficiency of Cory's work, it would be damaging to his efforts to land future assignments elsewhere.

Cory has some explaining to do about that $25,000 "overrun," particularly since he didn't give Alice any advance warning about the extra time he was running up. In order to end up with a satisfactory settlement, he has to be able to justify his fee. And the real key to that is the usefulness of his work. As Alice said, no one likes to pay for something that's worthless. Admittedly Alliance could be using this argument as a bargaining chip. But if Alice is serious, Cory has to persuade her that at least his *analysis* is valid and useful, even if Alliance chooses not to adopt his recommendations.

So Cory should suggest to Alice that they put aside their dispute for the moment, sit down together, and give him a chance to understand why she feels his report is worthless. And, by the way, he won't charge her for *this* time! He may find, after hearing Alice's objections, that without too much additional work he can recast the report so that it becomes more helpful. At that point its settlement value would go up sharply.

A possible scenario. Here's the way the bargaining might go from there. Alliance makes the first offer, which is to let Cory keep the initial $50,000 and take another $10,000 for his trouble. Cory's counteroffer is to accept $112,500—the number that is halfway between the disputed $100,000 and $125,000 figures—as payment in full. If Alliance's first offer were really chintzy, such as one that called on Cory to refund $25,000 of the $50,000 in his pocket, he would be better off not to counter. At the same time he could suggest that if Alice were to offer him something reasonable, he would be willing to enter into serious negotiations.

Alliance now edges up to $70,000, while Cory comes down to $100,000. If Alice can persuade Cory that his reputation is at stake, and if he can persuade her that he wasn't wasteful and the report is usable, they should ultimately strike a deal in the vicinity of $85,000.

How do you think this might differ if Cory hadn't received *any* down payment up-front? Now Alliance wouldn't be one cent out of pocket, while all Cory has to show for his trouble is the threat of a lawsuit. Alliance would probably hang a lot tougher. (Shades of your dealings with Walter the waiter back in the introduction!) If Cory still prefers not to sue, he might have to settle for something in the neighborhood of $62,500, roughly half of his $125,000 demand.

Let's face it, the old saw about possession being nine-tenths of the law is right on the nose. This is something that must *always* be factored into the equation—and not just when you're trying to resolve a dispute. You should have it very much in mind when you're negotiating the original business deal that could end up *resulting* in litigation, particularly in addressing such issues as how much of the money will be paid in advance and how much held back pending performance.

NEGOTIATING POINTERS

Here are a few pointers on conducting negotiations to resolve disputes.

• Make an effort to persuade your adversary that it's in his best interests to settle. It must be in *your* interest, or you wouldn't be at the table; but your adversary may not yet be convinced that settlement is advantageous for him, too. Probe to find out why he's reluctant and then deal directly with the problem.

• Be persistent. There's no quick fix in settlement discussions. One case I handled involved settlement talks, interspersed by litigation maneuvers, that went on for a number of years. You simply have to stick with it, no matter what the frustrations. Instant gratification is for bowlers.

• Be creative. There may be things other than whacking up a pot of cash that can bring the parties together. Say, for example, there's a question about the value of disputed property. The property happens to be a natural resource that's divisible. It may be possible to transfer some of the property itself in the settlement, instead of reaching an impasse trying to agree on an equivalent dollar value.

• Appreciate the significance of time. Payments spread out over a number of years contain both a financial and psychological dimension. The recipient can say "I settled for fifty thousand dollars," which is the face amount of the payments. The payor can say "I got rid of the case for thirty-five thousand dollars"—the net present value of the future installments.

• Try a piecemeal approach. If your initial discussions have isolated several difficult issues, attack them separately. By chopping the overall settlement into parts, you may achieve a series of small accords that, taken together, pave the way for the ultimate resolution.

ALTERNATIVE DISPUTE RESOLUTION

There is another process that, although still far from realizing its full potential, has enjoyed burgeoning popularity in recent years: alternative dispute resolution, or ADR for short. In many disputes you're caught between a rock and a hard place. The rock is *litigation*, which as a means of resolving a dispute is frustrating, time-consuming, expensive, and full of friction. Furthermore, the parties surrender their ultimate control over the outcome. The hard place is *negotiation*, which can often prove unavailing as a means of reaching accord between two disputants, each of whom has strong feelings about the matter.

The purpose of ADR is to escape from this dilemma by using neutral third parties in a variety of ways to help resolve disputes— mediating, facilitating negotiations, rendering advisory opinions, and so on. Unlike arbitration (which is basically a substitute for litigation), the parties to the dispute who invoke ADR still retain the right to say yea or nay. If ADR fails to produce a mutually acceptable settlement, the parties can then resort to litigation or binding arbitration.

The availability of ADR depends on the willingness of both parties to consent to its use. That consent may be hard to come by at the time the dispute ripens. Thus it makes sense to include in the written contract governing the deal a provision mandating the use of ADR should a dispute arise.

In my view the most significant role a neutral third party can play is as an agent of reality. This works best if each side has had an opportunity to present its best case to the neutral. When the neutral then tells the decision maker for one of the parties that *his* case is a loser, it represents the most sobering kind of judgment; and the party so advised is likely to adopt a much more reasonable attitude toward talking settlement from that point on. This happened to a giant financial institution in a case where, fortunately, I was representing the other side! We had been miles apart in the initial negotiations. But once the neutral spoke, the institution quickly saw the light, and we were able to settle the dispute on terms favorable to us.

DISPUTES WRAP-UP

Keynote

Be cognizant of the two big differences between negotiating disputes and deals. One is the heightened emotion usually present in the dispute, which requires a real effort to keep tamped down. The other is the omnipresent litigation alternative; like it or not, the caliber and probable outcome of your case furnishes a major leverage element that's central to determining your realistic expectation.

Blunder

The mistake is in demanding unconditional surrender, or close to it, as the price for resolving a dispute. This virtually guarantees that no settlement will result. Don't let your heart rule your head.

Lapse

The omission is waiting around for the other side to blink. Each side is fearful of displaying weakness; as a result no settlement dialogue ever takes place.

13 TOUGH TACTICS, GOING TO CONTRACT, AND MORE

As both a negotiator and teacher, I'm often asked questions about many of the situations and tactics people encounter at the bargaining table. Let's look now at some of these, and I'll try to answer the queries most commonly posed.

PSYCHOLOGICAL WARFARE

I haven't stressed the various psychological ploys that some negotiating pundits exalt, because I've never put much stock in them. But since your counterpart might be one of *their* disciples, I should comment on a few common varieties.

IS THE PLACE OF MEETING SIGNIFICANT?

The general view seems to be that there's a home court advantage to negotiating a deal at your place rather than the other side's. I've never quite understood this. Is it because the visitor is viewed as a supplicant, or his willingness to meet on the host's turf as a sign of weakness? Personally I don't buy it.

I might prefer being on home grounds, but only for reasons of convenience unrelated to the outcome of the negotiations. If it's just as easy to meet at my counterpart's office, I readily acquiesce in his suggestion to do so—and sometimes I even propose it myself. In any event, most negotiations require multiple sessions, so the venue can be varied to balance things out.

Geography can be harmful, however, if you make a big deal about where the meeting is going to take place and *then* acquiesce to your counterpart's demand. This may suggest to him that holding his ground on *substantive* issues will eventually produce similar results.

How about the number of people present?

Some negotiators think that the side with more people at a bargaining session enjoys an advantage. As a result there's sometimes a lot of jockeying over the permissible number each party can bring to the table. This has always struck me as foolish. In fact, I'll let you in on a secret. My favorite negotiating lineup is when I'm alone and the other side has several people present. Not that I'm attracted to the role of underdog; rather, it's because I can now control what *my side* says, which isn't the case when I'm accompanied by clients or colleagues. Meanwhile the other side, speaking through multiple mouths, is more likely to let slip useful information or inadvertently expose conflicting viewpoints.

Two caveats here, however. First, it's not a good idea to let the other side possess particular weapons you lack. If your counterpart has a lawyer present, you should probably have one, too. If the subject matter is technical and his technician is seated at the table, call yours in. If taxes loom large, match his tax expert with your own.

Second, there are certain times when more progress can be made in a session limited to just a few key people, rather than enduring the crosscurrents generated by multiple participants. In those instances, don't hesitate to restrict the guest list to each side's decision maker and most significant adviser.

What should I do about a stressful atmosphere?

Some people fret over working conditions that affect their stress level: a seat with the sun in their eyes, a chair lower than their counterpart's, no food or drink in sight, and so forth. Suffice it to say, don't let anyone put you in an uncomfortable situation. Move your chair; stand up tall; ask for a glass of water.

What if I run into a "good cop–bad cop" routine?

Sometimes you come up against a team of negotiators—Victor and Victoria, for instance—who use a routine in which Good Victoria almost appears to be on *your* side against her stubborn or obstinate cohort, Bad Victor. Ultimately Bad Victor proves to be so unyielding that Good Victoria is "reluctantly" forced to suggest further concessions on your part in order to satisfy Bad Victor's insatiable appetite.

Be alert to such assaults on your intelligence. Don't take your negotiating advice from *anyone* on the other side.

THREATS

The most common pressure tactic in negotiating is the threat. In its general form the maker tells the target that unless he acquiesces to the maker's demands, the maker will take some action—perhaps in regard to other existing relations between the parties—that will harm the target. It's a means of gaining one's objectives that relies less on persuasion and more on intimidating the other side into surrendering something of value.

WHAT'S THE MOST EFFECTIVE WAY TO GO ABOUT THREATENING?

For a threat to cause trepidation, it has to possess three attributes:

- The threatened consequence has to *worry* the target, at least in private, even if he feigns public indifference.
- The target has to believe that the maker is *capable* of implementing the threat.
- The target must think there's a good chance that the maker actually *intends* to carry it out.

In many cases the first two attributes are present, and the real key becomes the issue of the maker's credibility, a subject we explored previously in other forms in chapter 4. If he doesn't get his way, will the maker do what he says he'll do—or is he bluffing?

To achieve credibility you can't threaten to do too much. People are more responsive to realistic threats than massive ones. Unless the threat bears some reasonable relationship to the situation, it simply won't be believed. If, for instance, you threaten to abort a thriving business relationship over some minor disagreement, your counterpart is unlikely to lose much sleep. Even worse, you leave the impression that anyone who would even *think* of such a thing must be nuts—and who wants to do business with a lunatic? So make sure that the issues on which you bare your teeth are significant—not some mere sideshow.

The timing of the threat can also be significant. A threat issued *after* some real (but unfruitful) effort to resolve the deadlock is usually more meaningful than one uttered at the outset of the negotiations. I've also found that a logical explanation, if one exists, as to why you'll be *forced* to take the threatened action, increases the likelihood that you'll be believed. It further serves to blunt some of the target's negative reaction to the threat.

In order to be taken seriously on a major threat, you may have to build up your credibility with a lesser one or two. Several years ago, when I represented TWA against Carl Icahn's takeover, we engaged in some spirited negotiations. Icahn, a tough negotiator, uses threats as one of his tactical mainstays. He would frequently tell us, in the course of bargaining over some collateral issue, that the proposal he was making was available only if we agreed to it on the spot, or within the next twenty-four hours, or over the weekend.

The first few times Icahn used this tactic, we ignored the threat, taking whatever time was necessary in order to reply. Icahn must have realized the need to do something that would lend more credibility to the subsequent threats he would undoubtedly be making over larger issues. So one day he actually *withdrew* a proposal that we hadn't acted on within the prescribed period. After that, when he employed this sort of pressure, we had to assign the threat a relatively greater degree of credibility.

The most important single element in making a threat credible is that it be one you're *prepared to implement,* even though you might prefer not to. It's hard enough to convince the target that you mean business when you really do; it's a tough uphill battle when you're bluffing. My advice here is simple: *If you're not prepared to carry out the threat, don't threaten.* Given the combative way many people respond to threats, there's too much risk that your bluff will be called—at which point, you'll be revealed to the world as a paper tiger.

Should I use threats as a bargaining tactic?

In case you haven't guessed it by now, I don't like to bargain by using threats, even if I'm not bluffing and have the power and will to carry them out. A threat often angers the target, and it's more likely to cause him to harden his position than to do what the maker demands. Worse still, the target's frequent response to a threat is a counter-threat, to which the maker replies in kind, and away we go—with no one wanting to cave in to the pressure.

Still, I'm in favor of using legitimate leverage in negotiations, and the underlying subject matter of the threat often falls into this category. Perhaps it's something that the other side isn't aware of, or hasn't focused on, or doesn't think you would resort to. If so, you may want to devise a nonthreatening means of getting the point across, perhaps a more subtle link that doesn't provoke a direct confrontation. A word of caution, however. If you're going to be subtle, just make sure you're not *so* artful that the target doesn't even know he's being politely threatened!

One way to proceed here is by issuing a *warning* instead of a threat. A warning is intended to caution your counterpart about the negative consequences that may flow from certain conduct or inaction. Those consequences should appear to be *independent* of your will, as contrasted with repercussions that you're threatening consciously to bring about.

I confess, however, that the distinction between warning and threat may be more apparent than real. I recall another session with Carl Icahn when he really got under my skin with several outright threats and I finally exploded: "Carl, I'm not going to listen to any more of your threats. Unless you stop that, we're just going home."

"Okay, Jim," Carl said soothingly, "I promise there won't be any more threats. Let's keep going."

Five minutes later he said, "Now, Jim, this isn't a threat, but I just want you to know what could happen if you guys were to do that," at which point he proceeded to spell out exactly the same kind of threat he had been using all day! Fortunately, instead of blowing up, we all enjoyed a big laugh—Icahn included—which served to break the tension and enabled us to get down to real business.

WHAT SHOULD I DO IF SOMEONE THREATENS ME?

Let's imagine now that you're the *target* of a threat that carries real weight, one that the maker is capable of implementing and, for all you know, intends to carry out. How should you respond?

Assume first that the threat is uttered in a bullying manner: loud voice, purple face, fists pounding the table. The temptation is to scream right back. Don't do it. It's much more effective to stay cool, admonishing the maker to "dispense with the theatrics and get back to business." If he persists, you may be "forced to call it a day," thus leaving him without an audience to intimidate.

Now, assume the threat is more run of the mill—overt, but with no melodramatic effects. One way for you to react is simply to ignore the threat. This strikes me as dangerous, however. Your lack of response could be misinterpreted by the maker as fear, suggesting that his threat has struck a nerve and achieved the intimidation he sought. Another possible reaction is to claim that the threat has no value. This is effective, however, only when it's believable. If implementation of the threat would clearly harm you, I don't recommend this reply.

I also don't encourage the common response of a counterthreat, which escalates the confrontation in a dangerous way. The original maker is now tempted to up the ante, and who knows where it will all end?

Here's how I handle threats directed at me or my client, distinguishing between the subtle and overt varieties. When I pick up a *subtle* threat, I decide among three courses of action. The first is to ignore it, showing by my subsequent actions that it hasn't affected me. The second is to call attention to the threat, but with a light touch to show it has no value. "Do I detect a veiled threat in that last soliloquy," I might say, "or is my natural paranoia just showing through?" The third is to force the maker to make the threat explicit and thereby provoke a confrontation. "What did you mean by that last crack?" I may state sternly. "Are you threatening me?" Which of the three I choose depends on the threat, the maker, and the context in which the threat is issued.

When the threat is *overt*, I favor a two-part response. First, I always reply to the threat; I don't just let it hang there. For example, take the threat frequently made in a dispute situation: "Either agree to our terms or we'll sue you." Anyone with a typewriter and postage stamp can bring a lawsuit; you can't stop someone from suing. But since the implication of "we'll sue" is "we'll sue *and win*," the way to handle this threat is to assure the maker that he'll be clobbered in court, even if the outcome of the case isn't quite so clear. Don't ever let your counterpart feel you're cowed by his litigation threat. That may blind him from seeing the need to compromise his position.

Then, after countering the threat, I like to move things to a more practical plane by saying something like this: "We could discuss the merits of a lawsuit all day. But wouldn't it be more constructive for us to focus on whether there's some way to resolve our differences?"

NEGOTIATIONS BETWEEN CORPORATE AND MULTIPLE PARTIES

In the business world negotiations aren't always of the one-on-one variety, and the individuals who conduct them often represent organizations. Needless to say, this can add to the difficulties.

WHAT'S DIFFERENT IF ONE OF THE PARTIES IS A CORPORATION?

The major distinction in negotiating with a corporate party (or any large organization) is the necessity to consult various constituencies to obtain the corporate seal of approval. Each of the staff functions—tax, accounting, legal, employee benefits, and so on—is likely to have a say; and several echelons of corporate hierarchy may have to sign off before the deal is sealed. As a result, when you're sitting opposite a representative of a corporation, don't let yourself get too far out in front. Be careful about signifying your willingness to accept terms that, although agreeable to the corporate executive across the table, haven't yet been confirmed by the requisite authorities.

The ultimate frustration occurs in those significant matters where the corporation needs the approval of its board of directors (or a committee of the board) to conclude the deal. The board or committee meets only at periodic intervals and prefers to address fully negotiated transactions. Under these circumstances you may find that by agreeing to the deal terms, you've given the corporation—which isn't even morally committed until its board acts—an informal option. And the worst part is that you won't even be present at the board or committee meeting in order to influence the outcome.

The best way to equalize this kind of corporate leverage is to stipulate that the deal you've negotiated is indissoluble, that the corporate hierarchy or board has to vote it up or down as a package but can't pick and choose among the elements. And where a board is involved, don't be bashful about insisting that the corporate management go on record formally as recommending approval. None of this wishy-washy neutrality. You want the board to have to *override* the judgment of its hand-picked officers in order to nix the deal. On the other hand, when you find yourself on the *corporation's* side, you'll undoubtedly want to use this institutional process to your advantage, maneuvering the other side into precisely these kinds of snares!

Whenever the real decision maker for either side isn't present for the bargaining, you have a situation sometimes dubbed "the empty chair at the table." If the absent decision maker is on your side, you may use that circumstance to your advantage. When the other side takes an unacceptable position, you can say "I *know* our CEO and what his thinking is. There's no way I'm going to be able to get his approval of anything less than five hundred thousand dollars." Or, under a different set of facts, "My boss is going to need something a lot higher than the four hundred thousand you're offering if you expect her to do this deal." If the other side's decision maker isn't there, don't let yourself be manipulated by reason of the resulting imbalance. That empty chair often turns out to have an insatiable appetite, but keeping it gorged isn't your responsibility.

WHAT COMPLEXITIES RESULT WHEN MORE THAN TWO PARTIES ARE INVOLVED?

Multiparty negotiations often get tricky; two may tango, but three can entangle. Still, the basic principles remain the same as for two-sided bargaining. Without delving too far into the complexities, let me identify three common situations and offer a helpful tip for each.

The needed consent. You're doing a deal with Victoria that requires her to get the consent of Victor, who has contractual or other rights against Victoria or the property involved in the negotiations. Victor, as you might expect, has his hand out; you can bet that his consent is going to be costly.

This may look like *Victoria's* problem, not yours, but unfortunately the cost of Victor's intransigence is often passed on to you, directly or indirectly. Be alert to this; and if you sense it happening, then make sure to get *yourself* involved in those Victoria-Victor negotiations, lest you find your bucks being dispensed unwisely.

Divvying up the damage. Victor has a claim against you and Victoria, which you both dispute but recognize will have to be settled. In addition, however, you and Victoria disagree over what portion each of you will bear of the amount ultimately needed to resolve Victor's claim. This raises plenty of issues and can place you in some uncomfortable positions. For instance, what you say to rebut an argument from Victor might actually strengthen Victoria's hand vis-à-vis you.

To my mind, however, the key issue here (as in many three-party situations) is *sequencing.* Do you *first* reach agreement with Victor on what he'll take by way of settlement and *then* work out the split between you and Victoria—or vice versa? Your goal is to avoid the discomfort of hammering out a difficult agreement with the first party, only to find the second party unwilling to accept terms that fit your first deal, forcing you then to go back and renegotiate with the first party.

There's no all-purpose answer to this common multiparty issue, but at least in *this* scenario I know what my typical advice would be. Before commencing serious negotiations with Victor, you and Victoria should work out jointly your realistic expectation and starting point for the Victor talks, as well as how the two of you will share any ultimate payment to him under various probable outcomes. Otherwise you'll have lots of trouble figuring out where to begin with Victor, what concessions are appropriate, and how to arrange the ultimate compromise.

Whacking up the pie. You, Victor, and Victoria are negotiating an agreement that would redound to the benefit of each of you in varying degrees. An example here would be combining your three businesses in order to gain an added degree of clout or avail yourselves of certain synergies.

In my experience this kind of situation seldom remains purely triangular. More commonly, two of the parties get together in a two-against-one alignment. If you're the *one*, this kind of pressure can prove hard to resist, particularly if the other two have the additional leverage of being able to accomplish most of their goals without you in the picture. So my advice here is simple: Don't fly solo! Make sure you're part of a twosome, even if that requires some generous concessions to your would-be partner.

BARGAINING ON THE TELEPHONE

In an ideal world, all negotiations would be conducted face to face. You can learn a lot sitting across a table; you're likely to be more persuasive looking your counterpart squarely in the eye. But in today's fast-paced world, things don't always work out that way. The telephone may be impossible to avoid, especially when the parties reside in different cities.

SHOULD I SHUN NEGOTIATIONS ON THE PHONE?

The literature and the lore of bargaining used to caution against reliance on the telephone. In my experience, however, although working by phone is not as effective as negotiating in person, there's no reason to shy away from it, particularly now that fax machines and overnight mail delivery enable you to have the document under discussion in front of you while you talk.

Of course, there are shortcomings. The worst of these occur when there are a number of people at different locations. Although everyone can be plugged into a conference call, it becomes very disconcerting when several people try to talk at once. You can't confer with your own side as developments occur; and there's no telephonic substitute for those sidewise looks, or handwritten notes, or caucuses outside the conference room. But in the end you really have no choice. The telephone has become essential to fill the gaps of a multisession negotiation. So you may as well master the technique.

WHAT SHOULD I BE PARTICULARLY CONSCIOUS OF ON THE PHONE?

Let's say things begin very casually. Your counterpart calls you on the phone and starts in to negotiate. This can be dangerous. You should be just as prepared on the telephone as you would be for a meeting. If you're unprepared, don't negotiate. Hear your counterpart out; but before conceding anything or taking a step that could cause trouble down the road, tell him you'll call back later. This suggests that it may be to *your* advantage to initiate the call, at a time of your choosing. If you do, who knows, maybe your unprepared counterpart will then plunge ahead to his detriment.

If you're like me, the minute you hang up a telephone you remember something you wanted to say during the call. So when I'm the one initiating a negotiating call, I generally jot down in advance a list of the points I want to make, just so nothing slips between the cracks. Also, although I don't usually take many notes in face-to-face meetings—preferring instead to observe what's going on around the table—I feel no such restraint on the phone. These notes can prove helpful during the post mortem briefing session with other members of your side who weren't privy to the conversation.

Make a special effort to be clear on the telephone. Misunderstandings occur more readily when you're speaking into a machine; unintended ambiguities and secondary meanings have a way of slipping in. So don't be reluctant to repeat yourself, to ask your counterpart to reiterate his proposal, and to summarize what has been agreed upon and what's open.

The importance of being a good listener applies in spades to telephone negotiations. You may be able to pick up clues from the content or tone of what's being said: pregnant pauses, agitation in the voice, and other verbal equivalents of body language. Resist the tendency to talk too much yourself, a temptation especially prevalent when you've initiated the call. Don't be so anxious to reply to your counterpart's arguments that you interrupt all the time. It's bound to irritate him; besides, he has to finish speaking before he'll be ready to listen.

Silence, which can be a powerful negotiating weapon, is particularly potent on the phone. Your counterpart may feel compelled to fill the conversational void with implicit concessions or disclosures of helpful information. Conversely, if he tries to give you the silent treatment, don't feel compelled to accept responsibility for keeping the conversation alive. Should silence prove too difficult, you can pose questions that bring your counterpart back into the dialogue, questions that can't be answered "yes" or "no" but require some elaboration on his part.

PUTTING IT IN WRITING

Even when a basic deal has been struck, going to contract is no picnic. The parties may have *agreed to agree*, but people can change their minds, particularly if a major development occurs during the time it takes to complete the contract. A purchaser, for example, may lose heart watching the financial condition of the business he's buying deteriorate. A seller may think seriously about reneging on Buyer 1 when Buyer 2 appears out of the blue, ready and willing to pay more for the seller's property.

Even if nothing changes, difficulties can arise when the parties attempt to "put it in writing." Invariably the major deal terms turn out to be more complex than they seemed when negotiated initially, leading to further conflict as each side jockeys for position. The same jousting occurs over those issues that the parties have deliberately left to be negotiated during the contract phase. And sometimes one party is just looking for an edge or trying to retract a point conceded previously.

If the effort to reach agreement in principle has been arduous, the parties may be only a stone's throw away from saying "To hell with it." Then, when those inevitable second thoughts intrude, it doesn't take much to push them back over the line. Negotiating the proposed contract often provides that push. It is, in fact, a project that can bog down the best of negotiators, not only in coping with the real issues, but also in dealing with the mountain of minutiae. The currencies in which a formal contract trades—representations and warranties, covenants and conditions, tax and accounting matters—lend themselves to discord. And the lawyers, who should be a positive factor, can also be a real pain in the neck.

So, for various reasons, many deals come unglued at this stage. This is particularly true in the case of a *dispute* whose resolution isn't simple. All the distrust and paranoia and ambivalence come to the fore ("I *told* you that son of a bitch never intended to settle!")—and as Yogi Berra warned us, "It ain't over 'til it's over!"

GIVEN THE RISK OF THINGS UNRAVELING, DO I NEED A WRITTEN CONTRACT?

My general advice is to get it in writing, painful as that process may be. Of course, an *oral* agreement can sometimes be binding, although in most cases it's safer to assume that a written agreement is required. But the real problem with oral agreements, as someone once observed, is that they're not worth the paper they're not written on! People recall things in ways that suit their advantage; the passage of time can impair relationships; the individual who negotiated the original deal (when a company is involved) may have moved on to greener pastures. Bottom line: it's your word against your counterpart's.

Contracts aren't perfect and can themselves generate disputes over what was intended. But by and large they form a bulwark of stability in the commercial world. In my experience most contracts are honored—whether out of a sense of moral commitment, or the residual threat of legal enforcement, or a little of both. Still, there are times when you've negotiated a favorable deal that you fear will disintegrate under contractual scrutiny. If you consider your counterpart an honorable person, you might choose to rely on the meeting of minds, at least until the moment for going to contract seems more propitious; but you should be fully aware of your vulnerability if your counterpart later suffers a change of heart.

IF I'M GOING TO CONTRACT, SHOULD I SIGN A "LETTER OF INTENT" FIRST?

There's no invariable answer here. The letter of intent (sometimes called a "memorandum of understanding" or "heads of agreement" or "deal memo"), although typically not binding, serves to codify the basic terms you've agreed to in principle during protracted contract negotiations. It represents an explicit moral obligation of the parties, which principled businesspeople take seriously. (You might even call it a cheap form of antirenegotiation insurance.) On the other hand, going directly to contract may make more sense than expending energy to negotiate a letter of intent, especially when the contract shouldn't take too long and you want to get the other side bound as soon as possible.

In deciding which course to follow, be sure to give special weight to the psychological and leverage factors. The individual who has just agreed to sell his business, for example, often suffers a major psychic wrench—the familiar "giving up his baby" syndrome. This is a bad time for the buyer to send over a one-hundred-page definitive contract, replete with legalese. A two-page letter of intent, which morally binds the seller to complete the deal, better serves the buyer's purpose at this juncture.

As for leverage, always consider whether having a letter of intent in place will improve or worsen your bargaining strength for the contract negotiations to come. For example, buyers like to insert a provision in the letter of intent which restricts the seller to conducting exclusive negotiations with this buyer until a final contract is either signed or the deal abandoned. As the seller, you may feel this undercuts the leverage you would enjoy if the buyer had to worry about your holding concurrent negotiations with other potential purchasers.

DOES IT MAKE ANY DIFFERENCE WHICH SIDE DRAFTS THE CONTRACT?

It sure does. If you're looking for an advantage, make certain your side seizes the opportunity to draft the contract. Why do I say this? Because drafting offers you so many options: choices in how to introduce and phrase a concept, the ability to omit points or language, the deliberate use of ambiguity, and so on. At least *some* of your edges are bound to slip by the critical gaze of the other side. And since the other side doesn't necessarily know what's troubling you, it's possible to draft around your own concerns.

Another real plus from being the draftsman is the control it gives your side over the *timing* of the deal. It's easier to push your own lawyer to turn out the next draft of the contract quickly than to get the other side moving. Conversely, when delay suits your purpose, your lawyer is a more malleable culprit.

Some businesspeople worry that it will cost them more in legal fees for their lawyer to do the drafting. That may be true, although not necessarily, especially if your lawyer has to spend hours sanitizing the other side's overreaching draft. But all I can tell you is that this will be the best extra money you've spent in the deal.

In certain transactions an etiquette has developed over who handles the initial drafting: landlords draft leases, financial institutions prepare loan documents, and so on. In other situations the identity of the appropriate draftsman isn't clearly defined, so you can seize the baton. Since most experienced lawyers are aware of the drafting advantage, you may run into some opposition here. But others don't think about it, or are too busy (or lazy), or consider themselves smart enough to catch any curveballs that might come their way.

Remember, however, if the people on the other side think that letting your side draft the contract would work to their disadvantage, they might feel obliged to volunteer for the task. So it behooves you (and your lawyer) to introduce the subject in a way that masks your desire. Don't look as if you're salivating for the assignment. Simply make it appear that you're willing to undertake a necessary evil.

WHAT'S THE BEST WAY TO REPLY TO THE OTHER SIDE'S DRAFT?

There are various means of response. A common method is to go over the draft with the other side at a meeting, enumerate your suggested changes orally, negotiate the substance of the provisions, and then have the original draftsman revise the draft to reflect any modifications agreed upon. If your revisions are numerous or complex, you may want to incorporate them in a memo which you deliver prior to or at the bargaining session. Nowadays, however, the recipient frequently just "marks up" the original draft with handwritten suggested changes, plus typed riders containing longer provisions, and sends it back to the draftsman.

This last method has the virtue of seizing at least part of the drafting impetus. But unless the original draftsman is hapless, it's not wise to revise his contract completely—or, worse yet, put it on your own word processor! In the friendly adversarial world, it's considered bad form to press for *stylistic* changes. Save yourself for the *substance*. The fully negotiated contract is unlikely to be enshrined in the National Archives.

Just one caution to those who subscribe to the mark-it-up-and-send-it-back school of response. Always consider the other side's likely reaction to your markup. Are you introducing some new concepts that haven't been discussed previously? Have you included provisions that, on the surface, might seem onerous or overreaching but could be made to seem more benign and "ordinary course" with appropriate explanation? If so, you might want to raise such points for the first time at a face-to-face meeting. It's a setting in which you can be persuasive and responsive to the other side's concerns, as contrasted with the sterility of inserting a significant new wrinkle via the fax machine.

WHAT ARE SOME OF THE MAJOR BLUNDERS AND LAPSES EACH SIDE MAKES IN THE COURSE OF DRAFTING AND RESPONSE?

Here are a few, keyed to the party identified:

The draftsman. In drafting a contract, the draftsman typically marks up a prior model rather than starting from scratch. But when using a previously signed contract as the model for his markup, he often forgets that what he has in his hands represents the *end product* of the previous deal. As such, it bequeaths to the present recipient, gratis, the other side's work product from the prior deal! All those pesky revisions that were conceded back then are now fixed firmly in place, often defying efforts at excision. What the draftsman should do, of course, is go back to the *first draft* of the prior contract (which is buried somewhere in his files) and mark *that* up. But, believe me, this blunder happens time and time again.

The draftsman's client. Many businesspeople, appalled at the wordiness of a contract, are convinced the lawyer drafting it must be charging by the pound. To the client it appears that the draftsman is dredging up everything that could possibly go wrong and providing for it in explicit fashion. Just keep it nice and short, says the client— but that's his line *today.* When the day of reckoning comes, the lawyer had better beware if any normal protection was omitted.

To do his job properly, the lawyer has to advise the client what he thinks should be included in the draft. But before it's sent to the other side, the client should have an opportunity to make the business decision of whether to delete certain portions for the sake of brevity or to avoid confrontation.

The draftsman (again). Every draftsman (as well as the draftsman's client) should learn to appreciate the value of subtlety in shepherding a beneficial provision through the other side's review. Hit the other side over the head with a crowbar, and it's bound to react. Yet many lawyers can't help being tendentious in pounding home a point. Here's the way I look at it: I would much rather that my 75 percent–perfect provision remain in the contract intact because it's never opposed than have my 100 percent–perfect provision get watered down to 50 percent as a result of some hard adversarial bargaining.

The recipients of the draft. When you receive a draft contract, you must go over it thoroughly, searching for provisions of surface innocence that might prove onerous or omissions that have to be rectified. Never assume your counterpart has done your work for you; rather, speculate on just what edges he may be trying to take.

The big blunder occurs when the recipients examine the contract in the privacy of their respective offices. The lawyer has a good feel for the legalities but sparse factual background. The client has plenty of business know-how but not much appreciation of legal significance. Important matters may fall between the cracks. To avoid this, lawyer and client should always coordinate their review *before* going to meet with the other side.

THE LAST WORD ON SMART NEGOTIATING

I think you can now understand why, at the outset, I emphasized that negotiating is a *process.* The challenge to you as a negotiator is how skillfully you manage that process—beginning at a point prior to the actual talks, through the twists and turns of the bargaining cycle, to the successful completion (or abandonment) of the deal. I've outlined the major steps in "The Smart Negotiator's Checklist" at the end of the book. That's as far as I can take you. After that you're on your own.

I believe the approach to negotiating I've described in these pages will work well for you. You should have a good feel now for the positional dance that borrows the best aspects from both competitive and cooperative modes of bargaining. You're aware of the key skills needed. You have a game plan and a grasp of some of the special situations and complicating factors you may have to face.

I urge all of you to seek out new situations in which to test your negotiating skills. In this field, experience is the master teacher. You'll discover techniques and tactics that appeal to your instincts. If they work well, by all means use them. We each have to find our own way.

For example—I can't resist the temptation to provide you with just one more example—I'm particularly partial to stratagems that set things up for an amicable resolution. Let's assume you've concocted a solution to an issue on which the parties have clashed. You want it to be accepted by the other side as *the* solution, not as the prelude to another round of bargaining. My favorite technique to accomplish this is the "petard hoist": using your counterpart's own words to render your proposal irresistible.

Many negotiators are verbose, making unnecessary statements that seem innocuous when spoken yet return to plague them later on. Others are unaware that what they're saying in support of one objective may have potential negative significance elsewhere. Either way you can't afford to pass up the opportunity to foil your counterpart, right out of his own big mouth.

Sometimes the opportunity falls into your lap. If not, a little staging may be in order. A seemingly innocent line of questions can be useful here, but don't let your interrogation suggest cross-examination, which will put your counterpart on his guard. Above all, you have to plan ahead, knowing where you want to end up before the other side figures it out.

Let's take a simple example. Say you're negotiating the purchase of a used truck from Victor. Tentative agreement has been reached on a price of $8,000, but your inspection reveals the need for some work on the transmission. Although Victor has been downplaying this problem, you suspect it may be significant.

Now you could take the position right from the outset that Victor should get the transmission work done before the deal takes place. But he might well refuse, and then there's no telling where things will end up. After all, Victor never warranted to you that he was delivering a truck in perfect condition. And nothing has been said about his taking steps to put the vehicle in tiptop shape. The better tack is *not* to disabuse Victor of the notion that it's *you* who will have to get the transmission work done. You want him to think that if you're satisfied the needed repairs are minor, you won't let them stand in the way of the $8,000 deal.

So you patiently lure Victor into the trap. He goes right along, flaunting his vast mechanical expertise to convince you that the transmission isn't a major job. Finally he puts a mere $100 estimate on what it should cost. At that point you have him. "Okay, Victor, I want to receive a clean truck, not one I have to take to a garage for repairs the first day. *You* get the transmission fixed, and I'll increase the purchase price to eighty-one hundred dollars."

That does it. Victor is hard-pressed to dispute your compromise, since he made the repair estimate himself. Your only concern now will be that Victor's garage may do a halfhearted job—the old $99.95 special! But, remember, if you try this kind of gambit, don't let Victor suspect from the outset that *he* will have to pay for the repair, or you'll never generate his lowball estimate. And don't blow the punch line by implying that you'll increase the price by the *actual* repair cost, which presumably will be a lot higher.

With time and experience, you'll discover the negotiating stratagems that work for you. Above all, keep alert and focused, think ahead, don't let the pressure get to you, and enjoy what you're doing.

That's smart negotiating.

POSTSCRIPT

Do you remember the warm-up negotiating exercise in the introduction—"The Case of the Torn Twenty"? For our wind-up, let's
return to that fanciful restaurant and see how the bargaining has
progressed.

For this excursion I want you to pretend that you're Walter the
waiter and you've recently finished reading this book. Charlie Custer,
the customer, has just delivered the bad news that your tip will be
$12 rather than the $20 you anticipated. Back in the introduction I
estimated that you would end up with $14 from the negotiations. Can
you do better than that *now*?

For openers you have to assess your realistic expectation. Pocketing $20 would be terrific, but you quickly realize there's little chance
of receiving the whole amount. Custer seems to have a real need to
pay something less, either to validate his perception that the service
wasn't first class or to keep from feeling foolish about handing over
half the twenty-dollar bill before he even ordered his appetizer. And
he doesn't seem excessively bothered by the prospect of not getting
your half of the bill back should negotiations fail.

Still, you sense that Custer isn't wedded to his $12 offer; there's
room for him to move. The problem is, however, that the *leverage* is
definitely working against you. Custer is under no legal obligation to
tip, you have more to lose, and your desire for the money is greater.
So weighing all these factors, you set your realistic expectation at $16,
a 20 percent tip that's halfway between the parties' initial positions
and, all things considered, not a bad night's work.

Starting out at $20 was the right thing for you to do, and you
shouldn't come off it right away. Your best rationale here is the "ex-
pectancy" factor, and your $20 posture underlines the moral fervor
you're trying to bring to bear on Custer. If possible, you would like
him to make the first concession. In fact, you're hoping that he'll offer

to "split the difference" at $16 right off the bat, in which case you're likely to make out even better than your expectation.

Perhaps you can do something to help that happen, like dropping a hint along these lines: "Look, Mr. Custer, you yourself set the boundaries for this negotiation at twelve dollars for ordinary service and twenty for excellent service. We happen to disagree on the excellence of my service. So shouldn't the ultimate tip reflect the fact that there's an honest disagreement here?"

This is definitely worth a try, but let's suppose it doesn't work. In fact, Custer replies, "You're right, Walter, I'll give you thirteen dollars," at which point he reaches into his pocket, pulls out his money clip, and adds another single to the bills he's proffering in exchange for your half of the twenty.

In the process, however, you discover some useful *information*. You notice that there are no more dollar bills in Custer's money clip—only a few fives. So although he certainly *could* make a subsequent offer of $14, a settlement on that basis would require him to ask you for change. For psychological reasons, given the circumstances, you sense that this isn't too likely. You surmise that Custer, in violation of the rule against *increasing* the size of concessions, may jump to $15 on the next round, provided you can offer him some incentive to take that step.

With that in mind, now that Custer has made a concession—albeit only a dollar—it's your turn to make one. If you don't, given Custer's leverage, you're unlikely to get a higher offer from him. What should your move be? Say you come down only $1 from your starting position to $19. Assuming that Charlie is unlikely to respond at $14, he may then stick at $13 rather than go all the way up to $15. So your best bet may be to counter at $18, a $2 decrease that makes Custer's $1 increase look chintzy and points him in the direction of a $2 jump to $15.

You can't just throw your $2 on the table, however; you need a plausible rationale. Here's a possibility: "I realize, Mr. Custer, that I was slow in getting back to take your dessert order. The entrees for another of my tables had gotten bogged down in the kitchen, and I was fighting to unclog the bottleneck. I have a hunch that this single glitch is at the heart of your dissatisfaction with my service. So I'm willing to be docked ten percent of my expected tip, or two dollars, for this lapse. Give me eighteen dollars, I'll return the half of the bill, and we'll shake hands on a deal."

Unfortunately, Custer is unwilling to shake on the $18; he does, however, bite at the $2 carrot. He pulls a five from his money clip, returns the singles to his pocket, and says: "Look here, Walter, I'll give you a tip of fifteen dollars—but that's it. And the fifteen is only available if you accept it right now. Otherwise I'm out of here, and you'll have nothing."

Now you're facing a very specific *threat* from Custer. You need to reply to it forcefully, while still trying to move the discussion onto more constructive grounds. Remember, your worst fear is that Custer will walk out of the restaurant with you holding nothing but the torn twenty. You also have to convey to him, in *credible* fashion, that you won't accept $15 as a settlement, which he might otherwise presume is very much in your best interests to do.

I can think of more plodding routes to take, but what about a creative (if unhygienic) way to abruptly turn the tables and put the pressure on Custer. You say, "Mr. Custer, the fifteen dollars is not acceptable. You should be willing to do better. But if you're not, and if this is really your final offer, than I have no recourse but to . . ." And now, with a dramatic flair, you take the half of the twenty out of your pocket and start to put it in your mouth, with a gesture that clearly suggests you're about to swallow it!

Charlie is appalled. "Wait!" he cries. "There's no reason to do that."

You agree immediately. "You're right, Mr. Custer," you respond, removing the undigested bill from between your teeth. "So why don't you make me a decent offer."

Now, *at last,* Custer says, "Okay, Walter, let's split the original difference at sixteen dollars."

There it is: your realistic expectation. But perhaps you can do a little better. So, like a flash, you close in for the kill. "All right, Charlie—I hope you don't mind if I call you by your first name—you're at sixteen dollars and I'm at eighteen. What do you say we leave it to *Mrs.* Custer to decide what the tip should be?"

Guess where you'll end up?!

THE SMART NEGOTIATOR'S
CHECKLIST

For ready reference, here is a synopsis of the book's principal points in the form of a checklist. The dozen major subjects are arranged chronologically, as they would arise in the process of a deal. You may find this checklist useful to consult before starting out on a negotiation, as well as during later stages of the talks (just to make sure you haven't overlooked anything).

PREPARATION BEFORE THE NEGOTIATION STARTS

1. *Information.* Collect and evaluate information on leverage, values, sale prices, competition, and other factors that will have an effect on the negotiation (chapter 3).

   - Determine *what* information you want to know about the other side and *how* best to get it: a direct question to compel a straight answer or an indirect probe to expose collateral facts.
   - Work out a defensive plan to protect sensitive information that the other side is likely to inquire about—blocking techniques to avoid the unappetizing extremes of lying and harmful disclosure.
   - As negotiations progress, keep your eyes and ears open for additional helpful information about the other side's position. Hold debriefing sessions after meetings to draw inferences "while they're hot."

2. *Agents.* Decide whether and how to use an agent to represent you in the negotiation (chapter 11).

- Evaluate the pros and cons (such as the agent's emotional detachment vs. the principal's possible loss of control).
- If you use an agent, communicate with him or her early, often, and candidly, to be sure you're both on the same wavelength.
- Always exercise judgment as to what weight the agent's advice deserves in your decision-making process, based in part on your relative degree of expertise.
- Decide who will handle the actual bargaining, based on such factors as comparative negotiating skills, the issues at stake, and the potential impairment of ongoing relationships between the principals.
- Give your agent adequate authority to negotiate, unless the other side's agent lacks it.
- For meetings of principals *and* agents, work out your strategy in advance to protect you from having to respond where inappropriate.

3. *Expectations*. Develop realistic expectations on price and other key issues prior to commencing negotiations (chapter 7).

- Start by determining your *aspiration*: an amalgam of *objective* value (get professional advice if needed) and *subjective* worth to you.
- Temper your aspiration with *feasibility*: an amalgam of what your counterpart is likely to have in mind (with the possible need to combat unreality on his part) and the relative leverage of the parties.
- Reassess your expectations along the way, as new information becomes available and leverage factors change.

4. *Disputes*. In a dispute, take the special factors involved into account in setting your sights and mapping out a strategy (chapter 12).

- Decide whether to sue before negotiating—whether it's a lawsuit or the *threat* of a lawsuit that will bring your adversary to the table.
- Try to lower the emotional temperature by focusing less on history and more on "What can we do about this *now?*"

- Evaluate (with your lawyer) the alternative to a negotiated settlement: what's the court likely to decide, what are the odds of it occurring, how long will it take, and what are the costs of litigation?
- Determine who should handle the negotiations, the lawyer with the big stick or you with the big grievance.
- Let the other side know you're willing to fight, but don't demand unconditional surrender.
- Consider the possibility of using alternative dispute resolution (ADR) if neither negotiations nor litigation appear palatable.

ONCE THE NEGOTIATION BEGINS

5. *Starting Point.* Prepare your strategy on how and where to start out (chapter 8).

- Determine *who* should go first on particular issues.
  a. On *price*, choose between the conventional wisdom ("let the other guy go first") and the attempt to take control of the negotiation by putting your own number on the table (but only if you know values and have determined your realistic expectation).
  b. On *nonprice* issues, go first where the issue is important to you, *unless* you don't want your counterpart to realize its importance, or it comes out your way by operation of law.
- If you're going first on a nonprice issue, decide *when* to raise it: during *price negotiations*, before the parties' minds have met, or during the subsequent *contract negotiations*.
- When you're going first, decide how much "room" to give yourself.
  a. On price, always give yourself *some* room, except when you're trying to make your expectation an objective lodestar for the negotiations.
  b. Don't overreach, but don't underachieve; for example, in a sale, use the 15–25 percent rule of thumb.
  c. Treat nonprice issues similarly, but avoid taking illogical positions just to create some room.
  d. Buttress your first position (and all *subsequent* ones) with

an appropriate rationale, especially if your proposal is much lower (or higher) than the other side anticipated.
- If the other side is going first, prepare your *reaction* in advance, characterizing the proposal in a manner consistent with how you'll respond to it.
- Respond to the initial proposal in a way that's supportable by a plausible rationale and best serves three functions:
  a. to establish a helpful bid and asked range;
  b. to send the right kind of message;
  c. to induce a constructive second proposal from the original bidder.

6. *Concessions.* Actively manage the concession process to set things up for the final compromise (chapter 9).

- Reciprocity is crucial; you have to move to generate movement from the other side.
- Send a three-part message with your concession: it's meaningful, but there may not be many more, particularly if it's not reciprocated.
- Don't be afraid to make the first price concession if it's "your turn," but not at the same meeting as your initial bid. If your counterpart's counteroffer is off the wall, try to get him to bid against himself.
- When making *price* concessions
  a. do so in a few meaningful strokes (rather than multiple small ones);
  b. decrease the size of each subsequent concession;
  c. don't feel you have to match your counterpart dollar for dollar (especially if he started "way out");
  d. don't adopt an invariable, recognizable pattern.
- With respect to concessions on *nonprice* issues
  a. rank the issues in terms of significance to you and their likely importance to your counterpart;
  b. determine plausible intermediate steps from the opening proposal to your expectation;
  c. try to make your concessions do double duty, resolving this issue *and* furnishing trading bait on some other issue.

7. *Leverage.* Understand and deal with the leverage factors affecting the negotiation (chapter 2).

- Assess the relative impact on the parties of the four key elements (*necessity, desire, competition,* and *time*) and others.
- Keep in mind the importance to leverage of *appearances*— and remember, looks can be deceiving.
- When the balance tips your way, communicate your strength credibly and quietly and get the deal done quickly, because leverage can change.
- When you're at a disadvantage, put your main energies into those issues where you can wrap yourself in a cloak of reasonableness or conventional practice.
- Where the factors are in conflict, get those favoring you out in the open, keep your counterpart from becoming aware of the ones that work against you, and generate new favorable leverage, where possible.

BRINGING THE NEGOTIATIONS TO A CLOSE

8. *Credibility.* Make a real effort to achieve credibility for yourself, while being alert to whether or not your counterpart is bluffing (chapter 4).

- In terms of transmitting and receiving positive *information*
  a. work hard at convincing your counterpart that your information is credible through specificity and detachment from the negotiations;
  b. always assess the reliability of what you're being fed: the more significant the information, the more skeptical you should be.
- In terms of buttressing the firm *positions* you take that are *genuine*, you need to show that you've "gone the distance" and also how meaningful the issue is to you.
  a. Distinguish between blue chips (both *immovable* and *staunch*) and bargaining chips (both *malleable* and *pliant*), sending appropriate messages and articulating a "sticking" rationale on the blue chips.

- In deciding whether to bluff, be concerned about the two (out of three) possible negative outcomes:
  a. You're not believed, so your bluff is called.
  b. You're believed, and the other side then walks away—even though you would have accepted their last position.
- If you do bluff, try to "follow the rules": choose a significant issue toward the end of the negotiating process, extend a compromise proposal that is consistent with prior expressions, and make sure you offer a plausible rationale, coupled with a show of flexibility, the ability to back down, and a story to cover your retreat.
- If you think your counterpart is bluffing (but if not, you would yield), you have to transmit evidence of your own (nonexistent) resolve in order to force him to back down.

9. *Endgame Tactics.* As the negotiation moves into its final stages, be aware that such tactics as *threats* (chapter 13) and *deadlines* (chapter 9) become more tempting to employ.

- Generally avoid the use of threats, which can cause hardened positions and counterthreats.
  a. Consider use of a warning about negative consequences that may occur independently of your will.
  b. If you do threaten, don't bluff—and enhance your credibility by the proportionality of the threat and your consistency, timing, and reasoning.
- When someone threatens you, distinguish between subtle and overt varieties.
  a. If the threat is subtle, you can ignore it, handle it with a light touch, or ignite a direct confrontation.
  b. If the threat is overt, always reply to it (showing you're uncowed), but then shift the discussion to a more constructive level.
- Since deadlines can create (and can be manipulated to create) pressure:
  a. Keep alert for clues that indicate the other side is feeling some heat.
  b. Conceal any impending deadline pressure on your side by moving things along briskly from the outset.

   c. If your counterpart attempts to impose a deadline on you, test how real this is; and where it's onerous, resist it as unrealistic or unnecessary (or "we have our own deadline").

10. *Judgment.* Remember that the key to good negotiating judgment is keeping yourself in balance (chapter 5).

- In terms of *substance*:
  a. Strike a balance between what you do to get a leg up and what you do to compromise.
  b. Try to balance persistence with perspective; you can't win 'em all.
- In terms of *style,* adopt a manner that feels natural, is consistent, and conveys the message you want to send.

11. *Compromise.* To make deals, you have to be willing to compromise (chapter 10).

- Search for that favorable middle ground, while helping your counterpart solve *his* problems.
- Keep in mind that each good compromise has two aspects:
  a. finding the precise formulation that works;
  b. introducing it in such a manner that it becomes the solution.
- Watch out for prematurity, as with a rush to split the difference.
  a. Follow the ground rules for splitting: small gaps, patience, finality, caveats, "Are *you* willing?" and so on.
  b. Remember, the split does *not* have to be fifty-fifty.
- Reduce principles to dollars (plus throw in a face-saver where needed).
- Be creative, both in terms of
  a. dividing issues to satisfy your counterpart's *real* concerns while protecting your *essential* interests, and
  b. expanding the pie.
- With respect to a package deal:
  a. If proffering, remember to label it as such, so the other side can't pick and choose.
  b. If receiving, don't be afraid to reformulate your own package.

- In the final moments, consider the need to *stretch*, if all else fails (chapter 7).
  a. Ignore emotions and use this test: If I stick on my terms and lose the deal, will I regret not having paid (or accepted) the stretched terms available?

12. *Contract.* Don't relax once there's a meeting of the minds, but turn your full attention to the problems of negotiating a written contract (chapter 13).

- As a general rule, put it in writing.
  a. Make a possible exception for the favorable deal with an honorable counterpart that you fear will be lost in the contract negotiations.
- In deciding on the advisability of a letter of intent vs. going right to contract, assess the psychological aspects of the situation and its leverage effect on the contract negotiations.
- Be alert to the advantages of drafting, but don't salivate over the opportunity.
- If you respond to the other side's draft by "marking it up," be careful about introducing explosive new issues into the negotiation in this sterile fashion.
- Avoid the recurring blunders and lapses:
  a. marking up a previously negotiated contract as a first draft;
  b. omitting significant protections by "keeping it short";
  c. ignoring the value of subtlety as a means of avoiding hard adversarial bargaining;
  d. letting matters fall in the cracks between lawyer and client.

ACKNOWLEDGMENTS

I'm grateful to a number of people for their help on this book. Here are a few I particularly want to single out: Marguerite Millhauser, who inspired me to start on the project, helped me think through the basic approach, and critiqued the early returns; my partners, Rich Easton, Dan Stoller, Paul Schnell, and Brian McCarthy, who read the whole manuscript and offered so many insightful suggestions; my friends, Bill Silver, Fred Gerard, Peter Goodson, Bill Jacobi, and Dick Schmidt, for taking the time to share their wisdom with me; my wife, Barbara Fox, who scrutinized every word for anything that sounded pompous and has put up with the time demands imposed by the book for lo these many months; my mother, Marcy Freund, and my brother-in-law Joe Hilton, for helpful commentary; my secretary, Chris Greges, and my former secretary, Nancy Martin, for moral support and herculean efforts in pulling the manuscript together through innumerable versions; and my editor, Fred Hills, and his colleague Burton Beals, for their continuing support, good advice, and sound editing.

Over the years I've encountered a lot of good negotiators and read many books and articles on the subject by other commentators. I'm sure their accumulated wisdom has made its way into my consciousness, and perhaps even onto some of these pages, for which I thank you all.

Jim Freund
May 1992

INDEX

ABOUT THE AUTHOR

A prominent negotiator in many of the major corporate takeover battles of the 1980s—from TWA to Federated Department Stores—James C. Freund is a senior partner at the eminent New York law firm of Skadden, Arps, Slate, Meagher & Flom, as well as an adjunct professor at Fordham Law School, where he teaches a course in negotiating. He lives in New York City.